12°

"A Rising Star of Promise"

The Civil War Odyssey of David Jackson Logan

17th South Carolina Volunteers,
1861-1864

*To Gordon
Brother in Arms
Hope you enjoy the book!
Sam Thomas
6-08*

Edited by

Samuel N. Thomas, Jr.
& Jason H. Silverman

Manufactured in the United States of America

A Rising Star of Promise: The Civil War Odyssey of David Jackson Logan, 17th South Carolina Volunteers, 1861-1864

edited by Samuel N. Thomas, Jr., and Jason H. Silverman

Copyright © 1998
Samuel N. Thomas, Jr. and Jason H. Silverman

Includes bibliographic references and index

Printing Number
10 9 8 7 6 5 4 3 2 1
(First Hardcover Edition)

ISBN 1-882810-29-5

Savas Publishing Company
1475 S. Bascom Avenue, Suite 204,
Campbell, California 95008
(408) 879-9073

For Lynn, my love forever;
and to Steve, the brother-in-law I never
knew and a true Rising Star of Promise

S. N. J.

As always, for Susan and Alex, with love;
and in memory of my father-in-law,
Jim Riel, truly *sui generis*

J. H. S.

A pre-war image of David Jackson Logan

Courtesy of the Historical Center of York County

TABLE OF CONTENTS

South Carolina and York County

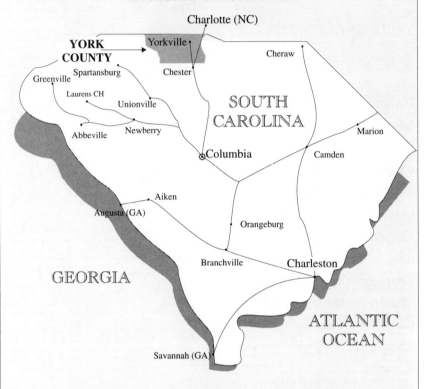

NORTH CAROLINA

Charlotte (NC)

YORK COUNTY

Yorkville

Cheraw

Greenville

Spartansburg

Chester

Laurens CH

Unionville

SOUTH CAROLINA

Abbeville

Newberry

Marion

Columbia

Camden

Aiken

Augusta (GA)

Orangeburg

Branchville

Charleston

GEORGIA

ATLANTIC OCEAN

Savannah (GA)

By 1850, York District was developing into one of the largest and most prosperous regions in the upper Piedmont of South Carolina. The population by the beginning of the decade topped 15,000 residents, of whom over 40% were slaves. A decade later on the eve of the Civil War, the county's population had expanded to some 21,500, nearly half of whom were slaves. The white male population numbered 5,500. During the 1850s, York District was heavily tied to agriculture. Ninety-three percent of the work force was involved in raising crops. By comparison, 78% of the nation's work force was employed in agricultural pursuits. Only 13% of the District residents were involved in industry of one form or another.

By 1850 York District was the largest cotton producer in the upper Piedmont, and the second largest in 1860. It was the third largest producer of corn in 1850, and the second largest, per farm, by 1860. With its growing share of the agricultural market, York District experienced an increase in wealth during this period. Indeed, it enjoyed the highest wealth, per capita, of the free population in the upper Piedmont in both 1850 and 1860. By 1850, the farmers of the upcountry were becoming increasingly dependent on merchants for such items as ready-made clothing and even foodstuffs, such as meat and grain.

To the surprise of few in the state, South Carolina called for a Secession Convention when Abraham Lincoln rode a divided field of candidates to victory and the White House in 1860. There was virtually no opposition in York District and the rest of the South Carolina upcountry to secession.

Theodore P. Savas

LIST OF MAPS & ILLUSTRATIONS

Foreword

All of us know the feeling. You pick up a book, peruse the introduction, and shuffle through some pages. Slowly but surely you begin to realize that the book has it, that ineffable combination of subject matter, style, and revelation. You take it home and spend a couple of nights in a row with it. When you're finished, you find room on your shelf for it. Before you put it away, you hold it one more time, look at the cover, maybe flip it around a bit. Finally, you slip it in between two other books about which you harbor similar feelings. And every time you peruse your library, you glimpse the title and remember how happy you are that you read it. There's even a little self-assuredness in there somewhere because, really, you knew it all along.

You are holding one of those books now. *"A Rising Star of Promise": The Civil War Odyssey of David Jackson Logan, 17th South Carolina Volunteers, 1861-1864*, is an absolute bounty of fresh information on a previously unknown Southern officer and a little-known South Carolina regiment. Logan's observations are all the more important since they appear at a time when interest in the wartime Carolinas is swelling. For years, emphasis in Civil War historiography has unaccountably avoided South Carolina and her soldiers. Few regimentals exist detailing the state's combat units, and not a single study examines her storied brigades. *"A Rising Star of Promise"* goes a long way toward remedying that deficiency, offering for the first time keen insight into both the 17th South Carolina Infantry and Gen. Nathan "Shanks" Evans' Tramp Brigade. The word "groundbreaking"—so bandied about in publishing these days—finds proper application here.

When South Carolina left the Union, David Logan enlisted in the Carolina Rifles—"without waiting for any Call from Constituted authorities"—and received assignment to the 17th South Carolina Volunteers, whereupon he began his march into the hell of war. Logan's writings carry us to Columbia and Charleston, South Carolina, then to Virginia as part of the aptly-named Tramp Brigade. Logan subsequently serves in Wilmington, North Carolina, and in the battles around Kinston before heading west to Jackson, Mississippi and the Vicksburg Campaign. After the fall of the river citadel, he returns to Charleston until, finally, he and the "Tramps" head north to burrow into the trenches of Petersburg, Virginia. Obviously, the sweep of Logan's narrative is immense.

Like many Carolinians, Logan went to war with high spirits and firm convictions. Unlike most, he had a way with words, and he put his descriptive talents to good use. Still, with a plethora of interesting letter collections and memoirs flooding the book market, you may ask what recommends this particular publication. The answer is plain. Editors Samuel N. Thomas. Jr. and Jason H. Silverman have brought together a cornucopia of material—David Logan's letters, his insightful diary, and a series of in-depth articles he wrote for a local newspaper—and skillfully melded them into a coherent, eyewitness history of Logan and the 17th South Carolina. A daunting task, but Messers Thomas and Silverman have succeeded beautifully.

The editors' own work is thankfully transparent. They provide just enough connective material to keep the narrative flowing, and include plenty of end notes for those wishing to dig deeper. Thus we are allowed to focus on Logan's own words. Therein lies the reward. The young Carolinian's ability to succinctly state his mind is demonstrated time and again. "(G)o forth with the resolution calmly taken," Logan writes, "to die or be free." At another point he freely admits, "The yankees have the whip hand of us badly now, and in the language of Old Abe 'we must keep pizzing away' or submit which I hardly think will be done." Numerous incidents come under the scrutiny of Logan's sharp observation: his near-surreal encounter with his Federal counterparts during a cease-fire; a meeting between Jefferson Davis and P. G. T. Beauregard on the ramparts of Fort Lamar outside Charleston; and Logan's excited sighting of European royalty. In each instance, Logan's colorful description renders an historical immediacy that flows like a good novel.

When Logan puts words to his deepest emotions, we get a revealing glimpse of the awful bill the Civil War presented. He left a wife and two small children behind when he marched off, and he quickly confessed to his beloved Sallie, "I did not know how much I loved you and our dear little babies until I came to leave you." This longing resurfaces time and again, and its intensity increases as Confederate fortunes plummet. Although consumed by military issues, Logan is forced to deal with a variety of problems on the homefront. His need to stay connected with his family becomes terribly apparent when he complains, "You have not answered all my questions again. . .I have that awful humor worse than ever." But, he never ends a letter without imploring Sallie to "Kiss my babies," without assuring her of "My love to all."

Based solely on Logan's observations of camp life and his own revelations of the war's steep emotional price, this book would have much to commend it. But, being privy to the Tramp Brigade's operations and important battle descriptions elevates *"A Rising Star of Promise"* beyond the typical soldier gossip. On the little-known operations around Kinston, North Carolina in December of 1862—which Logan describes in depth in an article for his local newspaper—the young man's diary entry tersely propels the reader into the furnace of combat:

> The work is getting hot. Mullinax of Co A killed just to my right. Firing becomes furious on our right. We retire over the crest of the hill. The Legion is sending death into the enemy. Reinforcements are heard coming. . .

And again, during the fighting at Bermuda Hundred, Logan gives us this nugget:

> The boys pressed onward shouting as only rebels shout, until we reached to within 30 paces of the works, when the Yanks probably having a vision of Fort Pillow cross their minds, ingloriously fled. . .

If one more reason to recommend this work is required, I can offer this: Logan's writings allow us to share the thoughtful reflections of an intelligent, committed Southerner who watched the fire of his cause slowly extinguish. Like most soldiers, he developed opinions concerning the Confederacy's prosecution of the war, and we again benefit from his literary skill. He eloquently argues for a system of regular furloughs since "the prospect of a future return to the homes of the loved and cherished will sweeten the bitter cup." At one point, he almost humorously concludes that the Union barrage of Fort Sumter will soon bankrupt the Federal government, and he gives us the math to prove it. As the Tramp Brigade marches away from a desolated Jackson, Mississippi, Logan poignantly concludes, "The fall of the place was unavoidable. A natural result of the fall of Vicksburg. How far we are yet to retreat is hard to state." General Joseph Johnston couldn't have said it better.

Logan reemerges from the shadows of history to remind us all of the deep strength a Civil War soldier had for his cause. While we learn about the campaigns of the 17th South Carolina, we also discover much about those who stood in the ranks. As another who has read Logan's correspondence commented to me, "You really end up liking him." I agree. But, more than that, you gain insight into a man and a unit that has eluded history for more than one hundred and thirty years. Logan's perceptive powers give the reader a soldier's view of the conflict, a soldier who served in almost every major theater of the war.

As fitting as it is that David Logan's story is now published, it is we the readers who benefit from the telling. *"A Rising Star of Promise": The Civil War Odyssey of David Jackson Logan, 17th South Carolina Volunteers, 1861-1864*, is a simply great book.

Of course, you knew it all along.

Patrick Brennan
December 21, 1997
Skokie, Illinois

Editor's Preface

The Search

While sorting and cataloging a local collection for the Historical Center of York County in 1992, I came across a small group of letters written during the Civil War by a local Confederate soldier. Reading through the letters David Jackson Logan had written to his wife Sallie from 1861 until the middle of 1864, I became impressed both with the style of writing and depth of information imparted in the correspondence. Clues in this correspondence led me to believe that the collection was not complete. In several letters Logan asks Sallie to search for his articles in the *Yorkville Enquirer,* their local newspaper. In still another letter he asks his wife to save his articles. Did these articles still exist?

In the hope of locating these articles or additional correspondence, I sought out the Moore family of York County, the donors of the Logan letter collection. This request uncovered an old family scrapbook, which the Moore's graciously allowed me to view. My hope turned to elation when nearly thirty newspaper articles, together with a number of Logan's pre-war writings, were found inside amongst the scrapbook's loose and sometimes brittle pages.

Additional family members were located in both North and South Carolina in an effort to gather background information on this intriguing Confederate soldier. Several family members told of having heard of a diary which had been written during the war, but they could not remember the author (several members of the Logan, Moore and related families served in the war). Encouraged by the possible existence of a diary, I decided to backtrack in an attempt to locate more information on David Jackson Logan.

David and Sallie Logan had two children, John ("Johnnie") and Lula, both born before Logan left to join the army. David's letters were donated to the Historical Center of York County through the family line descended from his daughter Lula. If one side of the family had letters, certainly it was also likely the other side might have something of interest. Perhaps the family line descended from Logan's son John had the diary? Unfortunately, an obstacle arose. I learned that David's son John had several children, but the last two surviving daughters had passed away several years ago. The sole surviving son had moved to New York City and had lost contact with the Moore family. Now the historical detective work began in earnest.

I began searching for and contacting individuals in two states who had known these three children. After numerous and largely fruitless conversations which did not seem to be getting us any closer to discovering the diary—except for finding out that John's last son in New York City had probably also passed away several years earlier—I came upon one person who thought he remembered his widow and son (John's grandson and David's great-grandson) had moved to North Carolina some years ago. Several more phone calls turned up another clue when a family member remembered the same story and named Raleigh, North Carolina, as the likely location.

Aided with this new information, a number of phone calls were made late one Wednesday evening to every "Logan" listed in the Raleigh directory. As luck would have it, on the third try a gentleman answered the phone and, when asked if his family had originally been from York, South Carolina, answered in the affirmative. When asked if his great-grandfather was York County's David Jackson Logan, he again answered positively. Indeed, he even mentioned that he had his great-grandfather's diary, but that he had never been able to read it. Somewhat nervously, I inquired if it would be possible for me to see the diary and perhaps copy it. The welcome reply was a very kind "yes."

Soon after I arrived at the Logan home in Raleigh, I discovered that not only did this gentleman possess David Jackson Logan's diary, but he also had the *other half of his personal letters to Sallie!*

After copies were made of all of this memoranda, transcriptions were completed and copies were sent to each side of the family. In the meantime, the Logan family in Raleigh decided that after nearly 100 years, the writings of David Jackson Logan deserved to be reunited. The diary and letters so lovingly kept for so many years were donated to the Historical Center of York County, guaranteeing the preservation of Logan's writings. It was at this stage that my friend and former professor, Jason Silverman, agreed to collaborate with me on this project. And thus, a "Rising Star of Promise" was born.

Samuel N. Thomas, Jr.

Editorial Method

We attempted to preserve the integrity of Logan's original work while simultaneously producing a text with consideration for the contemporary reader. The latter objective was achieved by presenting David Logan's writings, i.e., his letters, diary and newspaper articles, chronologically. Interspersed therein, where appropriate, is information relating to the general course of the war and its effect on Logan, his family, and his regiment. Hopefully, this method will assist the reader by placing Logan's informative memoranda into historical context.

Preserving the integrity of Logan's work proved to be a more vexing problem. Unfortunately, David's original correspondence is almost entirely without punctuation. As such it is often cumbersome to read. In order to assist the reader, punctuation has been standardized to currently prevalent styles. Thus dashes, which he sometimes placed at the end of his sentences, have been converted to periods. David's spelling has been retained. Although he occasionally made use of phonetic spelling, he relied on this method of spelling less frequently than did most Confederate soldiers. His educational background is aptly demonstrated through the use of Old English spelling and Latin phrases. Many Southern writers of the mid-1800s used capitalization as a completely arbitrary literary function, and Logan was no exception. Capitalization, or lack thereof, was retained with the exception of the beginning of sentences. Extraneous marks that appeared within the text and margins have been omitted for the sake of clarity. Abbreviations have been left undisturbed, in keeping with the intention of the author.

As far as Civil War letters go, Logan's are in amazingly good condition. Other than an occasional indecipherable word due to a stain, missing section or extensive over-handling—or his own haste in writing—they were relatively easily transcribed. As was common with letters written during the latter years of the war, David often wrote sentences in the margins, between lines, or even in the opposite direction of previously written text. These actions made it occasionally difficult to transcribe these sections. This was especially the case when ink bled into earlier text. The legibility of David's writing frequently varies, as did his use of writing utensil. Letters written in ink, as opposed to pencil, did not fade nearly as badly and were considerably easier to read. Illegible words have been replaced by a question mark [?] inserted between brackets. Logan's diary presented related problems, and the same editorial conventions were utilized.

Many individuals mentioned by David were from York District, with a few from other areas. They have been identified, whenever possible, in the Biographical Roster printed as an appendix in this book. Officers, especially generals and line officers, were easily identifiable. Only brief information has been provided for these men, usually in the form of their involvement with the event Logan mentions. Cursory data is presented about many others, often merely their rank, company and regiment. Where more than one person may be the individual to whom Logan is referring, brief information about each is presented. Invariably, the lack of data made it necessary to list some individuals as simply "unidentified." All bold-faced names are spelled in accordance with Logan's original; corrected spelling is used within the biographical entry.

Below is a list of the abbreviations used by Logan in his writings:

agt: agent	Dist: District
amt: amount	Cola: Columbia
Bal: balance	Dolls: dollars
Bro: brother	Esq: Esquire
Capt: Captain	Genl: General
Cts: cents	Lieut: Lieutenant
Co: Company	Lt: Lieutenant

Maj: Major	Sergt: Sergeant
NCV: North Carolina Volunteers	Sgt: Sergeant
NERR: Northeastern Railroad	SCM: South Carolina Militia
prchd: purchased	SCRR: South Carolina Railroad
prs: pairs	SCV: South Carolina Volunteers
pvt: Private	TO: Turn Out
QrM: Quartermaster	yds: yards
Regt: Regiment	

Acknowledgments

As with all scholarly projects, many others contributed their time, resources and interest in the preparation of this manuscript. No historian has ever completed a work without the assistance of others, and we hope we pay proper homage to our predecessors in the notes to this work.

We are particularly indebted to the two individuals who so generously made available their private family papers: David L. Moore of York County, South Carolina, and Thomas J. Logan of Raleigh, North Carolina. Both of these gentlemen provided materials of such value that without them, this work would not have been possible. They also proffered valuable assistance in locating additional information and sources. Betty Logan Wilcox of Charlotte, Virginia Logan Sams of Winston-Salem, Marilyn E. Logan of Shelby, and Frances L. Carpenter of the Broad River Basin Genealogical Society in Shelby, all contributed tremendous amounts of valuable information. Many seemingly blind alleys were opened with the assistance of these four women. Rececca Williamson, Bert Carroll and Sarah Kennedy Tyler also provided assistance by contributing a variety of "leads."

One of the greatest contributors to historic preservation in this country are professional archives. Foremost and unique among these preservation facilities in the Carolinas is the Historical Center of York County, and its sponsor, the York County Historical Commission. The former is a county-supported public facility, and through its efforts the papers of David Jackson Logan have been reassembled and preserved for future generations.

Two additional archival facilities also provided much needed assistance. Gina White at the Winthrop University Archives in Rock Hill, South Carolina, has more knowledge of collections housed there than anyone else, and was very helpful in pulling records together and answering questions concerning these holdings. The Learning Resource Center at Lenoir Community College in Kinston, North Carolina, was extremely useful and informative concerning operations in and around Kinston during the period when the 17th Regiment was stationed there in 1862-1863.

A number of friends gave freely of their time and assistance whenever called upon. We thank Dr. Paul C. Whitesides of York, South Carolina, for his assistance in co-compiling *Under the Leaves of the Palmetto: York County's Confederate Veterans*. This work helped us tremendously in identifying names mentioned throughout Logan's writings; Ruth Dickson Thomas and Jo Roberts Owens, also of York, provided help through their transcription of the *Confederate Veteran's Enrollment Book of York County, S. C.—1902*, and through their answers to our numerous questions; Susan Silverman, Head of Public Services, at Dacus Library of Winthrop University, pointed the way and acquired substantial amounts of obscure information, without which this work could not have progressed; Leon Sikes of Kinston, North Carolina, assisted us in locating sites mentioned by Logan while the 17th Regiment was "in that corner of the world"; Dr. Robert L. Seymour offered his expertise on matters dealing with medicine and disease; Scott Coleman of the Chester County Museum, and Patrick McCawley of the South Carolina Department of Archives and History, were extremely instrumental in identifying certain individuals and sites mentioned within the writings. Both of these exceptionally gifted experts on the Civil War went well beyond simply replying to our numerous inquiries; Wade B. Fairey, executive director of the York County Historical Commission, located additional information and furnished tremendous support and encouragement; Fred C. Holder of Seneca, South Carolina, is one of the most gifted editors and researchers on the Piedmont of South Carolina. Fred answered and asked numerous questions, read through portions of the manuscript several times, and offered much needed criticism of the work; Iva Jean Maddox, archivist at the Historical Center of York County and a superb researcher, edited portions of this manuscript, furnished additional identification of individuals, and provided useful suggestions and sources to fill in gaps in the work; Dr. Thomas H. Appleton of the Kentucky Historical Society, Mr. Robert M. Gorman of Dacus Library, Winthrop University, and Dr. Robert Poch of the South Carolina Commission on Higher Education, provided friendship and assistance that were both invaluable and sustaining. To all of these individuals, we can not begin to express our sincere gratitude.

We would also like to thank Patrick Brennan, the author of *Secessionville: Assault on Charleston* (Savas Publishing, 1996), for his willingness to write the excellent Foreword to our book, and Mark A. Moore, for his exemplary cartography. We also wish to thank our publisher, Theodore P. Savas, who somehow manages to give editors, publishers and lawyers a good name.

Finally, to our families we wish to express our appreciation for the assistance and support they have shown in this project. Without support from one's family, a work such as this could not move forward. Sam Thomas' mother-in-law, Estelle Camp, was the first reader of "A Rising Star of Promise," and offered many corrections and suggestions. Sam's sister-in-law, Susan Elaine Camp, assisted with a number of medical questions. Jason Silverman's in-laws, Jim and Eloise Riel, provide support and encouragement in virtually everything he undertakes.

Sam Thomas would like to thank his parents, whom he cannot begin to repay for the many years of love and support they have given him. Their guidance encouraged him to develop and pursue his individual goals at his own pace and in his own way. Through them the seeds of history and heritage were planted. He also thanks his brother and sisters, Gigi, Jim, and Beth for their support, and his nephews and neices, Maggie, Scott, Rollie, Stephanie, Maria, Ian, Drew, Hanna, Ada, Samantha, Thomas, Eliza, and Janey. Perhaps through them a new historian will emerge.

Lastly, we have received the greatest, and most important, encouragement from our wives. Lynn Thomas typed, read, criticized, pushed, and endured. Susan Silverman provided the support, encouragement, and patience for which she has become legendary. Five-year-old Alex Silverman always and happily demonstrated what, and who, was truly important in life. We both want to express our love and appreciation to our families; they have contributed more to this project than they will ever know.

Sam Thomas knows his brother-in-law, James Steven Camp, only through stories and photographs. Just as with David Jackson Logan, Steve's life came to a tragic and untimely end on a distant battlefield while performing his duty in the service of his country. Jason Silverman's father-in-law, Jim Riel, did not live to see this book published. His unabashed pride in introducing his son-in-law, "Dr. Silverman," to anyone and everyone he could, however, was truly sustaining when energy and enthusiasm faltered. It is to our loved ones and to the memory of those who have gone before that we dedicate this book.

Samuel N. Thomas, Jr.
Jason H. Silverman
December 1997

Prologue

etween 1861 and 1865, three million men of the thirty-one million residents of the United States fought in the Civil War. More has been written concerning this conflict than any other single event in American history. Americans entered into the struggle on both sides with strong convictions and the belief that theirs' was a just cause.

Following the war and the creation of the "Lost Cause" myth, many former Confederate soldiers wrote of their wartime experiences as a means of vindication. As a result, much of the written material available today was produced from memory and often pursued to explain one's actions in that conflict, so that in the end, the record was more often than not, erroneous. Published memoirs considerably outnumber published diaries and letters. These contemporary sources, of course, often offer new light on old subjects. Many of these excellent documentary materials have not been accessible to the public because of the private nature of the records. Most literate soldiers wrote to family and friends about their experiences during their service; soldiers who were illiterate usually had others write for them. These documents are among the richest sources of first-hand accounts of this turbulent period. Sadly, only a small fraction of them survive.

The correspondence of David Jackson Logan, as presented in "A Rising Star of Promise," is composed of three intertwined sets of writings: personal letters, diary entries, and newspaper articles. The letters, fifty-two in number, comprise the largest of the three segments and were written by Logan between 1861-1864 to his wife Sallie, in York District, South Carolina. In addition to his thoughts of home and other related issues, David's diary provides useful and often in-depth accounts of his military experiences. Lastly are David's twenty-nine newspaper articles, most of which were mailed to his hometown newspaper, the *Yorkville Enquirer*. These articles are gracefully written and cogently presented news reports from the front, and were intended to keep people back home informed about, and engaged in, the activities of the regiment. Their historical value is difficult to overstate.

Background

The first permanent white settlers into the upper South Carolina piedmont region west of the Catawba River did not begin arriving until the late 1740s. Predominantly Scotch-Irish, with sprinklings of French, German, Swiss, Welsh, Scots, Irish and English, they migrated there from former homes in Pennsylvania, Maryland and Virginia, traveling for the most part along the Great Wagon Road through the Shenandoah Valley to their new homes along the Catawba and Broad Rivers. They were mostly allied by both blood and religious affiliation, and settled in small communities along a number of creeks which flowed either west into the Broad or east into the Catawba.

Strong Presbyterian influences permeated this area and lent itself to two strongly held beliefs: separation of church and state, and an educated electorate. Both of these convictions contributed to the defeat of British forces in the region during the American Revolution. They also became deeply ingrained in the descendants of the Carolina Piedmont during the next century to the eve of the Civil War. The resultant society was thus built upon a foundation of honor and patriotism, as many writers on the South have so aptly noted.[1] These were the traits of the region into which David Jackson Logan was born in 1837.

The Family

David Jackson Logan was born in Cleveland County, North Carolina on September 22, 1837, to John Randolph Logan and Sarah Patterson Jackson.[2] David, or "Davy," as he was sometimes called, was the oldest of ten children in an upper middle-class family. Both of David's parents were from York County, South Carolina. His father, John Randolph Logan, grew up on the family farm in Cherokee Township (what is now Cherokee County, SC), while his mother, Sarah Patterson Jackson, was born in the Bethel section along the Catawba River and later moved to the Beersheba area in western York County. John and Sarah moved to Cleveland County in 1836, just one year before the birth of their first child.

John rose to prominence in the political and religious affairs in Cleveland, Rutherford, Lincoln, and Gaston Counties of North Carolina. Although his first calling was as a teacher at a number of schools in the northwestern section of York County, thereafter he turned to surveying. In that capacity he laid out the town of Shelby, North Carolina. In addition to surveying, he wore a number of different hats over the years throughout the region, including sheriff, judge, tax collector, and Baptist minister. David Jackson Logan hoped to follow in his father's footsteps.[3]

Little is known of David's childhood. Almost certainly his father's involvement in the region's social life had an effect upon his eldest son, for David developed passionate interests in religion, economics, and political issues. In 1854, David was licensed to teach school in Cleveland County, North Carolina.[4] Four years later, he married Sarah Catherine Rowell of York District.[5]

Sarah, or Sallie as David called her, was born to Benjamin Rowell and Elizabeth "Eliza" Catherine McFadden on February 15, 1836, in the vicinity of Smith's Turnout just above the York and Chester County line.[6] Shortly after the marriage, David and his new bride took up residence in the southern part of York County, where David continued to teach school. By 1859 David was teaching fourteen "free students" at Bratton's Academy at the Bratton settlement.[7] Much like contemporary educators, nineteenth century instructors also received low compensation for their work in educating the next generation. This might have been the catalyst that led Logan to seek out other career ventures. Or, perhaps it was the recent addition to the family of a son, John Rowell Logan, or "Johnnie," as David referred to him in his letters to Sallie. In all likelihood, low pay and a growing family probably made David realize how difficult it was going to be to raise a family on a teacher's pay.

The couple and their new son moved to the bustling courthouse town of Yorkville in the center of the District in 1860. With backing from B. T. Wheeler, a prominent local businessman, Logan formed a

Yorkville, South Carolina (circa 1870), where David and Sallie Logan resided.

Courtesy of the Historical Center of York County

partnership with Samuel Banks Meacham in the establishment of a new business in Yorkville.[8] On March 8, 1860, the grocery business Logan & Meacham advertised their store, which was located "near the Kings Mountain Rail Road Depot."[9] Although short-lived, the business operated successfully until the two partners enlisted in the Confederate war effort.

Life as a Yorkville merchant, however, did not utilize all of David's talents, including his considerable ability as a writer. About this time he began composing and publishing numerous poems, articles, and letters in local newspapers. He also found that with his unique talent for the written word, he was being called upon, from time to time, to compose obituaries for the *Yorkville Enquirer*.[10] As it turned out, writing proved to be one of David's strongest suits.

York County in the 1850s

By 1850 York District was developing into one of the largest and most prosperous regions in the upper Piedmont of South Carolina.[11]

The population by the beginning of the decade topped 15,000 residents, of whom over 40% were slaves.[12] A decade later on the eve of the Civil War, the county's population had expanded to some 21,500, nearly half of whom were slaves. The white male population numbered 5,500.[13]

During the 1850s, York District was heavily tied to agriculture. Ninety-three percent of the work force was involved in raising crops. By comparison, 78% of the nation's work force was employed in agricultural pursuits. Only 13% of the District residents were involved in industry of one form or another.[14] By 1850 York District was the largest cotton producer in the upper Piedmont, and the second largest in 1860.[15] It was the third largest producer of corn in 1850, and the second largest, per farm, by 1860.[16] With its growing share of the agricultural market, York District experienced an increase in wealth during this period. Indeed, it enjoyed the highest wealth, per capita, of the free population in the upper Piedmont in both 1850 and 1860.[17] By 1850, the farmers of the upcountry were becoming increasingly dependent on merchants for such items as ready-made clothing and even foodstuffs, such as meat and grain.[18]

Although Yorkville contained only 93 dwellings and about 500 inhabitants in 1850, its importance as the county seat contributed to the town's growth during the years leading up to 1860.[19] The expanding economic market may have prompted David to enter into the mercantile business in 1860. His decision to locate his new business across from the Kings Mountain Rail Road Depot was a wise move on his part, for most travelers departing or arriving in the town traveled by train.

By the second half of the 1850s, David was rising to a position of prominence in the community. In June 1857, he exhibited the strong religious convictions inherited from his father by joining the Sons of Temperance Movement soon after his arrival in Yorkville. Before long he was elected to lead the York Division, one of the first in the county.[20] As Worthy Patriarch, he was selected that same year from among the nine divisions in the District to act as Secretary of the Temperance Committee, York District. The organization was an active group, boasting seventeen divisions of the Sons of Temperance by 1860.[21]

York County Enters the Civil War

In the first secession crisis following the Compromise of 1850, York District, in keeping with the majority of the rest of the South Carolina upcountry districts, voted overwhelmingly for the "cooperation ticket."[22] Those who supported this belief held that South Carolina should secede *only* if joined by other Southern states. A national crisis was thereby averted, although nine years later the political winds of secession would return anew.

With the approach of the 1860 presidential election and the growing rift in the Democratic party, Republican Abraham Lincoln appeared to emerge as a serious contender for the presidency. Many Southerners were not willing to accept a Lincoln victory. Jonathan L. Miller declared in the October 4, 1860, edition of the *Yorkville Enquirer*, "We must be content with the mere shadow of a Republic, with every feature of republicanism completely obliterated, or we must reaffirm and re-establish the fundamental principles of our government in building up a Southern Confederacy." Miller's sentiment spoke for many of his brethren. To the surprise of few in the state, South Carolina called for a Secession Convention when Lincoln rode a divided field of candidates to victory and the White House. This time the results of the convention were far different than they had been in 1851. There was virtually no opposition in York District and the rest of the South Carolina upcountry to secession. A number of public meetings were held in different parts of the county to discuss the issue. The beliefs held by the attendees of most of these meetings can best be summed up by the resolutions passed by a citizen's group from the Bethel section:

> *Resolved*, 1st. That the ascendency of the hostile, sectional, anti-slavery party, known and recognized as the Black Republican party, is a sufficient cause, and loudly calls for a dissolution of this Union, and the formation of a Southern Confederacy.
>
> *Resolved*, 2d. That the sentiment of our sister Southern States tends to the consummation of the same end; and that we pledge our exertions for the accomplishment of the same grand object.
>
> *Resolved*, 3d. That we endorse the action of our State Legislature in calling a Convention of the people, with a view to the dissolution of the Union.

On December 20, 1860, by a vote of 170 to 0, South Carolina voted for secession. The Union was dissolved.[23]

When war broke out, men from all over the district enthusiastically rushed to join the plethora of forming companies in an effort to support their state and the new Confederacy. Enough men donned the gray to create fourteen infantry companies for service in the Confederate army, as well as a number of cavalry units and artillery batteries. The companies gave themselves colorful names, including: Jenkins' Light Infantry, Whyte Guards, Carolina Rifles, Kings Mountain Guards, Catawba Light Infantry, Bethel Guards, Lacy Guards, Indian Land Guards, Palmer Guards, Campbell Rifles, Turkey Creek Grays, Indian Land Tigers, Mountain Guards, and the Broad River Light Infantry.[24] Unfortunately for so many of these young men, a large number did not return home. York District would suffer during the war the highest death toll of any district in South Carolina.[25]

David Jackson Logan, Confederate Soldier

When his state seceded, David joined the Jasper Light Infantry. Sallie's pregnancy with their second child, however, temporarily kept David home when the "Jaspers" marched off for service in 1861. Soon after the birth of Lula Meacham, he enlisted in the Carolina Rifles, a new company forming in Yorkville. It was formally recognized later in the year as Company F, 17th Regiment, South Carolina Volunteers.[26] The 17th was soon brigaded with three other South Carolina regiments and a legion. Brigadier General Nathan "Shanks" Evans, one of the war's early heroes, was appointed its commander. Unlike most Southern units, Evans' "Tramp" Brigade spent much of the conflict marching and fighting across several theaters on an "as needed" basis. As a result, Logan and his comrades participated in numerous engagements in several states. His experiences in many of the war's most fascinating and yet overlooked operations were unique, and increase the historical value of his correspondence.

One of the most sustaining activities Civil War soldiers enjoyed was letter writing, and David was very prolific in this regard. Early in the war many soldiers obtained a supply of stationery—often embossed with patriotic themes—on which to write their loved ones back home. By 1863, a shortage of paper developed in the South. This dearth became more acute as the war progressed, and soldiers often relied on family members to send them writing materials from home. During the last year and a half of the war, the need for writing paper was so keenly felt that the men "made-do" by writing over previous correspondence, on the back of wall paper, or even on the torn pages of books.

David began writing about his soldiering experiences soon after he and the 17th South Carolina marched off to war. His letters to his beloved Sallie reveal his love of family and offer personal insights into his day-to-day life, as do his candid, revealing, and perceptive diary entries. David also provided reports for his home paper, the *Yorkville Enquirer*. His role as a nineteenth century "war correspondent" allowed the residents of York District to follow in the footsteps of their sons. These informative reports from the field offer a broader overall military discussion of his participation in the war.

CHAPTER 1

"This melancholy affair was the first time our Regt was under fire. They all seemed to acquit themselves bravely."

Palmetto State Soldier

February 1861 – July 1862

One of the first men to answer the clarion call to defend the state of South Carolina was 23 year-old David Jackson Logan of Yorkville. When Abraham Lincoln issued his call for 75,000 militia on April 14, 1861, to put down the rebellion, hundreds of the "Sons of York" flocked to the Courthouse to enroll in the various companies of state militia units then forming. Unwilling to remain behind, Logan initially joined the Jasper Light Infantry, which was destined for service along the South Carolina coast. When his wife Sallie gave birth to their second child (a daughter) shortly thereafter in March, Logan decided to postpone his service and remain with his family.

Logan's sense of honor and duty would not allow him to remain at home while his state was in need of his service. As soon as Sallie was able to care for the two young children, he began planning for a military career. In September 1861, Logan attempted to raise a company of cavalry at Yorkville by running notices in the *Yorkville Enquirer*[1] for "those interested [in forming a cavalry company] are to get in touch with Colonel W. B. Wilson, D. J. Logan, Dr. E. T. Avery, Reuben McConnell, and Captain S. H. Anthony." Failing to obtain the necessary interest, Logan joined a newly forming company of infantry from Yorkville, the "Carolina Rifles." Recognizing his abilities as an efficient and capable leader, Logan was immediately elected to the rank of Second Lieutenant. This company later became Company F, 17th Regiment, South Carolina Volunteers.

The 17th was brigaded with the 18th, 22nd, and 23rd South Carolina Volunteer Infantry, the Holcombe Legion (cavalry), and Boyce's South Carolina Battery of the Macbeth Artillery. The brigade was commanded by a fellow South Carolinian and hero of Manassas, Brig. Gen. Nathan George "Shanks" Evans, and would eventually become known as the "Tramp Brigade."[2] The brigade made up a portion of Brig. Gen. James L. Kemper's Division, which was part of Maj. Gen. James Longstreet's "Right Wing" of the Army of Northern Virginia. The brigade, however, spent much of the war operating as an independent unit (hence its nickname).

Also in early winter 1862, Logan succumbed to one of the "country" fevers. Being found unfit for service, Logan spent several weeks at the Home Hospital and a private home in Charleston before being furloughed home to continue recuperating. Two months later he returned to duty.

While in the Charleston area, the regiment saw its first "action" when they fired on their own men, after which time they settled down into a rather comfortable lifestyle of drill and guard duty. Aside from an occasional skirmish, the regiment saw little heavy action while on the coast. At the battle of Secessionville in June 1862, the regiment served in a reserve position and thus missed the majority of the fighting.

Yorkville, SC[3]
Feby 21st, 1861

Dear Sallie:

I arrived here safely and found all right at home. We have been very busy yesterday and to day. We have sold over $300 worth to day.

Pa has not come yet. I do not now look for him before next Monday or Tuesday. Pink has had a dandy stew and has been enjoying cards hugely. There has been nothing important taken place since you left.

Sallie Logan, a postwar image
Courtesy of Historical Center of York County

I want you to be very careful and dont let that young Logan[4] impose on you. Dont let him treat you as roughly as he did before I left you. I dont know whether I can get down before Sunday or Monday week. If Pa comes Monday or Tuesday I will probably get down before. I will write however for you to send to Guthries[5] for one Monday week. If I am sent down sooner I will be sure to come there unless something happens. If I go down sooner I shall trust to Providence for a conveyance. If anything happens be sure to have a Doctor. I dont mind the Expense as any thing that way. Your parents will of course not see you neglected.

You must not worry yourself in regard to me. I will be here doing all I can for you. If any thing happens, if you possibly can, let me know it as soon as possible. I will send you down some papers perhaps to morrow. Be sure to write to me if it is only a line.

Your husband

David J Logan

Diary of the Military Experiences of
Lieut D. J. Logan, 17th Regt S.C.V.

York District up to the date of 26th of November 1861 had sent into the field a large proportion of her able bodied citizens; but the Capture of Port Royal[6] and the occupation of a part of the soil of our beloved State aroused feelings of the most indignant character in the hearts of every true patriot in the District, and without waiting for any Call from Constituted authorities. There was a rapid rush to arms and in less time than 5 days our 300 stout hearts and strong arms were parting to meet the invader and drive him from South Carolina.

The writer attached himself to a Company raised from various portions of the district (but making the District town the rallying ground). It was without exaggeration or ostentation a noble and gallant looking corps. It received the name "Carolina Rifles" and left its cherished District Nov 26 1861 under the command of W.B. Wilson, Capt; J W Avery, 1st Lt; D J Logan, 2nd Lt; & R H Whisenant, 3rd Lt. The names of the whole will be appended. The first rendezvous was in Columbia where were gathering the injured Carolinians preparing to hurling themselves upon the vandal foes.[7] This company together with "Indian Land Tigers" Capt Meacham and "Lacy Guards" Capt Sadler were mustered into Confederate service by Col Jno S Preston. The Camp at Columbia was called "College Green" (in the rear of our state college) and often won our heart, cheered and Toil sentenced by the presence of the fair daughter of our beautiful Capitol.

The grounds around the city are becoming crowded by the incoming soldiery. It became necessary for us to remove to where more ample room could be found. We accordingly left our delightful Camp and proceded 4 miles down the SCRR to a place called Hamptons race paths on the estate of Mr Frank Hampton of Cola. This Camp was called "Camp Hampton" and soon became much endeared to the soldiers here. The organization of Regts &c began. Capt James of the old US Army soon organized a splendid battalion from Laurens Dist. A full Regt from Greenville Dist was organized by the election of Elfard, Col. These moved at once to the

threatened coast. News of a threatening character began to arrive from the coast
and we soon began to complete our organization, seven companies concentrated
upon Ex Gov J H Means for Col viz three for York, 1 from Lancaster, one from
Chester, one from Barnwell and one from Fairfield. Upon the basis our field
Officers were elected. Their names & position as follows Ex Gov J H Means, Col;
F W McMaster of Cola, Lt Col and Julius Mills of Chester, Major. Just before our
organization the great fire occurred in Charleston which destroyed a considerable
portion of the city.[8] As soon as our Regt was formed we moved to Charleston and
reported to Brig Genl Ripley who assigned us to a position just across the bridge
over the Ashley River near the mouth of Wappoo Cut, and here began the regular
routine of Camp life and here began the operations of the dreaded Monster disease;
Measles, Pneumonia, Fever, and Mumps. Here the writer was stricken with Fever.
He had felt unwell from the morning of the 19th December (the day this Regt
moved from Camp Hampton to Charleston) and having been appointed acting Qr
Master his labors were rather severe. He lingered in the Camp until the evening of
the 21st when he was removed to the "Home Hospital" in the city then under the
patronage of the "Ladies Christian Association" of which Mrs L Chapin was the
President.[9] The Surgeon in charge was Dr Mood. This hospital was situated on
Market Street and had been formerly an institution called the "Sailors home." Here
through the attention of the Surgeons and the unremitting efforts of the ladies every
thing was done for the suffering soldiers that could be done.

Here I must record an act of kindness performed towards me, which I never
wish my self or children to forget. In the darkest hours of Disease Mrs Chapin gave
me the most devoted attention and came in her carriage and conveyed me to her
own house where every thing that could minister to my welfare was performed.
Some few names I must record as endured to my memory by their many kind-
nesses such as Mr S Chapin and lady Miss Georgia Moore, Misses Brodie and the
venerable Mr G M Moore whose voice I often heard in the evening devotions
ascending to Heaven in my behalf. The Christmas and New Year Holidays of AD
1861 & 1862 I spent upon the bed of suffering. I remember the chimes of St
Michaels Church but knew that former gaities were not resumed as this was a dark
epoch in history.

I remained in Charleston three weeks. When I thought I was sufficiently
recovered to reach my home I did so but exposed my self to much and relapsed
from which I was long recovering. I finally proceeded to rejoin my Regt and did so
upon Johns Island. I met the Regt moving from "Camp Craft" near the village of
Rockville. I returned with them to "Camp Pillow" so named because reports had
reached us that we had gained a great victory at Fort Donaldson which finally

turned out the reverse. Camp Pillow was upon the estate of Dr Curtis six miles from Johns Island Ferry about nine miles from Legares village and fourteen from Rockville. A spell of rainy weather set in here and in one week I was sick again and compelled to return home where I remained four weeks then rejoined the Regt at the same Camp.

While at this Camp we could hear the enemys cannon every day as they shelled our pickets at Rockville, Bears Bluff &c. We could see the Camps of the yankees on Edisto Island and their Gunboats in the River and frequently listened to their bands playing old National airs. We then had abjured. We remained at Camp Pillow about three months expecting an attack at any time. The long roll[10] sounded several times but our foes were too wary to venture far enough from water for us to get a "pop" at them. We were greatly annoyed by sand flies, musketoes and Fleas. We found enormous Rattlesnakes plenty on the Island some with as many as 18 rattles and measuring over 7 1/2 feet in length. Several were stuffed and sent up the country by the soldiers. Alligators were plenty and many were killed for their skins. The skin tanned making an elegant shoe. There were also plenty of Deer, Turkeys and some Bear. Capt Walpole of the "Stono Scouts" killed a beautiful Doe one evening upon our parade ground.

The passage of the "Conscription Act"[11] took place while we were here and a reorganization of our Regt was ordered. A large number of the Officers over the age of 35 years with drew from the service & among the privates it was almost unanimous. In our Company only one remained over the age of 35 years. His name was WB Byers of Yorkville. Our Captain being over the age retired from the service. A new election was ordered to take place on the 28th of April on which day 1st Lt JW Avery was elected Capt; 2nd Lt DJ Logan, 1st Lt; Sergt EP Moore, 2nd Lt & Sergt WS Moore, 3rd Lt. Col JH Means & Lt Col FW McMaster were reelected without opposition. Maj Mills was opposed by RS Means and defeated by a majority of 62 votes. The Regt was now in for the war and at the Disposal of the Confederacy. Every thing passed off quietly and peaceably. Here the writer became afflicted with Dysentery and was permitted to return home again. A great favor as Furloughs were hard to get. He remained about ten days and returned much improved.

The Camp at that time (19th May 1862) was becoming very unhealthy and it was deemed prudent to remove so on the 19th of May we struck tents and left Johns Island. We all hoped we might soon have occasion to see it again during the war. Our next Camp was on the C & SRR near Rantowles station. We did not rest here long. The whining of the long roll roused us about Midnight on the 23rd and we Marched to Church flats on the Stono but as we had been treated before we got no fight. We remained at the Bridge on Stono for seven days and nights and then returned to Camp Simons the name of our Camp. Here we rested a day or two and for better health moved our Camp to a place called Ravenal on the same road near Logansville. Here we formed a pleasant Camp and some society. The citizens having altogether removed. This Camp also received the name "Simons." Here we obtained some rest and finding good water, our Regt improved in health rapidly.

The yankees about this time began their reconnaissances about Charleston and a considerable force was sent to take possession of the Rail Road at Pocataligo. We were hastily summoned to march against them. Took the cars, reached Pocataligo but found the yankees had been repulsed and were in retreat.[12] We took after them but after marching a greater part of the night failed to come up with their main body although we passed them closely. We followed them to Port Royal Ferry, fired upon their rear guard, then returned. The march was one of the most fatiguing we have had. We came all the way back to Camp that night having been under arms two days and nights and on the march all the time.

We were rested again for several days when we were ordered to Johns Island it being understood the enemy intended crossing the Island. This time we were absent one week with out tents and most terrible rain the whole time. We had to lie upon the naked ground. We were again unfortunate in not getting a conflict with our enemies but with sadness I relate a dreadful accident that occurred. Our mounted pickets were charged and driven in by about 200 yankee cavalry. A courier brought us the word. We sprang to arms — went off at the Double quick but had not proceeded far when we met our pickets coming like lightning, the yankees close behind with drawn swords. Our men deployed on the sides of the road. Unfortunately our pickets had become divided into 2 squads. The first passed through safely but the 2nd was taken for yankees, fired upon and 15 killed and wounded. Several of our own Regt were wounded. Our field Officers were not at their posts and no command was given. Whether the affair would have been better had they been at their posts we are extremely doubtful. A number of shots were fired at the yankees but whether any were killed or wounded or not we cannot say. The yankees seemed to indicate no intention of crossing Johns Island so we were ordered back to our Camps which was to us a luxurious habitation compared to our bivouack. This melancholy affair was the first time our Regt was under fire. They all seemed determined to acquit themselves bravely.

Camp College Green[13]
Nov 28th 1861

My Dear Wife:

We have all arrived safely and are doing finely. They have a lively time. Quite a number of the ministers hold prayer meetings and the songs of praise ascend together with shouts of laughter & merriment.

I drilled my squad this morning for the first time. I never drilled one before. I felt extremely "squemish," however I got along better than I expected. I thought I should have left home without its affecting me so much, but I was mistaken. It is a severe trial. A large majority of the men here are old men at least middle aged. I have not been out since I came down. I have come off without several things I should have had as I have now ascertained, but will get along finely after awhile. I hope you will be a brave woman and take our separation as one that is necessary to the common welfare of ourselves, our children, and our Country. I know the pleasure it has always given me to know that my ancestors were always willing to rally to the defense of their country and every Southern woman should imitate her spartan sisters in being rather the widows of brave men than the wives of cowards.

I came off with the safe key in my pocket. I hope, however, that Marion got the one above the clock before any inconvenience was created. I shall read your Bible daily and especially on the Sabbath, and will hear Dr. Breakes preach on Sunday.

I did not know how much I loved you and our dear little babies until I came to leave you. I want you all to go and get your pictures taken for my sake and have them sent to me. I want you to write often. You & Bro Marion too. Tell Ben to be a good boy and stay until his brothers come home and then they can get together, for the death of a private soldier, I do assure you, is any thing but pleasant. Standing guard all night in rain & snow would be too much, when Ben could serve himself & country so much better in other circumstances.

Give my love to all my friends. Kiss the babies for me and write soon and send those pictures. I did not get any writing material, ink, or pens before I left. Will you take care of my Gold pen?

In haste, Your husband,

D J Logan

*   *   *

Camp Hampton[14]
Dec 19th 1861

My Dear Wife:

I received yours yesterday arriving at the hands of Mr. Moore. Was very glad to hear that you were all well. You must not think that I will dislike your nonsense. On the contrary, I love to read and I read every thing I get from you. I am faring very well now. That quilt is a very valuable acquisition. It would have been some better if it had been thicker, but I can double it round me. I should like very much to have a small pillow, but no good chance comes to send one. I can do very well. I do not know when we shall leave here. It may be some time yet. I am inclined to think it will. We are having a very pleasant time now. Every one gets along agreeably and I think will continue to do so. I have not written Pa and my Bros. I think I will soon. We are having the most delightful weather now. I wish you could be here to walk with me round the encampment these lovely moonlight nights. Dr. Jordan's lady is in Columbia now. I think you could come down some time. You have not many more children than she has.

We have not engaged a Regt yet. Dont know when we will exactly. Today is the day for a Draft in York Dist. I wonder how they will come out. If we stay here until after Christmas I may get home soon. I dont think we will have a fight any time soon, although the present calm may forbade the coming storm. Tell Johnnie & Lula to be good children. I look at their pictures every night, and it affords me a great chance of pleasure. Give my love to Bro Marion. Tell him to write me soon.

I have been unable to get to Columbia yet. Have not been there since I came back. They keep me busy here as I can be. I think I will write in full to Mr. Wheeler in a day or two. Give my love to all friends and kiss the children for me & write often to me.

Your Husband

D. J. Logan

[January 10, 1862]
From our Correspondent

Dear Enquirer:—Your promised correspondent has finally (through the inter-position of Providence) undertaken to give you a word in regard to the "Carolina Rifles," although you may find in his communication more in regard to himself than the noble company for which he has promised to write.

The "Rifles," after the usual heart-burnings and parting regrets, left their loved homes-town-district and friends, and with as much cheerfulness as was possible under the circumstances, went forth to meet the ruthless invader who had dared to set foot on the soil of their native State.

A pleasant ride brought them to our beautiful capitol, where they were met at the Depot and escorted to their encampment by the "Indian Land Tigers,"[15] an-other noble company from Old York, who had preceded them. Arriving at the camp they found their tents had been pitched by the same generous company, a kindness long to be remembered. The Rifles then opened their provision boxes and charged upon their three days rations for the first time, when, with eating, joking, and preparing their soldier touches, the hour for tattoo soon came round, and then throwing themselves upon their humble beds the first day and night of soldier life was soon passed. The morning dawned, and as soon as all necessary preparations were made, the "Carolina Rifles" were made over to the Southern confederacy, and we now belong to Uncle Jeff and the Confederate States, since which event every-thing has gone on harmoniously and pleasantly.[16]

The continual pouring in of soldiers from the various Districts soon rendered it necessary that we should leave the pleasant and delightful camp at "College Green," and seek one where more ample room could be had. The orders were given, and with feelings of regret we prepared to leave. I say with feelings of regret, for it was so, for we knew that when removed, that our dress parades would become as irksome as our company drills, from the fact that lovely woman would not be present to cheer and urge us on, as was the case every evening at "College Green." But orders must be obeyed. We must leave. The remembrance of the past has much to do with the future. Thus we philosophized. Took heart, and with as good grace as we could muster of a rainy day, took up the line of march to "Camp Hampton," four miles below Columbia, where from 10 o'clock until 4 o'clock p.m., we enjoyed the soldier solace of standing in a continual rain, without shelter of any kind, save the foliage of the long leaf pine. But a brighter day will dawn, the morrow came—with it the sun—with it our wonted cheerfulness, and soon another local attachment sprang up, and "Camp Hampton" seemed the "dearest spot on earth save home."

At Camp Hampton our company improved rapidly in drill; we there heard of the great fire in Charleston, and I must say every one seemed anxious to go at once to the city, as we at first supposed it to be the work of the Yankees. We now began to receive items of threatening news from our coast, and events warned us to organize into a Regiment, and we have been fortunate to secure one by companies voluntarily concentrating, and still more fortunate to secure as our Colonel, Ex Gov. J. H. Means, a man whom we are sure is not after ambition or place, having already reached the summit in our glorious little State, and we all feel from the facts of his past position, and present age, that nought but motives of the purest patriotism have urged him to become our leader; and I was going to say that every man in the Regiment would imbibe the same spirit, and stand or fail by him, but I shall reserve the assertion to be vindicated by our future actions, firmly believing it will be the case. F. W. McMaster, Esq., and Julius Mills were elected Lt. Colonel, and Major respectively; they will make officers highly acceptable, and now have a strong hold upon the feelings of the men composing the Regiment.

Immediately upon our formation into a Regiment, we were ordered to report to General Ripley, in Charleston.[17] An extra train was provided for us, and on the 19th of December, 1861, we left Camp Hampton for the threatened metropolis of our State. We left with mingled feelings of regret and pleasure, regret, that we were leaving many pleasant associations; pleasure, that we were drawing near to that enemy who is seeking to ruin and enslave us.

We reached Charleston just after nightfall, quite a crowd of women, children and old men greeted our arrival with numerous expressions of gratitude. One old lady enquired of us where we were from, the reply was "from the mountains!" She invoked a very pious blessing upon the "men from the mountains," and we passed on. The people of Charleston have the new Freight Depot of the S. C. R. R. fitted up very nicely, and refreshments, such as bread and coffee, prepared for all troops who arrive there, or who may be in the city unable to procure them elsewhere. It is carried on in the best possible style, under the superintendence of Prof. Holmes.

Here your correspondent's intercourse with the 17th regiment, is about to be ended for a while. He had felt unwell on leaving Camp Hampton, and having received an appointment from the Colonel, which required him to exert himself to a considerable degree, when he arrived at Camp Lee, (the new camp of our regiment,) he was completely exhausted, and after "toughing it out" in his tent for two days, the surgeon considered it best to remove to the Home Hospital, an institution directly under the patronage of the ladies of Charleston, or a society of ladies of which Mrs. L. Chapin is President. This hospital is one which is entirely free from all the terrors of the customary hospitals. I had associated in my mind ideas quite different from the reality, as I found it there. The greatest attention is given to providing the best attendants and nurses, while all through the day the ladies are continually going from room to room like ministering angels, and everything a poor soldier could need or wish, for his comfort and health, is provided cheerfully and promptly.

Hundreds of poor soldiers from every point of the compass, will bless the efforts of these noble ladies, and recount their many acts of kindness to succeeding generations. Your correspondent, when he consented to go to the hospital, had no expectation of remaining longer than a day or two, thinking that his case was nothing more than a severe attack of cold; but a slow and continued fever seized him and threatened a very serious termination. It is here that he was made sensible of the existence of true philanthropy of that primeval virtue, which, in this latter day, has degenerated in so great a degree.

When his room became in the least crowded, and at a time when quiet was essentially necessary to a happy termination of his disease, a carriage was brought, and he was conveyed to a pleasant room in a private house, where every attention which could be given or desired by a sick man, was given and granted.

Under such attention and kindness, the fever[18] was soon broken, and the baffled soldier was allowed to walk forth in convalescence. The name of the family to whom I am indebted for so much kindness, I forbear to give, knowing the act was alone prompted by Christian feelings, which with numerous like acts will not go unrewarded hereafter; but will add stars to the crown of rejoicing, when we shall all hear of wars no more.

I must be pardoned, however, for mentioning the names of some who have shown me acts of special kindness, such as Dr. J. R. Mood, Mr. L. Chapin and his estimable lady, Miss Georgia Moore, Miss M. F. Brodie, and numerous others whose names I cannot now recall; but whose faces and kind deeds I shall long remember. To all I would say

"What can I pay thee for this noble usage,
 But grateful praise! As Heaven itself is paid."

Dear Enquirer, I must now bring my hurriedly written letter to a close, and beg pardon for trespassing so much longer on the time of your readers than I intended. I hope soon to be able to rejoin my regiment and assist in expelling from our shores the Yankee pirates.

Yours, L.

There is a gap in Logan's correspondence for more than two months, the result of his having contracted "country" fever (probably typhoid). He recuperated first in the hospital and thereafter at a private home in Charleston, South Carolina, before finally being sent home to York. Logan eventually regained his health and rejoined his regiment along the South Carolina coast, where his correspondence resumes once again.

While Logan was convalescing for his return to duty, important events were unfolding in both major theaters of the war. On February 6, Fort Henry on the Tennessee River fell to Federal forces under the command of Gen. Ulysses S. Grant, while Fort Donelson followed suit ten days later. Less than two weeks prior to Logan's return to his regiment the Confederates lost the Battle of Elkhorn Tavern, or Pea Ridge, a decisive engagement which solidified Federal control over much of Missouri and Northern Arkansas.

In the east, meanwhile, an important naval engagement was waged in Hampton Roads near Norfolk, Virginia, between the ironclads *CSS Virginia* and the *USS Monitor*. The metal-coated behemoths fought to a tactical draw on March 9 in a watershed naval battle that changed the course of sea warfare. A little closer to home, Maj. Gen. Ambrose E. Burnside's Federal forces captured Roanoke Island on the North Carolina coast on February 8. With the fall of Roanoke Island and the subsequent loss of New Bern, North Carolina, the Union effectively controlled the Pamlico Sound and nearly all of eastern North Carolina north of Wilmington.

Camp Pillow
March 27th 1862

My Dear Wife:

I received your letter yesterday and was glad to hear you and the children were well but sorry to hear that you are troubled with blues, I hope you will become in used to the times and have more cheerfulness.

We are having very pleasant weather and I am improving in health and flesh very much. I think if I have no back set, I shall weigh 200 lbs e'er long.

We are all exceedingly quiet here. The yankees seem to be willing to let us alone, or at least we can see no movements indicating an attack. I have been all over this Island pretty much. I was down at Rockville and had the pleasure for the first time to see a yankee army incamped. They seemed to be enjoying themselves very much on Edisto Island.

Our Regt is increasing daily. The health is now pretty good. Some typhoid fever and mumps. Wm Moore is pretty sick in our Company with Flux a little easier to day. W B Byers is getting along very well now. He is sometimes troubled with pain in his back.

Cols Dunovant Jones and Des sausure have assigned their Company uniforms on account of the appointment of S R Jist,[19] Brig Genl over them. I J V McL is quite well, seems to be enjoying himself finely. I find my self somewhat green in Drill but the Col is still a great friend to me and I think I will soon be proficent.

I have never written home yet but I wish you to write and let them know how I am. I will write them soon. I learn that 5th & 6th Regts[20] are gone to Cumberland Gap to be pressed to service 60 or 90 days. So Bro Pink may not be able to get home soon again. We have been defeated at Winchester.[21]

I am enclosing you a check on the Bank of the State for all the pay I have received—1 month & 4 days. I have endorsed the check to your Father and as soon as he goes to town which I hope will be soon after receiving, I wish him to present it to J A Brown agt and draw the money. I wish you to send me $5. or 10 of it by letter as I am out. You can also send me your note for bal if you choose. We can get no Furloughs now and I cant get to the city. I came strait to Camp. Kiss Johnnie & Lula. Tell them I hope to see them again when peace shall smile upon us, or before winter. I have sold my pistol to W B Byers for $30.00. I will send his note by next letter as I have not got it now. Write soon and give me all the news. You may send me the Enquirer occasionally. Send me a box if you can—Pone Bread, a Turkey, Butter, & cc. At morning-noon-& night I think of thee.

Your husband
D J Logan

[March 28, 1862]
From the "Carolina Rifles"

Dear Enquirer:—We send you for publication, at last, the roll of the "Carolina Rifles." This company has been in active service for the past four months, and, although the music from Yankee bands and kettle drums is distinctly heard from the enemy's camps on Edisto Island, yet we have never, up to this time, had the pleasure of an encounter with them. The Federals seem to be particularly cautious in their movements upon our coasts; how long we are to remain inactive we cannot tell, "we know not what a day or an hour may bring forth."

We are encamped on Johns Island, at this writing, having recently returned from Wadmalaw, an island separated from this, by Bohiket Creek, which at low tide we would consider rather a small affair, to give name to an island. Johns Island is separated from the main land by Stono River, (an arm of the sea, of considerable size) sufficient to float a gun boat, at least. We have faith in our defenses at either outlet, however, and sleep soundly after our daily routine of drills, &c.

Our regiment and company have had to encounter the ever to be dreaded enemy disease, and in the names below, to which is attached a star, the reader will see four noble volunteers of this company[22] who have offered their lives upon the altar of their country. Let not their names be forgotten, but let them live in the memories of those who love liberty.

Roll of the Carolina Rifles of the 17th Regiment, S.C.V.

Officers

W. B. Wilson, Captain.
J. W. Avery, 1st Lieutenant.
D. J. Logan, 2nd Lieutenant.
R. H. Whisonant, 3rd Lieutenant.
E. P. Moore, 1st Sergeant.
Perry Moore, 2nd Sergeant.
M. L. Randal, 3rd Sergeant.
E. G. Feemster, 4th Sergeant.
W. S. Moore, 5th Sergeant.
W. A. Moore, 1st Corporal.
W. M. Caldwell, 2nd Corporal.
R. McConnell, 3rd Corporal.
J. L. Moore, 4th Corporal.

Privates

S.H. Anthony,	Jas. Martin
Samuel Beamguard,	Thos. Martin,
Henry Beheeler,	Wm. Martin,
W.T. Beheeler,	Jas. McLean,
A. Beheeler,	R. McLean,
E.H. Bridges	W.H. Mitchel,
J.P. Burns,	Blanton Moore,
W.B. Byers	G.M. Moore,
Noah Bias	G.W. Moore,
R.P. Caldwell,	Geo. Morehouse,
Wash Carroll	J.C. Moser,
Ed. Carson,	W.R. Murphy,
J.P. Cavany,	P.S. Mullinax,
R.L. Cavany,	R. Mulholland,
W.H. Clark,	A. Neeland,
J.B. Collins	Ed. Owens,
W.W. Dameron	R.G. Parker,
J. H. Dixon	W.A. Parker,
Asa Dover	Jas. Plexico,
Felix Dover	J.A. Pollard,
E. J. Downy	R.F. Roberts,
J. W. Downy	Sam'l Roberts,
Wm. Dunovant,	J.L. Rainey,
S. A. Gallaher	R.S. Randal,
James Garvin	Joseph Scates,
O.R. Guntharp	M. Scates,
Jerre Green	Jacob Seapock,
F. Happerfield	Joseph Seapock,
J.J. Hampton	W.B. Sherer,
Robt. Hays	J.M. Sherer,
J.J. Hays	R.S. Stewart,
W.A. Hays	J.M. Sweeny,
Jas. Hetherington	T.S. Tipping,
J.M. Hope	J.A. Wallace,
Dudley Jones	O.L. Wallace,
A.S. Jefferies	John Weaver,
J.C. Kirkpatrick	R.W. Whitesides,
J.G. Latham	J.S. Wilkerson,
J.L. Love	D.C. Williams,
Sam'l Lowry	J.L. Williams,

[List of Privates, continued]

Geo. Wilson
A.L. Byers,
John Goforth,*
J.G. Mullinax,*
Pinckney Wilson.*

W. B. Metts, formerly Orderly Sergeant, is now Commissary of the Regiment.
March 28th 1862.

———

Camp Pillow
April 10th 1862

My Dear Wife:

I received your kind letter this evening. I had began to feel very uneasy. I also received a letter from my father. His family was quite well and in good spirits. They are looking for you to pass most of the summer with them, and I desire that you go up to see them if possible.

We are getting along here very quietly. We could imagine some to day that all was peace if not for the occasional booming of cannons from the yankee ships & batteries. I suppose you have heard of the glorious victory at Shiloh. I trust the tide of war has turned, and that we will not again become vain glorious, and proud, but continue trusting in that from which alone can save us.

Our Campaign will certainly end here in a few weeks and we will be either disbanded or ordered up the Country. J N Withers is Capt of the Jasper Lt Infantry; W B Smith, 1st Lieut; Jos W Carroll, 2nd Lt; James Black, 3rd Lieut. The 16th Regt & 5th Regt have united and made a Regt[23] & Jenkins is Col. York only made up 1 Company.

I wish you to write me, how the people are getting along volunteering. I suppose they will submit to a draft. The only state that has done it.

I sent you a long letter last week which I wish you to file away safely. If you have not received it let me know immediately.[24] You seem to have taken my jest about the "note" in cold earnest. I hope you will keep your temper as I seldom ever jest. I confide all such matters to you and if I thought you would do any thing wrong or imprudent I should certainly not trust them to you. If you can buy me any Hams cheap as 20 or 25 cts buy some and send them to me care of Graesur & Smith, Charleston S.C. Hams brought 72 cts in the city last week. We are hard run for some thing to eat now. Our men are living on nothing but Rice, scarcely no meat. I have attended preaching regularly ever since I came down. Every thing moves along harmoniously & pleasantly in our Regt. It is false about Conl Means having resigned. I do not suppose he has ever dreamed of it. I look at yours & the childrens pictures daily and think of you. I wish the war was over, but I would be dissatisfied any where else than in the service of my Country [when it] is in so much danger. I suppose Eugene enjoyed himself very much while up. The returned volunteers are likely to be Lions when at home. Bro Ben was well on the 26th prior. If you make me a box send a statement of about what worth. Dont cook the hams if you get them. You might send a good shoulder or so. If your Father has no need of Joe I will take him, and board & clothe him, so he need not hunt any one else. Price has gained a victory in Missouri also.[25] The war I began to hope will soon end. The Kentucky Thiefs are deserting Old Abraham. May the day soon come.

If you see Marion question him about the business of the store and so forth; also any one else. Ascertain if you can, how things are getting on, and write me.

The women will now began to have to look after their husbands interests if the war continues. I think our sales will decline soon but dont mention it. Kiss John & Lula for me. Tell them I hope to see them again and that I wish them to be good children. Give my respects to your parents and accept a husbands appreciation.

David J Logan

*   *   *

Johns Island S C
April 17th 1862

My Dear Wife:

I received your Kind letter Monday last. Was glad to see that you were in better spirits than when you wrote before. I am still improving in weight and have not been sick a day since I came down. I continue to increase in a knowledge of military also. I think I shall be very proficient soon. I get along much better than I expected. There is some effort being made to remove the word Local in our service. Wilson approves it. He is determined not to fight out side the state. One S C Regt was taken to Augusta on its way to Cornirth. When it got there it refused to leave the state. They teligraphed Adj Genl & Gov. They ordered them to be immediately arrested as traitors of the "deepest dye." This was the 19th Regt. Col Morquny.[26] They all finally went but 10, 5 of whom are in jail at Columbia.

Our Virginia boys are pressed into the service for ninety days. Our water does very well yet, but we are looking for single wells soon. Sand flies are awful.

This country is almost like it was when first discovered. There are numbers of deers. Any quantity of Wild Turkeys, Raccoons, and every other kind of game belonging to the climate. There is quite a stir in Camp this morning. One of our men has killed a monster Rattlesnake nearly 6 feet long, has 10 Rattles and 1 Button. It beats any thing I ever seen in point of size out side of a show. Venomous insects and reptiles abound here in great quantities. In fact this is not unlike the negro's native Africa.

You say you wish some snuff. I wish you to understand that I have had habit enough for the whole family and I shall make no promises about not telling the old folks; &c &c. I would like so much to see you all, but it is no use talking or thinking about such things as that now. If we are stationed at Sullivans Island I shall expect you to pass part of the summer or Fall in the City or Island, or if we are at Summerville the same in Summerville. We draw our next pay 1st May. I will send check for amt. We will draw 2 months then. Write me soon and at length. I have been very busy here drilling and reading and talking. W B Byers is much better. He says about well.

I would like to see that draft operating on some of the b'hoys up the country. Give my love to Mr & Mrs Rowell and all the friends &c. The Emancipation Act[27] has passed Congress. Kiss the Children for me and write at length.

Your husband

D J Logan

A substantial gap in the Logan–17th South Carolina paper trail exists during this period (April 18 through May 31, 1862). The utter lack of any correspondence or writings may have been due to a series of important events taking place within the region. On May 13, the steamer *Planter* was hijacked by several members of her black crew, who took her out of the harbor and surrendered the ship to Union blockaders. Robert Smalls, the *Planter's* pilot, revealed details about the Confederate defenses—including that much of the infantry had been removed to Tennessee and Virginia—that were unknown to the Federals. This intelligence coup, coupled with the additional knowledge that Coles Island and its batteries had been abandoned, exposed the precarious defensive state of Charleston.

As a result. Admiral Samuel Du Pont, commander of the South Atlantic Blockading Squadron, decided to test the Southern defenses by launching a series of probing actions to test this latest intelligence. On the 20th through the 22nd of April there was skirmishing on Coles, Battery, and John's Islands. This was followed on the 25th by skirmishing between James and Dixon's Islands. On the 29th, a much larger Union force marched inland and was on the verge of cutting the logistically significant Charleston and Savannah Railroad at Pocotaligo when sudden and stubborn Confederate resistence forced the Federals to withdraw.

While the Confederates debated where the next likely enemy threat would land and how to best deal with it, the Federals prepared for a direct move against Charleston with a thrust up James Island at Secessionville.[28]

From the Coast
Camp Simons, June 1st, 1862

Dear Enquirer:—Thinking some of your readers would like to hear from the 17th Regiment, I take an idle moment to give you a few items. We have at last been removed from John's Island, and after several counter marchings are now located near a little village on the Charleston and Savannah Rail Road, called "Ravenel." We are highly pleased with our present location; we have excellent water and unlike our old Island camp we have an occasional view of home scenes, (as many families are still residing near our camp.) It is decidedly refreshing and pleasurable to behold the joyous faces of children, and the lovely smiles of our fair country women, no one can appreciate the emotions produced unless they had been confined to an uninhabited Island as lonely as was our regiment. The health of our regiment is steadily improving, and if we continue long in our present camp, we will soon appear once more with full ranks.

Our Yankee friends, after a long silence, have again commenced operations on our coast; we have had two "long rolls" since we left the Island. My principal object in this letter will be to give you an account of our last operations: On the morning of the 29th ultimo, the Yankees landed at Port Royal Ferry, and took up line of march directly towards Pocotaligo station, on the Charleston and Savannah Rail Road. Our forces had all been removed from that point, with the exception of two companies of cavalry. The enemy had doubtless received information from the negroes escaping to them. At half past 2 o'clock, p. m. we received orders to march immediately to meet the enemy. A train brought the order, and without time to prepare a mouthful to eat, we were to be on the road, with the uncertainty of getting any thing at all for several days; but notwithstanding our men were ready to start, in 20 minutes, and anxious to be on the way.

At half past 3 o'clock we were on the road, as fast as steam could carry us. We reached Pocotaligo station just as the sun was setting, and found that the enemy had actually advanced as far as the causeway between "Old Pocotaligo" and the station, but had there been repulsed by our cavalry. A pretty sharp conflict had been kept up for several miles between our men and the enemy before they were repulsed. The force by three prisoners taken, and the observation of our men, was between 12 and 1400 men. In the fight along the causeway we lost two killed and several wounded. The Yankees loss was 3 killed and six wounded. As soon as we could get out of the cars we were ordered to push forward after the enemy, and attack them as soon as possible. We set forward in the best of spirits in pursuit of them. The Cavalry (5 companies) 2 companies of Infantry, and one of Artillery; the Beaufort [Artillery] had already gone in pursuit. We overtook them seven miles from the Station; our regiment was then halted, and arrangements were then made to attack them at three o'clock in the morning, they then being encamped within a mile and a half of us, at a place called Gardner's Corner. Two Compainies of our regiment were then detached to support a section of the Beaufort Artillery. Companies A & F were detailed, and Capt. Avery placed in command of the whole. Three companies were to move by a circuitous route, and come in the rear of the enemy, as they should have to pass to Port Royal Ferry. The other troops bivouacked until

3 o'clock, a. m. As your correspondent was with the detachment, he will speak of the route taken by it.

The road was principally through a densely wooded country, with all the superfluity of undergrowth common to the low country, and we knew not at what moment we might come across the enemy as we have not a single picket on before us. The night was so dark you could not see your hand before you, and our near proximity to them required us to preserve the utmose silence. It was certainly one of the most romantic marches your Correspondent has ever taken; the scream of the night birds, the multitudious frogs—the silent tramp—the thick darkness, all conspired with the contemplated death-struggle of the morrow to impress upon each one peculiar feelings of awe.

An incident served to increase it: As we were passing through a deep wood, supposed to be in less than 1 mile of the enemy, our advance came upon a horse grazing by the roadside, with sword, saddle and bridle all on him. We knew that no pickets were on the road from our men, and the horse with accouterments certainly indicated a rider, whether he was a Yankee picket who had fled without his horse or one of our town troopers we could not tell. We took the horse, however, sent forward pickets to scour the road, and marched on. We halted at a bridge and waited for the attack to be made by our troops; but unfortunately the enemy either ascertained that we were in force, or expected it, and left their camp between 12 M. and 1 p. m., and hurried towards the Ferry. The consequence was they had too good a start for us. Had we all pushed on and attacked them in the night we should certainly have whipped them easily, but our scouts were too tardy. As it was, we renewed the pursuit and rejoined our regiment where the Yankees had stopped in the night, and near this place we obtained the sequel to the mystery of our captured horse. On the side of the road (shot through the heart) lay the dead body of Dr. Godard, member of the Rutledge Riflemen. He had been to the Station with a dispatch to Colonel Walker, the commander of our expedition, and had taken the wrong road and was fired upon and killed by a Yankee picket stationed at the forkes of the road. As our men filed past his dead body, each quickened his step and grasped tighter his weapons. We pushed forward rapidly. Our scout soon reported the enemy only a few hundred yards before us, when our rifle companies and the cavalry were thrown forward to scour the woods and rouse the enemy. But whether the scouts were deceived, or a small detachment of the enemy were kept in the rear to cover their retreat, we are unable to say; but with the utmost exertion, we did not come up with them until they had taken their boats at the Ferry, and were making towards Beaufort. Our artillery unlimbered at the river, and sent the Yankee rear guard, "on the hills and far away" in double quick time. We fired on them as long as we could, and then, in our turn, made for Pocotaligo, which we reached before sun set, having marched upwards of thirty miles with nothing to eat, and without water fit to drink.

Our men were as cool as I ever could expect to see them. They were expecting the fight every minute, and I assert positively the men seemed anxious for the conflict, and chagrined when they found the Yankees had "heeled it" out of the way. Our men all stood the march finely; but 22 miles in a burning sun is no "child's play" I assure you. We have many a blistered foot in camp now, but our appetites are all good. I have troubled you too long and I will close abruptly, hoping the next time we have a "Yankee chase" we can report some good execution done by the 17th Regiment. The Yankees will never be able to earn their salt, on the coast of South Carolina.

Yours, L.

———

Church Flats
June 6th 1862

My Dear Wife:

I drop you this note that you may not be uneasy about me. The yankees have commenced their ground movements against Charleston. We were out all last week and every day this week. We have driven the enemy to his Gun boats once on Johns Island and we are nose before him daring him to reach Charleston. In this way we may have a big fight.

I am in the best health and spirits. I hope none of my friends are killed at Chickahominy.[29] Write soon.

Your husband
D J Logan

Kiss the Children for me.

*   *   *

Camp Simons
St Johns Colleton [undated]

My Dear Wife:

I have arrived safely in Camp and have enjoyed very good health ever since, my arrival. I am gradually improving. You will see that we have moved. We are now on the main land. We left Johns Island last Monday. We marched about 12 miles. I walked and stood it finely. We are now encamped in a very pretty place 12 miles from Charleston. We expect to move however tomorrow again to a place near Logansville, where I expect to find some people who I intend to claim Kin with if I can make it add to comfort &c.

The yankees are now on Johns Island. Since we left they have possession of Lagreeville and this morning at 1 o clock A. M. we were aroused again by the beating of the "long roll"; but as usual the yankees put back and we missed the chance for a fight. They will now take full possession of Johns Island as we have left it. It seems strange they did not attempt to take it before as they passed up the River the next day after we left. Our Batteries at Colles Island and Battery Island were abandoned and the guns all taken to Charleston. So if the yankees intend to take Charleston soon they must get to work immediately. We were under orders to march to Virginia when I got to Camp but Evans dont want to lose us, and wont let Genl Ripley have us if he can help it. So I fear we will have to stay here for sometime and perhaps not get to Va at all. Our Regt is improving in health. The men are all doing much better than I expected. I found no difficulty in getting to Camp at all and all was right with the Col.

I showed the vial of stuff I took with me to several salt manufacturers and others in Charleston and they all say it is undoubtedly "salt" and should be worked.[30] They think there must be a spring near the place. I would like for you to make the experiment with it. Take the earth and put it in a hopper and run water through it and then boil it and if a well could be dug about the place you could tell whether the water was such or not. Make a trial of it and wait and see what the result will be. I can buy salt at $25.00 in Charleston. I intend to send up 5 sacks when Uncle Henry can get his. I had to stay in the city on Saturday. I think Mr Wheeler is making us some money at the store from appearances. I staid all night with them. EP Moore got to Camp yesterday. R McConnell has gone home. I dont think he will stand it. WB Byers is in good health now. Uncle Jeff also is getting over the mumps finely. If you can make salt now you will be doing a cash business. I shall be anxious to hear of your sucess.

The news from the war I think is more favorable now than ever. Direct your letters to Rantowles station or Logansville via Charleston S.C. and I will get them. Kiss the dear little children for me and tell Johnnie I have had no chance to "Butt" a yankee yet. Write me a long letter and give all the items afloat. I learn that York is filling up very fast with down country people.[31] If we stay here long I may wish you to trouble with another box. I enclose the Recpt for our house rent which please file away and send me Byers Note as I for got it. I am strong in the hope we will yet have a better time. <u>Sil desperandum</u>.[32]

Affectionably Your husband

David J Logan

———————

Matters were much more precarious for Charleston and the defending Southerners than Logan imagined. Federal theater commander Maj. Gen. David Hunter was slowly but inexorably moving forward his plan to invade James Island and assault up the strip of land toward the city. On the morning of June 10 a large force of Unionists moved up the Stono River and landed near Grimball's Plantation. A sharp engagement ensued which threw back several attacking Confederate regiments. More Yankee troops poured ashore unmolested.

———————

Camp Simons
June 11th 1862

My Dear Wife:

I have arrived safely back to Camp again after one of the most fatiguing and disagreeable marches that has ever been performed on this coast. We got back to camp last night after having been gone 8 days. We bivouacked at night upon the damp ground, the sky our only covering and that sending down almost continually torrents of rain. It is perfectly useless for me to undertake to give you an account of all that has taken place. I should have to write pages. I may write it out for the paper. Then you will see it. Suffice it now, that we marched 6 times to meet the enemy and only met him once, when unfortunately our own men were mixed with the yankee cavalry and we killed and wounded 13 of our own men.

The yankees consisted of two companies of cavalry and had driven in our pickets and seemed determined to cut them down. We had just heard that the yankees were coming and only a part of the Regt had filed into the road. Just like lighting here came 15 horsemen with whips and spurs crying out "the yankees are behind us. Get ready and fire." Our men immediately fell into the bushes on the road side and here came another part of 15 horsemen hard as their horses could take them. I knew them to be our pickets but a great many did not and commenced the fire on them and in spite of all that could be done 13 were killed and wounded, several of our own Regt by the cross fire. I never saw saddles emptied so fast in my life and I was almost phasied to see it when I knew them to be our own men. I shouted to stop firing but I had just as well have shouted to the wind. The last party of our pickets was in command of Lt Crawford who passed the murderous gauntlet without a scratch. I saw him as he passed. He threw him self flat upon his horse and passed like lighting. The yankees were only about 30 steps behind him with drawn swords but when we commenced firing they drew up fired a volley at us and received one from us and then beat a hasty retreat. 5 men were mortally wounded and are now dead (of our cavalry pickets). Mr J L Love of our Company was severely wounded in the back but is doing well. Lieut Stephenson, Lieut Carlisle and Mr Randoll of the "Palmettoes"[33] from Charles[ton] were wounded. Stephenson & Randoll badly. A number of the cavalry were wounded besides those now dead but none thought dangerously. It is a very sad affair indeed but could not have been avoided by the best of troops. The enemy charging up among our own troops. I wonder when I think of it, how I escaped being shot as we were exposed to 3 fires and I was near to our man Love who was shot. I never once thought of being shot however during the whole action and was as perfectly cool and collected as I ever was in my life. Our Company every one acted nobly. Not one tried to get out of the way although this cannot be said of all the companies. We received the need of praise from the Officers for being the first Company formed in line of battle. We took the Colors and the other companies formed on us. We captured one yankee killed 1 horse and think we killed and wounded several others.

We have had very bad luck during the week past. Besides the fatal accident Capt Holly dropped dead without a struggle or a moment's reflection. He was Officer of the day and the Officer of the Guard asked him when they would post the guard. He remarked "in about 1/2 an hour" and dropped dead.

A Mr Bolezn of Witherspoons Company died just as suddenly. A young Mr Coleman from Fairfield was drowned in the Stono. We hope our luck may turn however soon. We have prevented the enemy from crossing Johns Island and dared him time and again to fight us. My health all through this dreadful march seemed to improve and I think I stand it better than any one else. I am feeling very well now. Have had a good Supper and Breakfast. We are expecting a fight on James Island. An artillery fight[34] is going on every day.

The grand crisis for Charleston is at hand. We will know very soon whether it will stand or fall. The enemy are thundering at its doors.

Logan was not exaggerating. The "grand crisis" erupted on the early morning of June 16 when Col. Henry Benham, in direct violation of General Hunter's orders, launched a vigorous attack against the Confederate Tower Battery position at Secessionville. The focus of Benham's pre-dawn thrust was Fort Lamar, a strong earthen fortification that guarded a direct approach to Charleston. After heavy fighting and a pitched struggle on the fort's ramparts, the Federals were driven back in confusion. The action was significant, for a Southern defeat would have provided the Federals with a water route into Charleston Harbor, bypassing Morris Island and Fort Sumter. The 17th South Carolina Infantry did not participate in the action.

Logan's casual reference in his June 21st letter to the Battle of Secessionville—the largest land battle in South Carolina's history—implies that he had already informed Sallie of the event in a piece of correspondence that has not survived.

Camp Simons
June 21st 1862

My Dear Wife:

I drop you a line this morning. I have nothing of interest to write. Every thing has been remarkably quiet hear since the battle of last Monday.

The yankees were so sadly disappointed. They are very cautious since. I hear an occasional cannon this morning, however. I look for the crisis here most any moment now. I feel that Charleston will be <u>hard to take now</u> and unless they come soon with tremendeous force I dont believe they will take it. Our Regt is very healthy now. We have several cases of Country fever.[35] A S Jefferies has been very bad off but is better we think this morning. My health has been very good since I came down and while on the march all the time I seemed to feel better than usual. We have all been accustomed to earth for a head & the sky for a covering for some time. I should like very much to be up the Country now to get cherries, plums &c, but cant well leave now. I think perhaps I may get up in time for some peaches & apples. Have you a "water melon patch?"

I hope Johnnie may not be badly poisoned. He must be careful about going into the dew. The news from Richmond & "Stonewall" seems to be improving. I hope the scales may turn soon and give us victory and independence. We all begin to believe as has always been believed although we may get badly deceived yet.

I want you to send 1st chance to the Grocery & buy me 10 ct coffee. Keep it at home until you can have a chance to send me some. There is none in the city now, and it is very hard to be without in Camp, where we are liable to get wet so often. I am troubled now with a very sore tongue & mouth.[36] It seems to be a Kind of an epidemic. Do you ever hear from Ben or Pink. The Conscripts are ordered down now. We are to send officers to Columbia soon to bring them to our Regt. It would certainly be very humiliating to any man to be dragged down and sent to any place he may be needed. We want 50 men more. I hope or wish the Col will send me as one of the officers to bring them down. I might get up home then.

I want you to write me long letters and give me news, prospect of crops & cc. I want you to get up to N.C. soon as you can, although I suppose transportation will be scarce until after crops are laid by. I know they will be so glad to see you, and next to getting up myself I want you and the children to go. Farm property about York has taken a sudden rise since the war. I guess a great many of the down Country people will be willing to live in the back woods now. I learn it is crowded from all quarters. My love to all. Kiss the children for me. I long to see you all, but dont wish to neglect the Call of my Country.

Yours

D.J. Logan

*   *   *

Camp Simons
June 28th 1862

My Dear Wife:

I take my pen this morning to drop a line to let you know I am still getting along finely in the way of health, although I am a little troubled with Diarhea. We have had very quiet times here since I wrote you last, no alarms or cannonading. The army on both sides seem to be very busy in preparations, throwing up entrenchments and preparing for a dreadful struggle. The health of our Regt is much better than I expected. We have some cases of Fever but very few deaths. I have received another letter from Pa. They are all well and he stated that he intended to go down or send down after you. I hope you will be able to get up there soon with the children.

Capt Metts came down the other day from Yorkville. Mr Meacham told him that he had sold out the store to Mr Wheeler. I suppose they have taken the stock this week. There has been considerable stealing in York lately. The Grocery was broken into and some salt &c was stolen. I am very glad the concern is off my hands now. I should have liked very much to have been present when the stock was taken, but I hope and think they will do me right. If there is any examinations to be made I want you & Pa to look over the matters. They will be able to send me a statement. However pay up all I owe Mr Wheeler. I think the stock on hand will. I should have written to you twice this week but had nothing of any interest to write. I would like for you if you can to knit me a nice pair of cotton gloves as light as you can make them. You can perhaps send them by W A Moore or A S Jefferys. I know you can by Jefferys as he will be home nearly a month from now. I think you dont write more than one letter a week now. If any thing important happens I shall write you twice a week if can get to office. If every thing is quiet I will only write once a week. We do not know how long we are to remain here. I am anxious to get away. The weather is entirely too warm. I begin to be very anxious to see you all again, but our country is in danger and we must stand it the best we can. I want you to write long letters. Give all the little items of news you can pick up. You can tell Mr Rowell I expect I have bought 10 sheep, if I can get them. I will have them driven down. I am getting them up on Kings Creek. Give my love to all the friends & neighbors. We have just heard that the great fight has commenced at Richmond.[37]

May God give us the victory. Kiss the children for me. Tell them to be good and they shall go to N.C. My best love to your Father & Mother.

Your husband

D J Logan

P.S. I send you a ring. You can send me my <u>hair ring</u>.

Camp Simmons,
St. Paul's Parish, June 28, 1862

Dear Enquirer:—We send you the roll of the "Carolina Rifles," as they now stand, reorganized for the war.[38] We have no stirring news to write you, but are in expectation of warm work at any moment, as the enemy, from best accounts, are making great preparation for the reduction of our metropolis.[39] We await their onset with confidence in our ability to maintain our position.

Yours, L.

OFFICERS

J.W. Avery, captain; D.J. Logan, 1st lieutenant; E. P. Moore, 2nd lieutenant; W. S. Moore, 3d lieutenant; O. R. Guntharp, 1st sergeant; J. A. Wallace, 2nd sergeant; Perry Martin, 3d sergeant; J. P. Caveny, 4th sergeant; Wm. Dunnovant, 5th sergeant; W. H. Mitchell, 1st corporal; G. W. Moore, 2nd corporal; F. Happerfield, 3d corporal; Robert Hayes, 4th corporal.

PRIVATES

Henry Boheler, Andrew Boheler, W.T. Boheler, E.H. Bridges, J.P. Burns, W.B. Byers, R.T. Caldwell, W. Carroll, Thomas Carroll, Edward Carson, J.B. Collins, R.L. Caveny, W.H. Clark, W.W. Dameron, J.W.Y. Dickson, Asa C. Dover, Felix Dover, E.J. Downy, S.A. Gallaher, James Garvin, J.J. Hays, W.A. Hays, James Hetherington, J.M. Hope, A.S. Jefferies, J.C. Kirkpatrick, J.G. Latham, James Martin, Thomas Martin, William Martin, James McLane, Robert. McLane, Blanton Moore, G.M. Moore, George Morehouse, J.C. Moser, W.R. Murphy, R. Mulholland, Edward Owens, R.G. Parker, W.A. Parker, James Plexico, J.L. Plexico, J.A. Pollard, R.F. Roberts, Samuel Roberts, J.L. Rainey, R.S. Randall, M.L. Randall,

Joseph Scates, Jacob Seapoch, Joseph Seapoch, W.B. Sherrer, J.M. Sherer, R.S. Stewart, T.S. Tipping, O.L. Wallace, John Weaver, W.R. Whitesides, J.S. Wilkerson, D.C. Williams, J.L. Williams, R. McConnell, Wm. M. Caldwell, C.F. Smith.

Since the reorganization, the following members of the company have been appointed to positions in the regiment, William Caldwell, Wagon Master; W. B. Byers, Ord. Sgt; A.S. Jefferies, D.C. Williams, Assistant Commissaries; J.P. Burns, W. B. Sherrer, J. M. Sherrer, J. G. Parker, George Morehouse, Regimental Band.

Diary of David Jackson Logan

Camp Simons St Pauls Parish, SC.

July 1: This morning we were all aroused by the most rapid and hardy discharges of Artillery in the direction of Charleston. It turns out to be an ovation in honor of the great battle of "Richmond"[40] of which we understand our forces have gained a glorious victory taking thousands of prisoners and routing Genl McClellan in every quarter, driving him in a word into the James River.

Our Col has suspended the usual drills in consequence. I am suffering some what from Dysentery. May God grant that we are triumphant at Richmond.

July 2: No news nor event of any importance has taken place to day. We commenced keeping up camp fires for the first time tonight all round the camp to prevent Malaria from inflicting the Camp. The fight at Richmond is still progressing in our favor. Several thunder clouds have passed over the Camp.

July 3: To day we have been designated as one of four companies from this Regt to go upon an expedition against the enemy on Edisto Island. Capt Avery having gone home to day I am in command of the company and am to lead it in the expedition. Our Genl commenced giving well Furloughs to day. The great battle of Richmond still progressing.

Camp Simons
July 3rd 1862

My Dear Wife:

I have barely time to drop you a note, as Capt Avery is going home on account of sickness. I have been suffering a little from Dysentry but feel better to day. We are all very quiet here. Nothing having been done by the yankees towards an attack. I know you have heard of the great battle of Richmond. We should all feel very thankful. I hope a better day may be dawning. I feel great uneasiness to hear from my Bros as I see their Brigade was in the battle.[41] May God have preserved their lives. If you hear from them write me at once as I may not hear.

I will have charge of the Company as our Capt is sick. I agree with you in regard to "Jno Starr." I was very wrong in sending home my old Jasper pants.[42] I am nearly out of pants. These summer ones wont do for Camp. I would be glad if you would send me those pants, the Dress A'ebe ones by Capt Avery or A S J.[43] Our Regt is in very good health now. I hope we will get Furloughs soon. I see Capt Wilson has accepted the appointment of enrolling Officer. I think he has made another bad lick. They will all say "you had better go your self." You will see a Roll of our Company in next York paper. I want you to preserve the Copy.

Negroes &c, Confederate bonds & cotton have all jumped up tremendously in Charleston since the Great fight.[44] I believe I wrote you before that we had sold the Grocery. I have not heard from the taking stock. I suppose it has been done. You say the wheat is not good. How much do you think you have made? Uncle Jeff is quite well. I dont think he knows Aunt Jane is unwell. I have never told him. You know I suppose that the yankees were in possession of Desota, Tippah & all the Counties where our Kins folk are in Miss. I will not be able to get up to Cola after Conscripts so I will have to depend on a Furlough to see you all again. Write me the news items. I will endeavor to write more again. Kiss the Children for me & my love to your parents & friends.

Yours

D. J. Logan

P.S. I have sent home by Capt Avery 2 Flannel shirts, 1 pr Drawers, scarf, vest, socks, &c. They will be sent to WP McFaddens[45] where you can get them. I leave for Adams Run[46] this Morning in a Sulkey.[47] Will be back this evening. Expect a pleasant ride if I dont get wet.

Diary of David Jackson Logan

July 4: To day we have passed without Drilling, it having been set apart for thanks giving and praise. This evening we are ordered to march at 7 o clock AM tomorrow on the expedition to Edisto.

July 5: This morning at 7 o clock AM we marched to Adams Run on expedition mentioned above. The forming companies were chosen, Co A Capt Culp, Co C Capt Witherspoon, Co E Lieut Logan Cmdy and Co K Capt Mills. We reached Adams Run but found the boats intended for our expedition not quite ready. We have therefore returned to our Camp to remain until Monday or whenever the Genl may be ready for us. The men were all in good spirits. We learn this evening of the victory of Hindman over Curtis in Arkansas[48] and the probable recognition of our Confederacy by France & England.[49] We are all very much fatigued with our march but feel like sleeping soundly.

July 6: Sunday, Our chaplain Mr Buist preached to a crowded house in the little church of "Ravenal." We hear now of our victories near Richmond.[50] I also hear that my uncle Andrew Jackson Col of the 5th Regt S.C.V. has his arm shot off and a minnie ball through his thigh. I am very fearful his wound will be mortal.

July 7: We started this morning for Edisto. Our Cols sent wagons to haul us to Adams Run. We had only proceeded a short distance however before we met a courier with orders for the whole Regt. We dismounted from our "carriages" and proceeded on foot. We halted at the "Run" and were there joined by the whole Regt. We remained until 4 o clock PM and then made for the crossing at Pine berry. The troops compossing the expedition were the Holcombe Legion, Nelsons Battalion, Jenkins Rebel troop, and our Regt. We reached the crossing about dark and were soon over and on Jehossee Island. The river crossed was the "Dawho." The Legion crossed first, Nelsons Bat next and Capt Culps, Capt Avery & Capt Stules Cmpy next. The troops had to march in single file along the Rice dams and the companies necessarily extended to a great distance. The narrow path was about 2 miles in length before any other company could cross except those mentioned. It was ascertained that nine Gunboats were lying at White point just above us and would probably cut us off and every thing seemed to indicate that the enemy was on the lookout for us. The remainder of the Regt was then detained but no orders reached the other troops until we had arrived at our places of Rendezvous, which was Gov Aikens plantation. He owns the whole of Jehosse Island and about 1100 negroes. His dwellings and negro quarters certainly exceed any thing in neatness and beauty I have ever seen. I was struck with one thing on this Island. I never saw such luxurious grass in my life. We had only got to our stopping place before a courier in post haste came, ordering us off the Island. We were soon on the narrow track again and after dreadful delay we were across the river again at three o clock in the morning as we have been disappointed again. No fight but all the labor attend with upon one. We stopped marching about half past 4 o clock A.M. having marched about 29 miles that day & night. The men were nearly worn out.

July 8: We returned to Camp to day nearly worn out. I stopped at Adams Run and received a very excellent breakfast at the Quarters of Lt G W Melton of the "Congaree Cavaliers," H.L. The Coffee was most excellent. I am disgusted with a number of field Officers. They seem to know nor care nothing for any thing except turning up their elbows & pouring down whiskey.

July 9: We have rested in Camp all day & begin to feel right. Had more peaches than we could eat to day.

July 10: Were all very quiet when up dashed a courier with orders from Genl Evans for us to leave at once for Pocataligo as the enemy had landed in force and were attacking our forces. We were on the way in a few minutes. Reached the place about dark, found the enemy had returned to their boats. We bivouacked all night on the ground.[51]

July 11: We remained loafing about the Depot at Pocataligo all day. Were disappointed in not getting a train in time. It did not come until 2 oclock AM.

July 12: We arrived at Camp about Sunrise very much worn and in need of sleep. I received the sad intelligence of the dreadful wound of my much loved and brave brother Ben F Logan Orderly Sergt in the Cleveland Guards 12th Regt N.C.V. I have not heard when he was wounded but suppose it was in the first encounters of the Battle of Richmond. He is shot through the lungs and I much fear is mortally wounded. The intelligence comes in a letter from EA Beatty to Sergt Martin of my Company. Orders were read this evening retaining all over 35 & under 18 years in service for 7 months. I was Officer of the Day to day. A position seldom conferred upon a Lieutenant.

July 13: I heard two good sermons to day from our Chaplain. Every thing quiet in Camp. Weather good.

July 14: No news to day. We learn that foreign powers are manifesting more interest in our struggle than heretofore. We begin to look for intervention.

July 15: Nothing important to day. Had a splendid dinner of Green Corn, apple pie, ochra soup, & water melons for which SC Lowery went to Johns Island, the plantations on the Island having been deserted. I heard to day in a letter from Maj Borders that my Bro is dead. Still have a hope it is untrue. Cant hear from wife & parents by letter.

July 16: In a letter from EG Beatty I learn that my bro Marion was also wounded in the face at Battle of Richmond. My Bro Ben not dead when he last heard. All quiet to day. Got more melons &c.

July 17: Nothing important took place to day. Lieut EP Moore got a furlough and leaves for home tomorrow. We had the best dinner to day we have had since in service.

July 18: To day we have been ordered to Virginia. We start Sunday morning. Genl Evans is to be our Brigade Commander.

———————

Camp Simmons
July 18th 1862

My Dear Wife:

We are ordered to Virginia and leave Sunday. We will be in Chester Monday or Tuesday. I don't know whether I can get to see you or not. If you can come to Chester, come, and bring me a pair pants. We have had the order now suddenly. I am feeling very well. I shall perhaps have a chance to avenge the blood of my brothers or shed my own.

Your husband,

D J Logan

Let E M Byers know if you can. Kiss the children for me.

———————

July 19: We did not start this morning. We Drew our pay and had to go to Adams Run. Qr Master absent.

*   *   *

A photograph of a July 27, 1862, letter from
David Jackson Logan to his wife, Sallie.

Courtesy of the Historical Center of York County

"I was entirely paralyzed in my right side and did not know but that the ball had passed directly through me."

Second Manassas

July – September 1862

The few months covered in this chapter of David Jackson Logan's life were of great import to the South Carolinian and his family. It began with news that Logan's 17th South Carolina, together with the balance of the brigade, would be transferred to Virginia. The news was greated with some excitement, for the journey promised a joyful reunion with families and friends in York County and the surrounding areas. Confederate authorities, however, were leery about the men traveling through their home areas. Fearing mass desertions, Richmond officials sent them north via another route. Instead of following the South Carolina Railroad through Columbia and Chester, the soldiers were sent on the Northeastern Railroad through Georgetown and Wilmington. The South Carolinians did not learn of the intended route until after the train had gotten underway and crossed the Ashley River. As one officer put it, "It was a dog-mean trick."[1] Indeed, men of the "Tramp Brigade" would not forget this heavy-handed move by the Confederate high command.

The journey to Virginia, while undertaken with mixed feelings by many of the men, dropped the brigade within the ranks of Robert E. Lee's Army of Northern Virginia. Lee had recently thrown back George B. McClellan's Army of the Potomac from the shadows of Richmond in the bloody Seven Days Battles. While McClellan regrouped south of the capital, Lee reorganized his army and sought reinforcements. Another Federal army, meanwhile, was coalescing in northern Virginia under John Pope. Threatened on two fronts, Lee determined to move a portion of his army under Thomas J. "Stonewall" Jackson against Pope before large segments of the Army of the Potomac could be transferred north to swell Pope's numbers. Lee's thrust into northern Virginia triggered the Second Manassas Campaign.

Diary of David Jackson Logan

July 21: We started this morning about 8 AM. The Engine became disabled and we were until 3 oclock PM getting to Charleston when there we were sadly disappointed by learning for the first time that we were not to go by the SCRR but by the NERR. Our families and friends we know are in Chester and along the Road waiting for us to pass. We were very busy loading our baggage until a late hour and working details for Sharp Shooters. Wash Carroll volunteered from our Company and we left him in the city.

July 22: We made a start at 10 clock AM this morning, crossed the Santee at Sun rise where I awoke from a very refreshing sleep. The country through which we passed has a very barren and uninteresting appearance. Very few houses, nothing but forests of pine and Turpentine Stills to relieve the monatony. We passed Florence about 12 M. A very pretty place. The ladies from this place seem to be entering in to our struggle with a hearty good will as we were cheered from every house until we reached Wilmington NC which we did about 8 oclock P.M. We crossed Cape Fear River in a splendid boat and procured quantities of melons &c on the city side. After getting a warm supper we bivouacked until day light.

July 23: We started for Richmond about 8 oclock AM this morning, the ladies cheering us on. The country is more interesting through here until we reach Goldsboro & Wilson where it is perfectly delightful. The ladies and citizens seeming almost ready to eat us up.

July 24: I reached Weldon NC whilst asleep but awoke after I had gotten there and made a fruitless search after supper. We found the ground covered here with soldiers.

July 25: We remained in the cars until morning when we were on the way to Richmond again. We reached Petersburg about 12M and were detained until 6 oclock P.M. Here I met Wm Hoey with his brother Capt Hoey who is very low with Typhoid fever. I learned from him that my two wounded Bros were at home and doing well. We started again and reached Richmond about dark when we were met by tremendeous crowds and cheer after cheer was given. Capt Meacham had been waiting at the Depot for some time for me and I left the Company with Lieut Moore and went with him to the Spotswood Hotel where we had a pleasant time.

July 26: I rejoined my Company this morning which I found encamped in front of the New Fair ground buildings. We were all delighted with the water we find here having had none except the surface water of the coast for months. I went down the city to visit the Hospitals and there found many wounded friends & neighbors. The Winder Hospital is one of the most extensive collection of houses I have ever seen. They are all large—neat & well arranged buildings, laid off in regular order, white washed, and were first built for winter Quarters for the army of the Potomac. I have found Col Jackson who is very seriously wounded through both thighs and left arm amputated just below the first joint or elbow. Capt Fitchett also badly wounded in the leg below knee, bone broken. I remained here awhile then went to Manchester where I found my bro Pinckney who at Williamsburg had injured his hand and was detailed as nurse in the hospital. I found him quite well. I visited several friends here and then brought my brother back to Camp with me. I was accompanied in those visits by Capt Meacham. I had chartered a carriage for which I paid $5.00. I returned to Camp where I found Capt Avery & Dr Lowry they having just got in by the train. All quiet in the Camp.

July 27: Nothing new to day. I was Officer of the Guard and did not go to the City but visited the Camp of the 42nd Miss Regt where I found many relatives and friends. T. P. McFadden, Poag, Mitchell, and Rowell relatives of my wife.

Camp Lee, Richmond
July 27th 1862

My Dear Wife:
I have arrived safely at this place and am in good health and spirits. You can appreciate the disappointment we all felt when we found we were ordered by the NERR. We did not know a word of it until we had crossed the Ashley bridge. We got along finely, had no break downs, and had a very interesting Country to pass through. The women, children & negroes

cheered us at almost every stop. Capt Witherspoon left us at Florence and married and caught up with us at Weldon NC. He had a short honey moon. I am very much in need of a pair of pants. If you have not sent them, please send them by Bro Ben, as I have just got a letter from Pa and he says he intends sending for you soon. Bro Pink staid with me last night. He is doing finely and I suppose you have heard all about Ben & Marion. I saw Sam Poag yesterday. He is well & Walker is very low. Uncle Andy is getting better but is not out of danger yet. Tom McFadden is here in the 62nd Miss. Uncle Jeff & I are going over to see him today. I am very much pained at not getting to see you, but perhaps it cost us less pain than to have just passed by you. I have a great chance to write, but are in a great hurry and will write you at length when I hear from you. We move tomorrow 9 miles below this city where we will be under Genl Longstreet. We will be close to all our friends. Uncle Jeff is wanting me to start, so I must close. Kiss the Children and give my love to all the friends. Write soon, and send my pants if you can as I will have to pay $40.00 for a good pair here. I have plenty money and wish to send some home. I will send it by Dr Loring. You can get it from him or he will leave it with Adicks. You call them and get it.

Your husband
D J Logan

Diary of David Jackson Logan

July 28: I remained in Camp all day. We received orders to report to Genl Longstreet to day down the James River.

July 29: I again visited Richmond my Brothers & uncle. I have bid them adieu not knowing when I should see them again. I returned to Camp and found it in great commotion about a citizen having charged some of the men with having stolen whiskey. He fared very badly being driven from Camp with sticks, brickbats &c.

July 30: We were aroused early this morning by reviele and started on our first march from Richmond. We passed down "Broad Street" to "Capitol Square" then down to "Ballard house" where we saw Genl Evans and were assigned our Encampment. We moved through the City passing by where hundreds of yankee prisoners were quartered. There were a great many fine looking men among them.

Others hard looking & disposed to make faces at us. We went down the River, the sun beaming down on us with all its power. Several men were entirely over come with the heat and a large portion of the Regt was compelled to remain behind. Just where the "River Road" loses sight of the James and where there is a noble Spring by the way side, there is a beautiful Mansion situated and here Capt Avery, Lt WS Moore & my self stopped for dinner. We were entertained a long time by the lady of the house a Mrs Eckles who we found from her conversation to be attached to the Old Flag as her relatives were all North. She provided us with an excellent dinner however for which we only paid $1.00 each. We here met Genl Greggs Brigade[2] among which we grasped the hand of many a dear friend. They were hastening to the "Valley" to join "Old Stone Wall Jackson" and meet the yankee Genl Pope.[3] We bid them a God speed and passed them by. We arrived at our Camping place about 4 oclock P.M. wet with perspiration. I took off my shirt and wrung about 1 qt of water out of it, then lay down and rested as well as I could ever present. Our mess is about 2 1/2 [miles] from Dury's Bluff and 6 miles from Richmond.

July 31: I visited the old Camp of the 12th Regt to day to see my uncle Dr Jackson who is left in charge of the sick of the Regt. They have about 85 unable to be moved. The sick of Genl AP Hills Division are all together and present a sad spectacle of human suffering. It was raining all day. I returned to Camp and found many old friends visiting us. We lay down in quiet to night but about 12 or 1 PM [AM] were awakened by a tremendeous Cannonading down the James River.[4] There is a dreadful conflict going on. We know not where.

Aug 1: The clouds have passed away and the sun shines beautifully. We hear the heavy firing was caused by an attack upon McClellans vessels in the river by our artillery. Loss unknown. Our first order from Genl Longstreet is to go tomorrow and throw up entrenchments upon our lines. All quiet to night. Mr Buist is praying fervently.

Aug 2: We repaired early to the place assigned us to throw up entrenchments. It is on the New Market road about 1 1/2 miles from Durys bluff. We worked at intervals of 1/2 hour and threw up quite a formidable works. In the evening we saw our Maj Genl Longstreet. He is an exceedingly fine looking man. One man killed & 6 wounded by the explosion of a Gun was the only loss we sustained in our night attack on the yankee fleet.[5]

Aug 3: Lieut WS Moore & my self visited HG Jackson this morning. Found his nurses laying out 2 dead soldiers. Went from there to the Camp of 5th, 6th & Sharpshooters.[6] Found many friends and enjoyed some pleasant home conversation. A yankee spy, a deserter was captured near the Camp this morning. We saw the "battle Flag" of the 5th Regt and counted 52 bullet holes. 1 hole made by a shell & one by a Grape shot through it. The staff was shot to pieces and nine men had been killed and wounded in carrying it through the late battles.

———

Camp Mary below Richmond
Aug 3rd 1862

My Dear Wife:

I have been looking anxiously for a letter from you every day and have been disappointed, although persons have been coming from York nearly every day. I have just seen Frank Clark & he says you sent by him a pair of pants but Mr Wheeler could not find them. I am in great need of pants and will have to pay 30. or 40 Dollars for them here if I cant get them from home. Please send them if possible to Richmond by any brothers if no other chance presents itself. I am at a loss to know where to write you as Pa said he intended going after you. I have had excellent health since I came here. We are now about 5 miles from the City down the James River. We are all at work on entrenchments. A complete fortification is being thrown up from the Chickahominy river to the James 10 miles long.

We had two little skirmishes the other night.[7] The enemy undertook to drive in our pickets but were repulsed. I see hundreds of old friends & neighbors here every day. I was with the 42nd Miss Regt the other day and passed a day with T P McFadden, McLure, Poag's son, two of the Mitchels & 1 of Randolph Rowells sons as many others of your friends. They are all well and in good spirits. There is no telling how many men are here. There are thousands & thousands. About 60000 have gone on to "Stonewall" Jackson and every train comes in loaded with more. If McClellan intends taking Richmond he will have a hard road to travel. I am going to see Uncle Hugh to day. His Regt is gone to Jackson but he is left with the sick. I have given out the idea of coming to see you now for awhile. I suppose I shall wait until the war is over or some unfore seen act takes place. We get plenty of milk & bread but that is about all. The water cant be beat. I sent you by Dr Lowry One hundred & eighty Dollars. He will leave it with Adicks as you can get it from him. Be sure to get it.

I should be happy to be with you all if the country was not in danger, but as it is, it is neither wise nor manly to grumble or complain. I have written to you in N.C. so you will excuse brevity. Direct to me at Richmond care of Col Means 17th Regt SCV. Be particular in writing the Regt & Co. We get all our letters at the City.

Kiss the children for me and tell them to be good babies. My regards to your Father & Mother.

Your husband

David J. Logan

Diary of David Jackson Logan

Aug 4: All was quiet to day.

Aug 5: We marched down New Market road again this morning to work on the entrenchments. We had got fairly to work when a courier with a foaming steed dashed up the road and reported the enemy advancing in heavy force. We redoubled exertions to complete the fortification, but an order from Genl Longstreet soon came for us to man the trenches and look out for the enemy. We occupied the trenches on the left of the road looking away from Richmond. We lay perfectly quiet until evening. Heard no guns of any consquence. The wounded began to pass up the road then reporting the affair to be a movement by the enemy in force on Malvern Hill. Our troops being only a few hundred did not contend with any hope of retaining the position but wreaked considerable vengence on them. Our loss was about 50 killed & wounded.[8]

I heard that a large number of prisoners were being exchanged and walked down to the River Road with Capt Durham when we had one of the most interesting sights I have most ever seen. About 4000 yankees were on the road and the same number of our own men returning from their confinement. It was interesting to see them meet.

Aug 6: We were ordered to prepare rations this morning and repair down the New Market road to the vicinity of Malvern Hill. We were soon on the road and found it filled with troops preparing down the road. We halted at New Market and remained until evening. About 5 oclock PM we received orders to march and were formed into line of battle near a factory where earthen ware is made. Our Regt was ordered to scour a dense wood on the left of the road. We went forward in good style and soon roused a picket of about 12 yankees who fled in a hurry leaving their guns, Knapsacks &c. We then hurried through until we came to cleared land where we halted and a yankee rode into the open space when several fired upon him but he rode off. Very soon another advanced towards us and was taken prisoner. We were then ordered to advance across the field which was done in a good manner. We halted in a hollow and Capt Culps company was sent forward to skirmish a piece of wood but before they reached it they encountered some yankee Cavalry and a conflict ensued. Another portion of the yankees were encountered by Gadberrys Regt. The yankees after firing a few shots turned and fled. Our troops firing volleys into them. 5 yankees were found dead. Several wounded & prisoner and quite a number were wounded who got away. Capt Stevens Regt was soon sent forward to skirmish in advance. They soon encountered the enemy and exchanged shots in which one of our men was wounded. Loss of yankees unknown. Artillery was heard advancing and it being late at night Genl Evans called off the troops and we returned to the Jug factory and slept behind our guns.[9]

Aug 7: Our Brigade lay quiet to day. Some Brigades however concentrated near this place. About 11 oclock P.M. a courier arrived stating that we had retaken Malvern hill without loss. The yankees leaving in good time. Our troops in other quarters capturing & killing quite a number of their rear guard & scouts. We had a pleasant time with our old friends of the 5th, 6th & sharpshooters. About 8 oclock PM we were ordered back to Camp and after marching several dusty miles reached Camp 10 1/2 P.M. and found one of our men, a Corpl Blanton Moore.

Aug 8: We have had nothing of note to day. I received first letter from wife since I came to Virginia. She has gone to No. Ca.[10]

Aug 9: We are working on the entrenchments today again. Had an excellent dinner at the house near by. Returned to Camp at 3 oclock PM. Two loaded guns went off and came near killing two of our men. We found orders to prepare 3 days rations and be ready to march Monday next. Our supper to night was 4 pieces of old bacon size of a plum & fried to a crisp and biscuit. The ration is becoming alarming.

Aug 10: Nothing important to day. Seven out of nine men died in one tent. At A P Hill's hospital the suffering and privation of the sick here is indescribable. There are over 1000 sick men in the sound of our Drum.

Aug 11: We start to day in the direction of the Valley of Virginia. We heard that Popes army had been repulsed by "Stone Wall" J. and driven back several miles.[11] Our army capturing many prisoners among them Genl Price. We record with sadness the fall of our Genl C S Winder.[12] The weather is extremely hot. McCLellan is reported to be leaving the James River. I suffered considerably from Diarhea to day but feel better. Became very weak. Rec'd a present from Mr Buist.

Aug 12: Left Camp Mary at 1 oclock AM. This time for an unknown destination. We reached Richmond after sunrise and found a Train waiting to take us to

Gordonsville, about 76 miles distant. Reached there late in the evening, bivouacked on the North West side of the Town near an old gentleman by the name of
King where we got an excellent supper.

———————

Richmond Va
Aug 12th 1862

My Dear Wife:

We are on the way to the Valley of Virginia. We will rendyvous at
Gordonsville. You can direct your letters as before to Richmond care &c,
also Genl Evans Brigade. They will forward to us. I am in very good
health. We have had another Victory[13] and I doubt not from the immense
numbers of troops going on, that a forward march will be made. I wish to
see my Bros & you very bad. I enclose to you Fifty Dollars ($50.) I sent
$180. by Dr. Loring. If you dont need all pay up SCRR & Co or KMRR
Co. Write soon. I am in great haste.
 Your husband
 D J Logan

I received your letter by Mother yesterday.

———————

On August 13, preliminary orders were issued for the balance of
Lee's Army of Northern Virginia to move from near Richmond toward
Gordonsville. Nathan Evans' Brigade—which contained Logan's 17th
South Carolina—was one of two brigades new to the army. Evans'
regiments marched and fought with James Longstreet's "wing," although for reasons unknown remained an "independent brigade" and
was not attached to any division. Ironically, the other reinforcing brigade, under the command of Brig. Gen. Thomas Drayton, had also
been transferred from to Lee from South Carolina.

———————

Diary of David Jackson Logan

Aug 13: Moved this evening 4 miles below Gordonsville near Mechanesville. Had one of the grandest scenes that night I ever witnessed. The Gathering of Longstreet's <u>Corps dance</u>. The bands of music, the camp fires on the hills will never be forgotten.

Aug 14: All quiet to day. More troops coming in.

Aug 15: Nothing new. 16th & 17th the same.

Aug 18: We are ordered to march against the enemy and are on the road.

Aug 19: This is early in the morning. We expect a grand fight to day. We are near the enemy. I do not know that I shall ever write another line in this book. If I die I wish this sent to my family.[14]

Aug 29th 1862

My Dear Wife: I am well. This morning passed thru my first fight. Yesterday under fire 8 hours. Yankees left burning their stores & horses. We are off in pursuit this morning. Our loss was from 200 killed & wounded. I am much cooler than I expected. I can get no mails. You must not be uneasy. My love to all. I am feeling very well this morning.

    Your husband

    D J Logan

Aug 30: On this day the <u>Grand finale</u> of the 2nd struggle of Manassas was consumated. About 2 1/2 PM a forward movement was made by our whole army. Our Brigade charged over the Texan Brigades of Genl Hood and driving in the "Fire Zouaves"[15] of Brooklyn fell with tremendeous force upon the main body of the enemy, driving them back but in doing so the contest was terrible. Our Company passed a piece of woods to the left of the "Henry (Chinn) House" and became somewhat scattered & massed in the woods during which time many were killed & wounded, among them OL Wallace, Jona McLean & James Hetherington were killed.

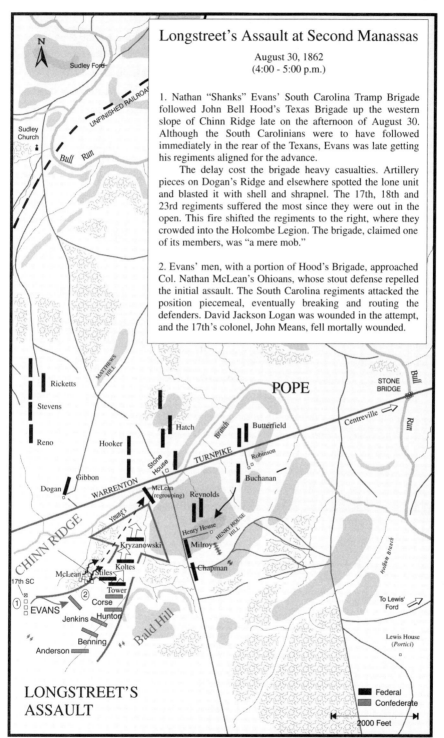

Longstreet's Assault at Second Manassas

August 30, 1862
(4:00 - 5:00 p.m.)

1. Nathan "Shanks" Evans' South Carolina Tramp Brigade followed John Bell Hood's Texas Brigade up the western slope of Chinn Ridge late on the afternoon of August 30. Although the South Carolinians were to have followed immediately in the rear of the Texans, Evans was late getting his regiments aligned for the advance.

The delay cost the brigade heavy casualties. Artillery pieces on Dogan's Ridge and elsewhere spotted the lone unit and blasted it with shell and shrapnel. The 17th, 18th and 23rd regiments suffered the most since they were out in the open. This fire shifted the regiments to the right, where they crowded into the Holcombe Legion. The brigade, claimed one of its members, was "a mere mob."

2. Evans' men, with a portion of Hood's Brigade, approached Col. Nathan McLean's Ohioans, whose stout defense repelled the initial assault. The South Carolina regiments attacked the position piecemeal, eventually breaking and routing the defenders. David Jackson Logan was wounded in the attempt, and the 17th's colonel, John Means, fell mortally wounded.

N

Sudley Ford

Sudley Church

UNFINISHED RAILROAD

Bull Run

POPE

STONE BRIDGE

Bull Run

Ricketts

MATTHEWS HILL

Stevens

Hatch

Branch

Butterfield

Centreville

Reno

Hooker

Stone House

TURNPIKE

Robinson

Gibbon

WARRENTON

McLean (regrouping)

Reynolds

Buchanan

Dogan

Young's

Henry House

HENRY HOUSE HILL

Holkam Branch

CHINN RIDGE

Kryzanowski

Milroy

Koltes

Chapman

McLean

Stiles

17th SC

Tower

To Lewis' Ford

EVANS

Corse

Jenkins

Hunton

Bald Hill

Lewis House (Portici)

Benning

Anderson

LONGSTREET'S ASSAULT

■ Federal
■ Confederate

2000 Feet

Mark A. Moore & Theodore P. Savas

We succeeded in getting the men from the woods forward upon the enemy and when we were driving the enemy before us & some 75 yds from the woods I received a wound in the right side of the chest knocking me down instantly. I was entirely paralized in my right side and did not know but that the ball had passed directly through me. I lay for some 20 minutes when fresh columns of the enemy coming up our Brigade was forced to fall back for reserves. I noticed that men were jumping over me and on raising myself up discovered that surely all of our men had fallen back & that the yankees were pressing forward. I was impressed with the idea that if I did not get away from where I was, I should be taken by the enemy. I threw away my Havesack &c and endeavored to get up which I did and succeeded in making my way through a most horrid fire to the woods where I fell from loss of blood and was carried off the field by Phillip Sassaugh & a Texan whose name I did not learn. The cannon balls & shells were playing havoc through the woods for some 2 miles.

Our Brigade was relieved by another as soon as it was compelled to fall back and soon the yankees were flying back across "Bulls Run" leaving their dead & wounded behind. I was met by Rev Mr Buist who procured a surgeon and stopped the flow of blood from my wound. (In the mean time I had fainted on account of its loss.) I was then borne from the field on a litter by the following soldiers, WB Shearer, James Hogue, Jno Meek & JP Burris to a Hospital in the woods near a little village called Gainesville. I was there met by a number of friends who did many things for my comfort, the principal being WB Byers. The surgeon came to me at once and examined my wound which was found to be directly under my arm and had broke loose my ribs fracturing them then glancing around my body lodged below my shoulder blade. The Dr., Wm Wylie, then gave me morphine and proceeded to extract the ball & probe and dress the wound which was done very well. I had great dificulty in breathing, my lungs being thought injured.

I remained in this place during the 1st, 2nd, 3rd, & 4th days of September all the time improving and was moved on the 4th in a wagon to Warrenton where I met with unbounded hospitality at the hands of the noble ladies of that place. Among their names I remember Norris, Weaver, Williams & Finks (& Hoover). Here I continued to improve until the 8th when Lts Moore, Nunnery, Carroll, Edwards & private SC Lowry & my self employed an Ambulance driver living near Gordonsville to take us to Rapidan River for which we paid $40.00.

We arrived at Culpeppers CH after dark and with much difficulty got into the Rail Road Hotel in that place. I was very much worn down by the jolting of the Ambulance. On the 9th we reached the Rail Road and got to Gordonsville about dark and lay on the Platform until morning. On the 10th we reached Richmond having met with Dr JM Lowry coming to meet us. We had to ride outside of the cars. Many well persons, sitting on good seats, but would give us none. Got into good quarters at the Columbian Hotel and remained until the next evening when we got to Petersburg. Met Rev Mr Anderson and got good rooms in the Hotel.

———————

Petersburg Va
Sept 12th 1862

My Dear Wife:

I am on the road to York. I shall reach there Saturday evening if nothing happens. I have a number of friends with me who are helping me along. I am sorry to hear that I was reported mortally. I am severely & near seriously but not near considered mortally. I would have gone by Shelby but I could not stand the staying. I must see all my Bros if possible. They must all come to see me. My love to all. I start in a few minutes.

Your husband
D J Logan

———————

Diary of David Jackson Logan

August 30, 1862 – ? (diary entry continued): We were much assisted all the way by Capt SB Meacham. Started early next morning for Home. Since learned that my Father passed me here on the way to the battle ground in search of me. I arrived at Charlotte NC on the morning of the 12th. Left on the Train for Lincolnton N.C. when I met a friend who conveyed me in a good Buggy to Shelby NC where my family was at the time. I took them with great surprise as the papers and &c had reported me dead. I here found my Brothers all at home. The first time we have all been together for several years. The wounded ones recovering.

I remained in NC about two weeks enjoying my self as well as I could. I then parted from my Parents and proceeded to Mr Rowells where I recovered rapidly. Winding up my business in Yorkville & visiting friends. I remained here until the 18th of Nov when I left Smiths T.O. to rejoin my Regt. I met with my Bro Pink at Charlotte NC and went on with him to Raleigh where my father then was in attendence on the Legislature then in session. He being a member from his county.

We remained with him until the 20th when I separated with Father & Bro and found my Regt near Kinston, capital of Lenoir County N.C. This is a very pretty place on the Neuse River. The country containing plenty of provisions we found much better than in the war worn country of Northern Virginia. I find our Company only numbering 34 men and most of them bearing the marks of hard service. There is one case of small Pox in the Camp. I have been vaccinated.[16] Capt Culp is promoted to be Major, caused by the death of Col Means at Manassas.[17]

CHAPTER 3

"Disease & battle have played sad havoc in our ranks."

Kinston and Court Martials

November 1862 – February 1863

The near-fatal wound suffered by Lieutenant Logan at Second Manassas kept him from rejoining his regiment until November 1862. The injury prevented his participation in the fight at South Mountain on September 14, as well as the bloodbath of Sharpsburg three days later. Logan was fortunate to have missed these actions, for Maryland claimed another 232 men from the ranks of the Tramp Brigade.

His return to active service was marked by fighting both on and off the field. In early November the Richmond War Department ordered Lee to transfer a brigade into North Carolina to help protect the Weldon Railroad from Maj. Gen. John G. Foster's threatening Federals. Lee left the choice of which brigade to send to James Longstreet, and before long the Tramp Brigade was riding the rails south. Upon reaching the Tarheel State, Evans' men took up a position east of the town of Kinston on the Atlantic & North Carolina Railroad between the Confederate held railroad junction of Goldsboro and Federal forces in New Bern. The men of the 17th South Carolina settled into camp life, their mundane routine broken periodically by the sound of artillery fire in the distance and the welcomed distraction of an occasional snowball fight.

This relatively quite winter sojourn ended with the December 14 fight at Kinston, in which the 17th played a pivotal role. Evans' outnumbered Confederates opposed Foster's advance in a running campaign to arrest his progress from New Bern towards Goldsboro. The Federals were attempting to cut the Wilmington and Weldon Railroad, the main supply route into Richmond from the port of Wilmington. Such a move would have prevented supplies from being brought in from Europe by blockade runners of the "Bermuda Line."[1]

During this period some of the officers of the Tramp Brigade became embroiled in a controversy with their commander, Nathan "Shanks" Evans. Many of Evans' subordinates accused him of being intoxicated during the Battle of South Mountain and in other actions that followed. Led by the 17th's Col. Fitz William McMaster, the officers signed a petition seeking Evans' ouster. The situation continued to escalate when an incensed Evans filed court-martial charges against McMaster for cowardice. Logan observed this fascinating chain of events while serving as secretary for the court martial proceedings.

Diary of David Jackson Logan

Nov 25, 1862: Every thing is quiet in Camp to day. The men are boiling their clothes in order to get rid of body lice which abound throughout our Virginia army.

Nov. 26: Nothing interesting to day. The Company was paid off. I was Officer of the Day.

Nov. 27: This is the anniversary of our going in to service. One year ago we were entering the "College Green" in Columbia. Now we are on the coast of N.C. about 3 miles South east of Kinston in Jones County. 30 miles above Newbern on the Neuse river. It is painful to contemplate the changes of the year. Disease & battle have played sad havoc in our ranks. More than one half of the gay volunteers who one year ago were buoyant with life are now missing from our Roll calls. Thanks to my Heavenly Father I am still spared through many trials. May I be permitted to record another year and prove a better man.

Nov. 28: Nothing interesting further than a report of a woman & her daughter being ravashed in the yankee lines by some of their soldiery. Lieut E P Moore returned to Camp to day.

Nov 29: No news to day. Several have returned from Hospitals.

Nov. 30: This is a beautiful Sabbath and I heard one of the best sermons preached by Rev Mr Gireaudeau, Chaplain of the 23rd Regt in the evening. We were inspected by Col Jennifer of Maryland.

Dec 1: I received a letter from my Father to day and was aroused at 2 oclock AM by the noise of couriers who brought news that our advance pickets at [Cog] Creek were driven in by the enemy. The "long roll" sounded and our Regt was ordered to proceed at once to the Front. We were on the March by day light and proceeded 5 miles down the Neuse road to Rouses Point where we learned the alarm was false and were ordered back to Camp. My feet suffered mostly as this was the first march since I returned to Camp.

———————

Camp Near Kinston, N. C.
December 1, 1862.

Dear Enquirer: As many of your readers will be interested in hearing from the 17th Regiment, I have concluded to consume a few idle moments in giving you a few notes. Our Brigade was detached from the Division of General McLaws, at Culpeper C. H. about the 5th of November last, and ordered Southward, a direction which was rendered peculairly attractive from the fact, that from Gordonsville to Richmond, our soldiers passed through a terrible snow storm, many being on platform cars, and but scantily clothed.

The announcement was made by our General, that we were ordered to "the coast" and the sanguine dispostions of our men interpreted his meaning to be "the coast of our own loved State" but in that we were disappointed. On arriving at Weldon, North Carolina, we were ordered to leave the cars, and after remaining there a day, marched to Halifax Court House, about 8 miles, where we remained two days, then took the cars for Tarboro', a distance about 35 miles, where we remained about three days.

In the meantime, General Foster, the Yankee commander from Newbern, had taken the back track and rendered our longer stay in Tarboro' unnecessary. I would here state that we were agreeable suprised to find, one of the most fertile sections of country we have ever seen, and evidence of much wealth. Tarboro' is a beautiful place. It is situated on the Tar River, and contains more fine residences, beautiful gardens, and hospitable inhabitants than any other place of its size we have yet seen—the same may be said of Halifax, though a much smaller place. I had almost forgotten to mention at Tarboro', there is now building a very superior "gun boat"[2] which we hope to hear much good from in future.

After leaving Tarboro', we took to the cars, and came to Goldsboro, then took the Newbern Road and came to the Town of Kinston on the 13th of November; here we left the cars again and marched five miles down the Trent road, and bivouacked. Kinston is the seat of Justis of Lenoir county, located on the banks of the Neuse River, thirty five miles above Newbern. It is a beautiful place, well laid out—has a number of fine residences and is in the centre of a small but wealthy country. The Neuse River is navigable for small boats as high as Smithfield, 20 miles from Raleigh. The channel for boats at Kinston is usually 6-7 feet water; at times a greater depth.

Our present camp is in Jones county, on the South side of the Neuse. We are partially supplied with tents and are receiving some shoes, blankets, &c. We learn that the Yankees are in heavy force at Newbern below us; but we cannot think they will attempt a movement up the river soon. They are carrying out their hellish proclamations upon all the citizens within their lines as is attested to us here every day by hundreds of persons who are leaving their homes and property and seeking asylum in the interior. They report the Yankee commander requiring all persons to enlist for the Union, take the oath, or leave, and this is the cause of the ceaseless rumbling of carts &c up the different roads from the unfortunate town, Newbern. These refugees report outrages which I forbear to mention. Our regiment is improving rapidly in health and numbers. We have 350 men for duty, our Brigade about 2000. Our General, Evans, commands this department. There is one Brigade of North Carolina troops and a force of Cavalry. What our whole force is, I am unable to state, but believe it suffcient to repel any force likely to come up the Neuse river.

There is considerable anxiety manifested by our soldiers in regard to our "Reserve Corps." We understand the "old fellows" are quite indignant at the idea of being thought unfit to select their own officers. We think they should have been entitled, and believe they would have made as good selections as the "Council." The "Council" seems to have as a morbid desire to create something whereby they could confer favors, create expense to the State, and produce us good results. In the appointment of officers they have ignord the choices of the veteran soldiers of Virginia, squandered money upon sin__curures and visionary projects, while other States have been contributing extra bounty to their soldiers and making provisions for their families at home. Had the money which has been uselessly expended in South Carolina, been appropriated to the use of families of poor soldiers in the service, there would be much more cheerfulness in camp and duty than there is. A man who does not know but his family may be suffering at home, cannot feel cheerful and happy around the camp fire. More *anon*.

Yours, L

Diary of David Jackson Logan

Dec 2: I went to Kinston to day. Rode in the Commisary wagon. Presented my "Pay Roll" to Genl Evans in person and drew my money from Capt Vardelle. Several yankee deserters were in Town who report Charleston & Wilmington to be attacked next week. Drunk soldiers & whiskey shops in abundance in Kinston.

Dec 3: It commenced raining about mid night last night and has rained on all day to day. We have been confined to our tents. For amusement I have played Whisk with Capt Avery, Dr Hall & Lieut Carlisle.

Dec 4: To day the sun shines beautifully. I have been unanimously called by the members of Capt Witherspoon's Company[3] to take the position of Captaincy. I am perplexed to know what course to pursue in regard to it. My own Company are relunctant to give me up. I must have time to consider. Rumors of French intervention are rife again.

Dec 5-8: No important event occurred during these dates except the breaking out of the Small Pox in Capt Crawfords Company.[4] Bratton & Patrick have taken it. All who have had intercourse with the persons are being quarantined. I have been appointed Judge Advocate of a Court of Enquiry by Genl Evans to meet in Kinston on the 11th Inst on the case of Maj Bryan Qr M. We have received Lincolns Message.[5] He is determined to carry on the war. Recomends the abolition of slavery by the year A.D. 1900.

Dec 11: I attended at Kinston but the Court was not ready for a trial. Capt Averys family is in Kinston.

Dec 12: Last night we were aroused by a courier stating that the enemy were advancing but all remaining quiet up to 9 oclock AM. I went to Kinston again but found reports of the advance of the enemy to strong. We held no Court again but returned to Camp. A number of wounded cavalry came up the road from Kinston who report the enemy advancing in force. Genl Evans was absent at Greenville during this time. Late in the evening Genl Gwinn came down and ordered us to retire to the North side of a considerable mill stream 3 miles from Town. We did so, leaving a guard under Lt W S Moore to protect the baggage left behind. We reached our Camp about dark & about the same time heard artillery & small arms down the road. A courier also notified us that the enemy's cavalry were between us and our old Camp. Great anxiety was manifested for our guard but about 10 oclock PM they came up all right, tho they had to elude the yankee picquets. We were considerably relieved when our guard came but Lieut Hilton and a company of the 22nd Regt were taken prisoners by the yankees 2 miles before our old Camp.

Dec 13: Morning dawned all quiet and several of our soldiers came in from our old Camp who reported no enemy in the way. Arrangements were made for sending after our baggage but no sooner made, than the sound of cannon away west of us, made us open our eyes with wonder. Very soon a courier came dashing in ordering us to proceed towards Kinston and take down the Wilmington road. When our forces were engaging the enemy we moved as rapidly as possible and came up with our forces slowly retreating before the enemy. Our force was a section of Capt Starr's battery, 4 Guns, one of which had been taken and 6 Companies of 61st NCT. We formed on the right of the NC Troops and retreated in good order firing occassional volleys at the enemy until we came back within 2 miles of Kinston when we made a stand and my Company & Capt Edwards Co A both under command of Capt Avery were sent forward to meet the enemy.

We advanced about 1 mile & deployed on both sides of the road where we could hear the vandals distinctly as they slowly advanced. We lay quietly. Presently we saw the vanquard in the distance and a party of horsemen galloped down the road towards us. We let them come within 100 yds when we gave the command fire and all were tumbled from their saddles but three. We then fell back to the edge of the woods where we heard their skirmishers advancing towards us across a cane brake. We fired a volley into them and joined our Regt when very soon the ball opened in good style and continued until after dark when the enemy withdrew to Camp and we retired to a Chapel[6] just across the bridge from Kinston, where we lay all night without fire. Here we were joined by the Holcombe Legion. Imagine our feelings lying upon the cold ground on a bitter December night knowing it would be a battle ground on the morrow and we having only some 500 men to contend perhaps against 25000 yankees.[7] Our minds perhaps would have been more composed at home in the chimney corner. We were here left without our Genl and no plans or dispositions for attack or defense were made known to our Regt officers. Take care of yourselves seemed to be all implied.

Dec 14: Morning dawned beautifully clear & bright. We awoke from our troubled slumbers around the temple consecrated to God, but now to angry Mars. It is a Sabbath morning too, but the voice of the man of God is not heard from the little "chapel." Instead we see the Artillery taking position on each side, an ominous silence prevailing. The morning wears away, no Genl comes. Our Col arranges a line of battle. The 61st NCT on the extreme right. Holcombe Legion Center. Our 6 Companies (I forgot to state that 4 of our Companies had been detached the day before up the "upper Treat Road") on the left. Capt Edwards of our Regt was sent forward to await the enemy, but our Genl comes "powerful for battle" (more whiskey aboard) orders another Company to be sent from our Regt to attack the enemy & to go on until we come up with them. My Company was sent again.

We proceeded forward some 300 yards to a tremendeous swamp. Crossed it, got to a fence, could hear the enemy coming, lay down, saw them crossing the fence opposite us then rose & gave them a volley and retired firing, across the swamp halted on the other side, gave them another round and then formed into our line of battle. This is 9 oclock AM and the work is getting hot. Mullinax of Co A killed just to my right. Firing becomes furious on our right. We retire over the crest of the hill. The Legion is sending death into the enemy. Reenforcements are heard coming. They charged into position on our right, and drive the enemy back. It is Col Mallett. Our artillery has exhausted its ammunition and 1 piece has lost every horse belonging to it and has to be given up. The Artillery has to leave but we still hold our ground nobly. More reenforcements to our left & right. The firing becomes hotter & hotter. It is One oclock PM. The enemy are Flanking us on the left. We are ordered across the bridge. We get across safely, are ordered to go back again, find every thing babel as confusion at the bridge. Orders given & countermanded every minute cussing & swearing. Meantime the enemy advancing up the road to our left. Capt Malletts Troops & Holcombe Legion fighting their way back to the bridge. The bridge is set on fire. Part of the Legion cross and a few of Malletts troops but most are cut off. Our Genl goes up Town. The enemy enfilade our batteries & troops and they are pushed back. Our troops after some good fires find things too hot, and the artillery gone begin to move up the river. The yankees press forward to the bridge leap on it. Kick off the light wood and some extinguish the fire then rushing across with their banners waving. They gain the bridge and Kinston has fallen.

Our Regt retires in good order through the Town which is now almost deserted. Cotton is burning in the streets. Shells are shrieking over our heads and knocking houses about behind us. We reach the Depot. The enemy are advancing in heavy Column after us. Genl Evans orders us to form line of battle, but the artillery is gone and the order is foolish and he finely sees it is so. We then retire up the RR towards Goldsboro. Presently three horsemen dash up the road with a flag of Truce. It is accepted and they demand our surrender. Evans tells them to "Go to Hell" and we continue our retreat. We march with sullen steps about 6 miles to

"Falling Creek" where we halt and determine to make another stand. I slept well to night for I was almost worn down. Our whole force in the battle of Kinston was not more than 2500 men. Of them, not more than 700 were actually engaged. The enemy according to the authority of one of the bearers of Flag of Truce had 11 Regts engaged and a large force in reserve.

Goldsboro N.C.
Dec 18th 1862

My Dear Wife:

I am here safely in Goldsboro. We have had some dreadful fighting. I have been in 3 fights and am unhurt as yet, for which I feel thankful to my God, but more fighting will evidently take place and I want you to pray for my preservation.

The enemy drove us from Kinston. They have taken the RR to Wilmington but we have driven them back. We have inflicted a great chance more loss on them than they have on us but they have overpowered us. We have now received heavy reenforcements and expect to push them back or let them push us. Dreadful fighting is going on at Fredricksburg.[8] I suppose you have full account of that. I have suffered a little from Flux[9] but feel better now. Be of good cheer and all will be well yet. Pray for me to come out safely.

Your husband
D J Logan

*   *   *

Kinston N.C.
Dec 23rd 1862

My Dear Wife:

I am back again at this place. The trials of Virginia are being nowhere in comparison with ours. Since last Thursday week we have not had a tent and only a Single blanket & been exposed to the worst incliment weather. We have passed thro three fights & thank God I am still unhurt. The enemy succeeded in getting within sight of Goldsboro and burning the RR bridge. Our force by that time became too large for them & they put back & we have followed them to Kinston. I learn that they are only Six miles from us now. I am one of the dirtiest looking <u>smoked</u> creatures you most ever saw. Our trunks &c are in Raleigh and I fear I will be full of lice before I can have a change. My Jeans pants which I have over am badly scorched and split open about the front. I am nearly out of shoes too. I am as you will see in a pretty bad fix, but I shall take it as best I can.

Capt Avery is sick & Pat Moore has resigned so we have no cook and have to do it ourselves. Capt. Avery may get home. He is now in Goldsboro. I am anxious to hear from my brothers since the fight at Fredericksburg. If you hear let me know. Direct to Goldsboro or Kinston. The "yanks" came on in too strong. We had to skedaddle over 30 miles, but we did it leisurly and am back again almost to where we started. They got all our Cooking utensils, pack of tents &c. They have left the Country a perfect desert almost. Carried off big quantity of negroes. I have not heard from you in nearly 3 weeks. Did brother Strait bring you the money I sent? I hope and pray the Lord may soon smile upon us in a more pleasant morning and may we live to appreciate the grace of humility of self denial. Pray for me. Give my best love to the children & write soon. Get me a pair of boots if you can. My love to your Father & Mother.

Write to mine. I am still safe. "Christmas Gift to you." We will not have much here but a happy one to you & all.

Your husband
D J Logan

ARMY CORRESPONDENCE

Correspondence of the Enquirer
Kinston, N. C., Dec. 29, 1862

Dear Enquirer:—Quite a change has come over "the spirit of our dreams" since our last letter to you. Up to the 12th instant, we were reposing in fancied security, upon the banks of the Neuse, dreaming of peace, and wars all over, &c.; but a most incorrigable Yankee called Foster, has recalled us to hard knocks and hard times again.

On the morning of the 12th instant, a company of cavalry were making reconnoisances in the neighborhood of Trenton, some 20 miles below us, where they ran full tilt upon the enemy, in heavy force, advancing towards us. We were only notified by the arrival of some of the wounded troopers, late in the day Friday. Gen. Evans, who commands this department, was absent on an excursion, in the vicinity of Greenville or Plymouth. Fortunately Gen. Gwin was in Kinston, and came down to our camp and ordered us to fall back to the north side of a creek[10] nearer Kinston, and where the numerous roads leading from below concentrate. We had hardly got away from our old Camp when we heard discharges of artillery and small arms down the road below us. We had left a guard at our camp, under Lieut. W. S. Moore, to protect our baggage we had left behind. We had hardly got to our new position when we learned from couriers that the enemy were already between us and our old camp. Great anxiety was manifest for the safety of our guard. I listened attentively for a discharge of small arms, for I knew "Bill Moore" was one of the sort who would give them a fire before he surrendered any way; but I only heard a few reports and about midnight we were much gratified by the an-nouncement "the boys are here," and sure enough they were. They had encouraged the advance piquets, fired on them, and then flanked the enemy and made good their retreat to the main body. We now felt much better, and although we looked for shells and minnie balls on the morrow, we have seen enough to know it is best to sleep when you can, and so at it we went. I regret to state that one company of the 22d S. C. V., suffered itself to be surprised and completely surrounded by the Yankee cavalry, 2 miles below our old camp, while on piquet duty; only some thirteen men escaped capture. They will learn to keep a better look out when they are released again, I doubt not.

We had a refreshing sleep the remainder of the night, and the sun arose clear and bright and everything seemed quiet and still. Our scouts had seen nothing of the enemy since day-light, and some of our men left behind with some sick near our camp, came in, and reported no Yankees between us and our camp. Everyone began to be cheerful and happy again, peals of laughter were heard over the Regiment—every one supposed it just a cavalry dash, and that the enemy had gone back during the night. The cry was "back after our cooking utensils!" The wagons were ready and about starting, when the sound of cannon away behind, or west of us, struck every one with wonder and astonishment; the wagons were stopped, and very soon orders came for us to repair, with all haste, towards Kinston, and go down the Wilmington road, as the enemy were engaging our troops stationed on it. Their direct movement from Newbern towards us having been a feint to mislead us until their forces could be pushed up the country by other roads, so as to attack Kinston from an opposite direction to the one would naturally anticipate. Their feint had succeeded, and now we were compelled to "change our base," and get to them as soon as possible, which we did about 1 o'clock, p. m., Saturday evening.

We came up with our forces which consisted of only a few companies of the 61st N. C. T., Lieut. Col. Lavaughn, and a section of Capt. Starr's light battery. The enemy had succeeded in crossing the creek, where our best chance of defense was, before the six companies of our Regiment came up, (the other companies under Maj. Culp having been sent down the upper Trent road). Our troops had been pretty roughly handled by the superior numbers of the enemy, and had lost one gun of the battery before we joined them. We formed on the right of the N. C. T., and sent forward skirmishers, brought out the enemy and then retired in good order, halting and firing volleys into them as they advanced. We continued to fall back to within two miles of Kinston, where we determined to stop them for the night, although we knew they outnumbered us 30 to 1. We took our position, and two companies of our Regiment, A and F, under command of Capt. Edwards and your correspondent, both under command of Capt. Avery, were ordered forward to meet the enemy and fight them back to our line. We proceeded forward across an old field, until we came near some out-houses, which were near a wood where the enemy would have to pass. We deployed there and waited for the enemy. Very soon we heard them coming along in "fine glee" hurrahing and laughing. I have no doubt it is so unusual of late for them to pursue a retreating foe, that it did them good to pursue four or five hundred men with some 20,000, which they evidently had.

We soon saw their vanguard debouching from the woods, and about the same time a party of horsemen galloped down the road towards us, we let them come to within 75 yards, when we gave the command "fire" and only three were seen to go back. We then fell back to a clump of old field pines, and drew up again. Very soon they were upon us. We fired into them and slowly rejoined our line of battle. Our artillery then opened and the balls flew thick and fast until darkness closed the fight of Saturday. We held our position until some eight o'clock, p. m., and prevented the enemy from advancing farther that day. The enemy overshot us badly, their balls mostly tearing off the limbs above our heads. We retired from this position to a church located on the road side, some half mile from the Kinston bridge. Here we met with a portion of the Holcombe Legion, and here every one decided that we must fight the battle of Kinston. We were driven to the wall. Some of our dinner table and chimney corner patriots can imagine our feeling if they choose, on Saturday night, the 13th of December. We had been on a forced march the whole day, many without a single blanket, and not allowed to kindle a fire, for it might serve to bring an angry bomb shrieking over your head; the bitter cold, the exhausted frame, and the contemplation of the fact that we numbered scarcely 500 men, and would on the morrow meet the horde of Foster in deadly conflict, were reflections which we have been unused to have, in days and nights so near to merry Christmas; but we will sleep despite it all and dream of warm beds and reinforce-ments.

In slumber I leave the actors of the first day's fight around Kinston, and will give you the grand final anon.

L.

* * *

Battle of Kinston.
Kinston, N. C., Dec. 31st, 1862.

The Town of Kinston is situated on the north bank of the Neuse River. Di-rectly south of the Town a bridge crosses the river and various roads lead off from the opposite side, to Newbern, Dover, Trenton and Wilmington. About half a mile from the bridge, down the Wilmington road, is a church, and around this church my last letter to you left the little band of Confederates, who were entrusted with the defense of the place. The morning of December 14 dawned upon them, in all the serene beauty of a December morning. They awoke from their chilly slumbers on the ground, and every thing seemed peaceful and quiet. The doors of the little church were open, the day was the blessed Sabbath, but the man of God was not to be heard to-day, counseling peace and repentance to day and the place were to be consecrated to angry Mars.

The morning wore away in fearful suspense. The near proximity of the enemy determined Col. McMaster to have arrangements made for an attack at any mo-ment, and he accordingly arranged a plan of battle. The detachment of the 61st N. C. T., were placed on the right, the Holcombe Legion in the center, and the six companies of our Regt. (the 17th) on the left. Four pieces of Capt. Bunting's N. C. Artillery were arranged in good positions, to rake an advance of the enemy from any quarter. Captain Edwards, of our Regiment was sent forward in advance to await the enemy. About 8 o'clock, a. m., Gen. Evans arrived on the ground, made no alterations in the line of battle, but ordered another company from our Regiment forward "to meet the enemy, and to go on until we did meet them, and then fight them back." Company F, Capt. Avery was selected, and the two companies pro-ceeded forward across a tremendous swamp, and then to an enclosed field, skirted with old field pines. The companies deployed in this field and very soon the long lines of skirmishers of the enemy were seen advancing. We allowed them to get within 150 yards, when we opened fire on them and fell back across the swamp,

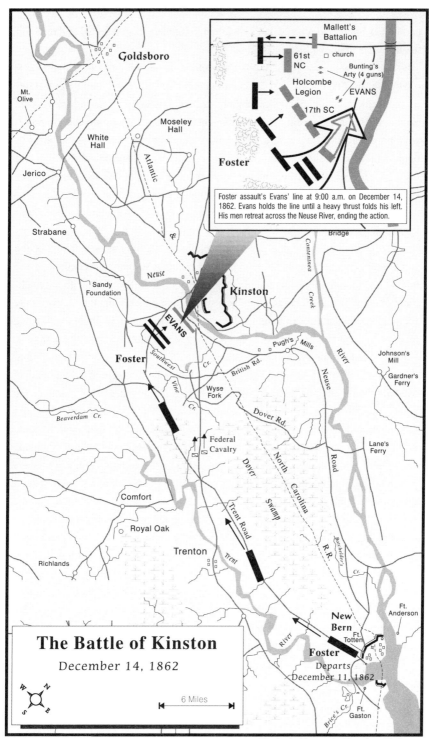

Mallett's Battalion

61st NC

□ church

Bunting's Arty (4 guns)

EVANS

Holcombe Legion

17th SC

Foster

Foster assault's Evans' line at 9:00 a.m. on December 14, 1862. Evans holds the line until a heavy thrust folds his left. His men retreat across the Neuse River, ending the action.

Goldsboro

Mt. Olive

Moseley Hall

White Hall

Jerico

Atlantic

Strabane

Bridge

Contentnea

Neuse

Sandy Foundation

Kinston

Creek

EVANS

Foster

Southwest Cr.

Pugh's Mills

British Rd.

River

Neuse

Johnson's Mill

Gardner's Ferry

Vine Cr.

Wyse Fork

Dover Rd.

Beaverdam Cr.

Federal Cavalry

Dover Swamp

North Carolina R.R.

Lane's Ferry

Road

Comfort

Royal Oak

Trent Road

Trenton

Trent

Batchelder's Cr.

Richlands

River

New Bern

Ft. Anderson

Ft. Totten

The Battle of Kinston

December 14, 1862

Foster Departs December 11, 1862

6 Miles

Brice's Cr.

Ft. Gaston

Mark A. Moore & Theodore P. Savas

and halted again; and when they came in range we gave them a volley and returned to our places in line of battle.

The artillery now opened and the fight commenced in good earnest at 9 o'clock, a. m. The enemy first attacked our right and were repulsed several times by our artillery and infantry. Our artillery did good execution, sending the vandals back at every onset, until its ammunition was exhausted and it compelled to retire, which it did about 11 o'clock, a. m. We were then left with only our small arms to oppose the overwhelming numbers of the enemy, with their splendid artillery in full play upon us. We still maintained our position, and Col. Mallett's battalion of N. C. Troops coming in at this juncture, charged the enemy on our right and drove them back some distance, the enemy continued to rally and return to the charge again and again, but were as many times driven back.

Fresh firing opened upon our extreme left and we soon became aware of the fact that the enemy were using their superior numbers to flank our position on the left, which they finally succeeded in doing, driving Col. Radcliffe with a detachment of the 61st N. C. Troops, from his position, and thus leaving the way open for pushing their columns up the upper Trent road to the bridge. Our Gen. foreseeing this, ordered our Regiment to fall back, leaving skirmishers behind, which we did. Why the same order was not extended to regiments on our right, I am unable to determine. The result was that many of the Holcombe Legion and a large part of Mallett's battalion were cut off by the enemy, and prevented from reaching the bridge in time to cross. Our Regiment crossed and found much wrangling and confusion. Troops were countermarching on the bridge, and we were ordered back, and then the order countermanded, and we took up a position on the River bank, above the bridge. In the meantime the bridge was fired and scores of our soldiers were dashing through the flames in order to escape the Yankees, who were pressing on behind them. Our artillery, some 20 pieces, now opened upon the advancing foe, but the close race made by the enemy, compelled our men to reserve their fire so long, that many of the enemy's sharpshooters gained the river banks and picked off the gunners in such a way that they were obliged to fall back, or lose all their guns, by having their horses and gunners shot. The artillery having again left us, the enemy bringing an enfilade fire to bear upon us, besides no enemy appearing where we were ordered to look for one, but all the troops left near the bridge leaving as fast as they could. There was no alternative left for the 17th but to retire also, which was done in good order, up the river-bank to Kinston. The enemy, as soon as we left, ran upon the bridge, kicked off the piles of lightwood, and extinguishing the fire, then crossed over in pursuit.

We marched through the Town in a very dejected manner, I assure you. Every house seemed deserted, piles of cotton, turpentine, &c, were burning in the streets, and the infernal shells of the enemy shrieked over our heads, splintering buildings in their course. We met General Evans at the Depot, in the Northern part of Town. He looked like one "out of soap," ordered us to form a line of battle, but the artillery was miles away, and there was no use in contending now, so we were ordered in the direction of Goldsboro. We set forward with heavy hearts, but better steps than one would imagine for broken down men. We had not proceeded far before two flags of truce were seen coming. We halted, and one being accepted, was taken to Gen. Evans, when the Colonel bearing it, notified Evans that Gen. Foster requested a surrender of his forces. Evans told him to tell Foster to go to the "hot regions," and the interview was ended.

We proceeded up the road some six miles and halted for the night, and determined to stand here again the next day. Thus ended the fight of Sunday, the 14th of December, and thus has fallen Kinston. Had we received a thousand men to our assistance at 1 o'clock, p. m., I believe we could have held the place. As it is, we fell back—were not driven back. Some orders, and firing the bridge, I think were not given and done at the right time. If they had, we should not have lost so many prisoners. Our loss in killed was small, our positions having been well chosen. Our Regiment was particularly fortunate, losing only some two or three killed and 8 or 10 wounded.

Our Colonel is a man respected and loved by every man in the Regiment. His courage is of the coolest character. He is always with his men, and selects himself, with a precision hard to be excelled, the best positions. The honorary fame of the 17th S. C. V., is secure, and fortunately, placed in the hands of the truely honest Scotch-Irishman, Fitz McMaster.

More *anon*.

L

Kinston,
Jany 4th 1862 [1863]

My Dear Wife:

I received your kind letter this evening of Jany 1st. I also received one by Moorehouse and answered it immediately. I am in good health & spirits this evening. I heard exclint Sermon from Mr Girardeau this morning from the Parable of the "Prodigal Son." He is an excellent preacher. Our Regt is in good health now. We number some 430 men. I am glad to hear you had a pretty good Christmas. Ours was pretty rough. I was over our battle ground yesterday. It is truly an awful sight. Every tree & bush is completely riddled with balls. Great pines are cut down like pipe stems and scenes of the death struggle are apparent every where. A number of huge graves are filled with our invaders and nothing but inscriptions upon board of their names rank &c are left to tell. As we were returning a yankee flag of Truce was at the river. They were after the bodies of some Officers killed there. We went with them and assisted them in raising them. They were in a good state of preservation. The enemy suffered <u>much more</u> here than we did. They had two Colonels killed and many other Officers.

We have good news from Murfreesboro.[11] I pray we may be successful throughout the West. We have rather exciting rumors here now, an advance is expected either upon us or Weldon but I am unable to say whether they are truthful or not. There is some movement going on however. I want you to come to see me and we may have rumors of this sent all the while. I have boarding engaged in Town, so if you are willing to risk the chances of a Skeedoddle you can come on. I wish you to have my boots however and write me when you will start. You can bring John & Cella, but had better leave Lulu. Mrs W S Moore will perhaps come. If so she will send word. Bill wants to get home himself but I think it doubtful about his doing so. I wrote you to get a sword. You need not do so now as I have one. Be sure to get me a pair of boots or I shall be barefooted. Send my blue coat. Be sure to let me know when you will start before you come. If you can come with Uncle Jeff it would be much better. You can bring a Trunk. I expect you can come on half fare on the N C roads. In regard to Uncle Jeff, if he is unable to perform Duty he must get an extension of his Furlough in Columbia. If he thinks they will not grant it, he had better come direct to his Regt and bring Surgeons Certificate or Family Physician. They are getting very strict about absentees, as you will see in papers.

You did not write me how much Mr Wheeler rented the house for. You ought to have made them one visit any way, if you had to stay another day. I expect it was well enough G R got a few wounds. He can now appreciate how bullets feel alittle. I fear we will have an active winter Campaign unless we can have course weather. It is very cloudy now. I would not care how bad the weather is now. Salt is coming down tremendeously. I see in Columbia it is only $12 Dollars per Bushel. In a short time it will be cheap enough. The people are getting supplied. The demand is falling off. I have not heard a word from my Brothers since the Fredericksburg fight. Write soon and give me all the news.

My love to all. Kiss the children & may I see you all once again.

Your husband

David J. Logan

W S Moore says to let his wife know when you conclude to come.

_____

The preceeding letter was the last personal correspondence between David and Sallie until January 30. It is probable that during this period Logan wrote and posted at least one letter which did not reach Sallie. At this time information began to circulate throughout the Confederacy of President Abraham Lincoln's Emancipation Proclamation, which had taken effect on the first of the year. Logan's correspondence is suprisingly silent on the subject. The "good news" from Murfreesboro, alluded to by Logan, was anything but for the Confederacy. In reality, Braxton Bragg's Army of Tennessee was beaten in the three-day battle and the Southerners were forced to retreat, giving up much of Tennessee in the process.

As Logan and his fellow South Carolinians marked time near Kinston, Union forces in New Bern launched a reconnaissance inland, triggering a series of skirmishes on January 19 at White Oak Creek and near Jacksonville, North Carolina.

_____

An Editorial to the Yorktown Enquirer

A Card[12]

Messrs Editors:

My attention has been drawn to the remarks of a correspondent of the Yorkville Enquirer, republished in your issue of the 10th instant, in which the writer, evidently, with a milicious intent, speaks of General Evans as being absent on an "excursion," at the time the enemy were approaching this place, and inferentially states that it was due to the presence of General Gwynn that the troops were brought from an exposed to a safer position.

I deem it due to General Evans to say that he was not absent in the manner indicated in the letter of the Yorkville correspondent, but was at the time on a tour of inspection, within the limits of his District. He returned, however, early on the morning of Saturday, and in time to make dispositions for the attack on that day. During his absence, Colonel J. D. Radcliffe, of the Sixty-first Regiment North Carolina Troops, a skillful, brave and prudent officer, was left in command with full instructions in case of an attack. The withdrawal of the troops from over the creek, spoken of in the correspondent's letter, was made in obedience to instructions left by General Evans, and by order of Colonel Radcliffe, and under his personal superintendence. The writer of this being present and cognizant of all the dispositions.

In describing the fight of Sunday, the "correspondent" says, that there were at the bridge "twenty pieces of artillery." I know not the manner in which the writer obtained his information, but as he is evidently a devotee of truth's the strange fact of seeing double may account for his coverting nine into twenty pieces.

The correspondent says, that the artillery having left their position it was no longer necessary for the infantry to remain. The artillery did not leave until the infantry had left them no support, or at least one battery did not and *all* left without orders from General Evans. As regards the "enfilade" fire of the enemy, one of the batteries in front of the bridge only had two men slightly wounded.

Further on the correspondent describes his feelings on the entering and traversing the town under fire of shell, and says that "he met General Evans at the depot in the Northern part of the town." The fire had ceased almost entirely before General Evans left the scene of action where he remained after all the troops had gone from their positions, and until the enemy had crossed one of his regiments. The writer was with General Evans at the time, and was sent by him to post the artillery on Washington's Hill. While the writer of this was absent to report this fact, the artillery under some misconception limbered up and left on the Goldsboro Road. It was subsequent to this that General Evans overtook the troops at the depot.

Lastly, the writer observes that "some orders and firing the bridge were not given and done at the proper time. If they had, we would not have lost so many prisoners."

I suppose the writer alludes to the order directing the troops to retire and assume position on the North bank of the river. In reference to this, I have only to say that had Gen. Evans' written orders been implicitly obeyed, the troops would have all passed the bridge unscathed, and the town of Kinston saved from the ravages of the enemy.

A STAFF OFFICER
Kinston, N.C., January 15, 1863

The above card and explination grew out of the letters in regard to the battle of Kinston. The "Staff Officer," I found to be Saml Carrie of Charleston S.C.[13]

*   *   *

Presentation to Colonel McMaster
Camp Kershaw, Near Kinston, N.C.
Jan. 17, 1863

Mr. Editor:—As hundreds of your readers will be interested in hearing from the 17th Regiment, S.C.V., I will state that we are pleasantly situated near Kinston, N.C., and with the exception of an occasional case of small pox, are enjoying excellent health. We have frequent rumors of the advance of the enemy from Newbern in this direction; but as Gen. Foster did not think it prudent to hold this place when he obtained possession of it a few weeks since, I think it hardly probable he will again attempt to take it.

The officers and soldiers of this regiment took their Colonel with a very agreeable surprise a few days since. In the short time of a few minutes, they had raised the handsome sum of near eight hundred dollars, which they determined should be applied to the purchase of a splendid horse and equipments. The purchase of this horse was committed to Adjutant J.W. Connor, who, after riding several days, selected a noble iron grey, sixteen and a half hands high, a complete animal, and fully worth the amount paid for him, (six hundred dollars.)

On yesterday, the 16th inst., at 10 o'clock, a.m., the regiment was drawn up in three-fourths a square, and Capt. E.A. Crawford, in behalf of the men, presented the horse to Colonel McMaster in the following words:

Colonel: The officers and soldiers of this Regiment, prompted by the high regard and esteem in which you are held by them as an officer and a gentleman, have placed in my hands for presentation to you this horse. The duty assigned me is a pleasing one, but it would be doubly so, could I but command a flow of language in which I could fully remind you of the many scenes of danger and death through which you have closely and unshrinkingly passed with us. From the green isles of our own loved State to almost the centre of down-trodden Maryland you have shared with us, without respite, the privations of camp, the suffering and fatigue of forced marches, and the bivouac upon the bleak mountains of Maryland and Virginia.

And there are spots consecrated in history, where we can testify in other places to the noble and heroic manner in which you stood forth our cherished leader. Yes, the "second glorious Manassas," the ill-fated "Boonsboro," and the long and terrible struggle of "Sharpsburg," with the more recent battles of "Kinston," all found you at your post, discharging your duty with calm and

determined courage, and blooded with courageous qualities, we have always found you the impartial and courteous officer, the humane and Christian gentleman.

Accept now, sir, this noble steed, and if destiny should decree that we must yet pass through the storm of battle, may that God who has so often protected you from the fatal shaft, still cover you with the same mantle of protection, and permit you to behold the blessings of peace, and return to your home and loved ones, honored by us all, as you now are.

Colonel McMaster then, in a very happy manner replied, accepting the horse:

Col. Fitz William McMaster

Courtesy CWTI

Officers and Soldiers of the 17th Regiment, S.C. Volunteers; More than twelve months ago you selected me, a stranger to the great majority of your regiment, and exalted me to the next highest office in your gift. The fate of war has removed him whom we and our State delighted to honor, and for the last five months it has been my privilege to be your chief commander.

During this eventful period, our country has passed through the keenest throes of the revolution, which is to declare her independence and establish your rights as freemen. In the conflict of arms which has moistened the fields of Virginia and the mountains of Maryland with patriot blood, you, with many other noble regiments of the South, have faithfully done your duty. Mournful and terrific have been your sacrifices, but alike honorable to yourselves and your country.

Upon the plains of Manassas, when the brigade to which you were attached was almost literally cut to pieces, five or six of your color-guard was shot down, and more than two-thirds of your number were killed and wounded. Amongst those who fell that fatal day was our noble chief, Col. Means, whose heart blood poured out on the field, attested his devotion to the principles of State sovereignty, which through life he had avowed. At Boonsboro, one half of your number engaged were disabled by the overpowering numbers of the enemy, but a large portion of the remainder still preserved the line of battle and presented a bold front to the enemy. In these engagements 258 of your ranks were killed and wounded. Reduced by the casualties of battle and the privations of the march to a little band of sixty men, your regiment three days afterwards, at Sharpsburg, engaged the enemy. Being detached from your brigade on the advanced line of Longstreet's division, that gallant little band, amidst the shot and shell of the enemy, for hours masterly maintained its position, until a Georgia and Carolina brigade on the right, and a Carolina brigade on the left, had been broken and driven back, and they were nearly encircled by the hostile hosts which opposed them.

The accidents of battle, the toilsome march, sleepless nights, and exposure to dews and rains thinned your ranks. Many with bare and bleeding feet, with scant and unwholesome food, with bodies weakened by disease and exhaustion, until they dropped in ranks—still they struggled on. For their hearts, stout and brave, were lightened with the fire of liberty.

When, in a measure, we had passed through the perils of the campaign and rested for a while on the banks of the Occoquan, our numbers were reduced to the size of a company. But now, thanks to a kind God for his mercies, the hospitals have been emptied, and many of our sick and wounded have returned, and our regiment begins to approximate the numbers we brought to Virginia, and perhaps is better prepared to do battle for our country than ever. It is not strange that I should be proud of commanding a regiment which has vindicated its honor and courage on so many battlefields. Adversity has welded our friendship, and it is natural I should feel interested in your welfare, for your honorable deeds reflect upon me, and if I do anything which deserves credit, it is by your instrumentality I am enabled to perform my part.

This day witnesses the appreciation you have placed upon my humble services. As a testimonial of your high regard and confidence, you have presented me with a noble animal, which, I understand, you have ordered to be equipped in the best style for my use. The gift of a splendid steed any one with ordinary feelings would highly prize, but the circumstances which surround this present, the alacrity and promptness with which the whole regiment have entered into this matter, shows it is a heart offering which would excite in a colder heart than mine, the deepest gratitude.

To you, Captain Crawford, I return my thanks for the complimentary manner in which you have bestowed the present. You are the only Captain in the regiment who, with me, have passed through the battles in which the regiment has been engaged, unscathed by the death dealing missles of the enemy. We have been preserved from the pestilence that walketh in darkness, and the destruction which wasteth at noonday. Let us continue to invoke blessings upon ourselves and our regiment, and let all the ends we aim at be our God's, our country's, and truth's.

My men, I thank you for your noble present. In future it will be one of the most pleasant recollections of my past history to remember this signal manifestation of your favor. And when grim visaged war has smothered its wrinkled front, and peace, like an angle of grace, will re-visit our country, stand redeemed and disenthralled from the foul tyranny of Yankee despotism. When God once more in goodness shall say to this Confederacy, "Peace within thy walls, and prosperity in thy palaces," It will always be a satisfaction to me to grip by the hand any member of the 17th and call him friend. Again I thank you heartily for your present, and pray that God's blessings may attend you in your future conflicts!

At the conclusion of the address, three rousing cheers were given, and the regiment returned to quarters.

Yours, truly, L.

*   *   *

ARMY CORRESPONDENCE[14]
Camp Kershaw, Near Kinston, N.C.
January 20, 1863

Mr. Editor:—I have been a constant reader of your paper for the last two months, and allow me to say that your course as a journalist has extorted admiration and praise from every officer and soldier in this department with whom I have conversed, although mostly natives of a different State. Your bold and manly course, in reference of the defense of your native State, together with the lofty feelings of State pride and jealous watchfulness you exercise in regard to her honor and fame, cannot but meet the approbation of every true hearted man, who loves his mother State as he should.

Although a citizen of South Carolina, I am free to admit, that the presses of the old North State have been tardy and slow, in rendering to her sons the glory which is richly theirs, on many a bloody battle field. There seems to be too much bickering and strife among political parties in your State; where the various organs which are, or seem to be, almost exclusively engaged in lampooning and belaboring each other, to display as much energy and zeal for the welfare of your soldiers and State, I doubt not, there would soon be but very few in your borders, but would glory more in the name of the old North State, and acknowledge her with much more furvor and devotion. I see that party feelings, or else a great (as I think) indifference to State defense still exists in your army in its "camps upon the Rappahannock." I am from another State, but for several months have been stationed on the coast of this State; I know (for I have seen) the finest portion of North Carolina is now in the hands of the enemy, and for a length of time, the invader has been threatening to extend his ravages, yet I see resolutions emanating from N.C. troops, counselling your Legislature to be calm and quiet, not to insist too strong upon a State force, "other States have suffered more than North Carolina, &c." We have a reserve force in our State, and I do not think President Davis or the other States would object in the least, for North Carolina to do all she can to stay the invader, and drive him back from such a fertile and productive portion of your State as is now in his hands, at least it is the duty of every State to be watchful and jealous of its interests; any other course would not be consistent with the feelings and State pride of an

Officer of Gen. Evans' Brigade

*   *   *

From the 17th Regt., S.C.V.
Camp Kershaw, Near Kinston, N. C.,
January 28th, 1863.

Dear Enquirer:—We have had quite a breathing spell since the raid of Foster, and have profited very much from the inaction of the enemy. When he came upon us before, we were reposing in fancied security. Now we have adopted the Yankee occupation of "digging dirt,"[15] and Kinston presents the appearance of a well fortified place. The works thrown up have inspired our soldiers with much better feelings of our ability to resist the invader, should he again attempt to drive us from our position. I think that the "dirt digging process" has proved to be of great service to the Confederates, in every instance where they have availed themselves of it; and great damage to them wherever they have allowed the Yankees to make use of it against them. As an illustration of the former, I would refer to James Island, Vicksburg, and Fredericksburg, and of the latter, to Malvern Hill and Corinth. There is no doubt about the question of a soldier fighting better and to a greater advantage when he is under cover, and feels some degree of security from the missles of the enemy; and I hope and trust our leaders will at all times, (for they usually have choice of position) look well to their ground and be well fortified. "Digging trenches" is a part of a soldier's duty that I have heard less complaining about than any other, from the soldier himself. He tires in the never ceasing "drill," and complains at the onerous guard duty; but put him to making a "breast work" and he goes at it whistling, and thinks of the advantage it may be to him personally, at some future time.

We have frequent rumors of the advance of the enemy towards us here, and to the *fresh soldier* these reports would be a source of never ceasing anxiety; but we have learned to be easy, and if we can't be exactly easy, we do like the Irishman "be as azy as we can." As to the probable advance of the enemy in this direction, I can venture no opinion of any worth. One thing we know, there is a powerful army in Newbern, and with a volcano so near, it is prudent at all times to be on the look out for an eruption. There is an unusual amount of desertion from the Yankee army. Some few arrive almost every day. One day last week as many as ten came in. They report dissatisfaction; but most of them are foreigners, and consequently not much can be gathered from them.

There is much bad feeling among the officers of our Brigade. Charges have been preferred against General Evans by Colonel Goodlet, of the 22d Regiment, S. C. V., and he in turn has several Colonels and other officers under arrest. Among

Brig. Gen. Nathan "Shanks" Evans

Generals in Blue

them our much esteemed Col. McMaster. What the charges are against him, he does not know, but seems to be resting very contentedly, and says the stings of conscience have not yet affected him for any known misdeed, and I am sure the Regiment with one accord sustains him, in all actions known to them. His offence is presumed to be a petition to be transferred to some other Brigadier General.

The action of an honorable court will soon decide the differences. In the meantime we are all united against the enemy and will fight as hard as ever if they come upon us.

Our Regiment has wonderfully improved in the way of comfort since my last letter. The Quarter Masters have been stirring, and all the wrath that I have been nursing for them has been cooled by the excellent tents we now have. Every private now has a canvass roof between him and the vault of Heaven, for the first time this winter. Choice English made shoes have been furnished in abundance too. As an acknowledgement to the ladies Soldier's Relief Societies at home I would state that our Company (F) has received the following articles, *gratis* from them, viz: One pair shoes, 2 pair drawers, 3 pair socks, 1 pair pants and 2 shirts. The same amount was received by the other companies in the Regiment, and was given to the most destitute. We begin to need hats about as bad as any thing else now. I see in Raleigh, N. C., that quantities of that useful article are manufactured by the ladies. They use a good article of casimere and make a very neat hat. I wear one myself for which I gave ten dollars. Our lady friends could make themselves very useful and subserve the good cause of Southern independence, if they would get up a hat factory in Yorkville, and send a few out occasionally, the soldiers will pay good profits and be glad to get something of the kind; and the reflection that they were made by our kind friends at home, would cause them to last much longer.

The health of our Regiment is very good. An occasional case of small pox occurs, but it travels slowly. The men are now well vaccinated, and the disease is very light, when it attacks those who have been so, causing them but little pain or apprehension. Quite a number of soldiers have recovered from the disease and act as nurses, thus rendering the situation of the sick much better here than it might be at home, and our Assistant Surgeon, Dr. Hall, although he has never had the disease, continues his ministrations as if it was a simple case of fever, and like other complaints. He has been well vaccinated and has, so far, escaped even the slightest varioloid.

The religious sentiment of our regiment is good, although we have no Chaplain at this time. It is delightful to hear, as the night is coming on, the cheerful voices of the soldiers, singing the familiar hymns of their respective sections. They gather into groups, and the old songs which are often sung at Antioch, Bethesda and Shiloh,[16] are reproduced with renewed fervor and devotion, as the minds of the singers recur to the scenes of home. There is not that wickedness which people usually think attendant with an army, here. The Bible is a constant companion, and the true appreciation of the daily jeopardy of life, is felt and considered by nearly all.

The spirits of the regiment are, also, good, as is attested by the crowds who fill the parade grounds during the interval from duty, renewing the sports of boyhood in the games of "Prison base," "Bull pen," &c.[17] The weary nights are shortened by nightly "auctions," where the "Ram" (the facetious name of the auctioneer) disposes of multitudinous articles of wearing apparel, knives, watches, &c., with all the grace of a Yankee "Razor strap man."

Although we are enjoying life as well as it can be enjoyed in camp, yet we would, above all earthly blessings, rather hear the word *peace* now, than any other, and be allowed to return to our homes and loved ones; but until we can be *assured* that we can return and "sit down beneath our own vine and fig trees, with none to molest or make us afraid," we shall continue to grip the weapon of war, and resist the invader until he is driven from our borders.

My space warns me to close. With the kindest wishes for the welfare of the good folks at home,

I am yours, truly,

L.

*   *   *

Explanation

Messrs. Editors:—My attention has been called to the publication of a "Card" in your issue of the 23d instant, signed "A Staff Officer," in which complaint is made in regard to certain statements of a correspondent of the Yorkville Enquirer. As I hold myself responsible for those statements I shall proceed to notice them.

First. The "Staff Officer" thinks that the statement that Gen. Evans was "absent on an excursion in the neighborhood of Greenville and Plymouth," was made with *malicious intent*. I disclaim any such intention. On the contrary, I remember that news reached our camp on the 12th of December that our forces were doing good work in that direction, and that General Evans was acting an important part in the programme, and at the time of my writing my mind was so impressed. Therefore I certainly think a "Staff Officer" must be particuliarly sensitive to construe my words into a meaning of that kind.

Next he infers that I stated that the removal of the troops to the North side of Southwest Creek "was due to the presence of Gen. Gwyn." I was certainly so informed by an officer who came to Col. Goodlett's camp with Gen. Gwyn; or at least was informed that a consultation was held there, the result of which was our withdrawal to the position before mentioned; but of course a "Staff Officer" would have better information in regard to the orders of Gen. Evans, and I accept his statement as correct. The account of the fight of Sunday was written hurriedly by me in pencil, and I asked, the question how many batteries had we? A bystander replied "four." I then wrote "some twenty pieces," and thus an error was made, which I have since ascertained to be such from other sources than a "Staff Officer." As to my "seeing double," I am very sure there were others than the "Yorkville correspondent" who had their sights raised on that occasion.

In the fourth place the "Officer" quotes me as saying that "the artillery having left it was no longer necessary for the infantry to remain." My statement was not so general as it is made here, but was confined to the movements of my own regiment in a great measure, as reference to my communication will show. The assertion "that the artillery did not leave until the infantry had left them no support, or at least one battery did not," I take it for granted is an unintentional mistake of a "Staff Officer," or at least has no reference to the 17th and 46th N. C. Troops, for every officer and soldier of these regiments will testify (I am sure) that their positions were maintained until *all the artillery had left*. Several members of my Company assisted at the wheels of the gun carriages of Capt Boyce's battery in getting *it* away from the scene of action, and I feel certain that *this* battery was the *last* that left. Our regiment was then occupying its designated position. There were two guns disabled and left by the gunners near the bridge, which were captured by the enemy. If the "Staff Officer" has reference to that battery, I *knock under*. The "Officer" goes on to state "that Gen. Evans remained on the scene of action until the firing had almost ceased," &c. I made no mention as to the "position of Gen. Evans" during the engagement, as I did not know where it was, but one thing *I do know*, the three regiments before mentioned were not *overtaken* by the General at any point between the Kinston bridge and Washington's hill, as every man will testify. They retired in good order up the river bank (as has been stated in your paper by the Colonel of the 17th regiment, S. C. V., in reply to the statement of "personne" some weeks ago,) and halted for some minutes opposite the residence of Gen. Cox in Kinston, and for orders; but not seeing the General or any of his Staff, they proceeded up the Main street to the railroad depot, where we saw Gen. Evans and he ordered us to "form line of battle." A "Staff Officer" then goes on to comment upon my remarks in reference to "orders," &c. As there is nothing conflicting there I leave the matter, hoping that my explanation will be fully satisfactory; and with the kindest wishes for the welfare and the greatest admiration for the courage and high social qualities of the gallant Captain, whom I have guessed as the "Staff Officer," I am done with the battle of Kinston in the newspapers.

Yours, L.

Camp Kershaw, near Kinston, N. C., January 29, 1863

———————

Camp Kershaw near Kinston
Jany 30th 1863

My Dear Wife:

I received your letter & box by Lieut Neely. The shoes are substantial & will certainly last well. They are quite large but that will be a good feeling. You complain of not receiving any letters from me. I am sure I write 2 or 3 for every one I receive from you. I received the one by Mr Black and one next day. Those are the last I received until this one. I have written 3 in the meantime. I received the gloves. We have had some dreadful weather here. Rain snow &c and an awful wind is blowing now.

Every thing is quiet at present as to the enemy. Our Regt is in very good health. No new cases of small pox. I wish your arm would take as I am very anxious to see you, but do not wish you to come unless your arm takes well. I think it best for you to have your teeth worked on if they can be saved & Dr Cravin of York is about as good a Dentist as you will get. Have them worked on by all means. I would like to have mine fixed but I dont fancy the operation in my mouth. I received a letter from Pa the other day. Ben was not so well and had been unanimously elected 2nd Lieutent. The other boys were in good health. I have not seen or heard from Uncle Tim, although he is near.

There is a large army all around us here, but we know but little of it. N B Bratton's marriage is certainly romantic. I am sorry to hear of the deaths you mention. We are fairing only tolerable now. Have to do our own cooking which you can imagine is none of the best. I wish I had got a boy while at home. I have some money which I would like to send home also some shoes. Write me how your arm progresses, and whether you can come or not. Write often and long letters. I would be pleased to have one every day. Is Mr Bratton <u>correct</u> in his reasons for your tooth ache? You have never informed me of your safety.

You will see a communication from me in Enquirer of next week. Also have presentation to Col McMaster in this week. I wish you to preserve all these papers. I sent by Sergt Mitchell a Pipe & letter last Monday. The pipe was a present from Col McMaster. I wish you to lay it away carefully. Your Father did not get full price for his corn as it is selling at $2.00 now in York. I have got a sword, as I have written 3 times now. We are having a <u>grand row</u> now among our big Officers. <u>I have got into a mess</u> in the "Charleston Courier" with "somebody." You may see the pieces copied in the York paper. I dont intend to get hurt bad in the scrape if I can help it. Include my congradulations in your letter to Mrs Neely. Capt Avery thinks he has Small pox.

My love to all. Mollie C had better look sharp as that McElwee.

Your husband

D J Logan

Write often. Kiss the children for me.

*   *   *

Camp Gregg, Kinston NC
Feby 5th 1863

My Dear Wife:

We have just received orders to march to Wilmington. Our place here has been taken by a NC Brigade & we leave on the cars as soon as arrangements can be made. I regret leaving here very much as it was a pleasant place and you might have come to see me, but is too late now. If there is any chance for you to stay near our Camp at Wilmington I will write you.

I am in good health. The snow is 8 & 9 inches deep and looks like it will snow again. I would like for you to pay the balance due on the Pagan house[18] & lift the deed and papers. I dont know how much is due on it. I will write Mr. Wheeler and inform him what you will do and to turn the papers in to you.

Write soon & direct to Wilmington NC. Give my best love to your parents and Kiss Johnnie & Lulu for me. I want to see you all very bad, but there is no chance now. Bill Moore can get no Furlough yet.

Your husband

D J Logan

———————

From the 17th Regt.,S.C.V.
Camp Gregg, Near Kinston, N.C.
February 5, 1863

Dear Enquirer:—Our hearts were made glad, on the evening of the 2nd instant, by the reception of the glorious news from our good old State. May the enemies of our country ever meet the same kind of disaster, in every operation against us. All hail to Ingraham and his gallant followers.[19]

After telling, and hearing the news repeated a hundred times, we retired to our soldier's couch, and fell into a sweet sleep, and upon waking, found the earth arrayed in the virgin robe of winter. The snow has fallen here to the depth of eight inches. Our soldiers, at the first peep of day, were up and busy in annoying their fellows with snow balls—not seeming to mind the cold. After much difficulty, we succeeded in raising enough wood, and thereby procuring a breakfast, and about the time it was over, we were aroused by the report that the 23rd Regiment, S.C.V., was approaching us in line of battle. We all rushed to our parade ground, and succeeded in forming a line of battle, in time to prevent a complete surprise. The Officers of the 23d, seeing us in active preparation for resistance, dispatched Capt. Duffey and Adjutant Richardson with a flag of truce, demanding "an unconditional surrender of our forces." They were met by Capt. Mill's and other officers of our Regiment, and informed that "the 17th never surrendered." They returned to their command, and hostilities immediately commenced.

Our skirmishers engaged, and the balls flew thick and fast. In a short time the whole line was ordered up. Your correspondent was sent with a detachment, to check a flank movement that was being made on our right. He succeeded in doing so, after desperate fighting, in which, for a time, he was a prisoner in the hands of the enemy; but our forces on the left, had overcome the opposition, and the enemy had "begun to waver." And about this time, the battle had rolled so much to our left, that the guard seeing the doubtful condition of their comrades, one by one, began to leave us, and finally so many had gone, that I looked round and gave the order to "overcome the guard," which was done in handsome style. The few remaining "guards" leaving at the double-quick, with innumerable balls exploding against them. (We did not consider the breaking away as *wrong*, from the fact that we were impressed by main force and not held by the same.) We then rushed to the assistance of our friends on the left, where we now achieved a complete victory.

The enemy retiring as fast as possible, but with occassional halts, and retiring salutes. Many were the exploits of strength and daring during the battle; but where all did so well distinctions would be invidious, as our Generals say. One incident I cannot pass over. Rev. Mr. Girardeau, Chaplain of the 23rd Regiment, was fighting manfully, and not being known by the 17th Regiment, was roughly handled at times. At one time I saw a Sergeant of our Regiment and another, gather him and hurl him to the ground, rubbing the snow into him very profusely, and occassionally asking him "if he gave up." The parson invariably replied "I never surrender." They would then "trounce him" in the snow again. Finally our men became informed who they were using so badly, when they restored him to liberty and joined in the pursuit of his then retiring comrades.

In the evening, our Regiment attacked the camp of the 23rd, and after a long and desperate engagement, were compelled to retire. The 3rd of February was rendered a gaily day by the "snow storm" and will often be mentioned with joy by the participants, in coming years, when their now youthful heads, shall be white as the snow of winter.

A very singular or unusual phenomenon was witnessed by us all here, on the evening of the 4th instant. The full moon had risen above the horizon in the East, and on either side, equi-distant from the moon itself, were representations of the same Luminary, as, in the language of the camp, three moons as plainly seen as could be desired. Many were the speculations indulged in regard to them in camp, but I shall refer the matter to philosophers and others, only marking it down as the first time I ever saw three moons. A very thin cloud covered the moon and the earth was white with snow.

Our Brigade has been ordered to Wilmington. Two of the Regiments have gone. We expect to leave on the morrow, and it is with regret I leave Kinston, for here we have enjoyed a soldiers life as well or better than the average. But we leave these scenes, and hope the new may be equally as inviting. Our Brigade has been relieved by that of General Daniel of North Carolina. You will send your kind favors, hereafter, to our new home, and the next you hear from me (if nothing breaks) will be from Wilmington.

Yours,

L.

"If the enemy ever attack us here [Wilmington], they will be welcomed, without doubt, with `bloody hands to hospitable graves.'"

Wilmington & Charleston

February – May 1863

avid Logan's 17th South Carolina Regiment spent the next four months at two different stations on the southeast Atlantic coast. The first was Wilmington, North Carolina, and then Charleston, South Carolina. The time spent in camp at Wilmington was rather mundane when compared to the previous months in the vicinity of Kinston and Goldsboro. While at Wilmington, Logan made several excursions into the countryside and recorded much of what he saw. It was during this period that Logan learned the Tramp Brigade's infamous commander, Nathan Evans, was found not guilty on the charges preferred against him. While in his mind such a ruling could only have been rendered by "a partial court," the brigade took a commander, albeit temporarily.

During the early part of May 1863, the regiment was hurriedly transferred to Charleston to strengthen the defenses there in anticipation of a Federal attempt to capture the city. When the attack failed to materialize, the regiment's brief stop on its home soil drew to a close.

From the 17th Regt., S.C.V.
Camp Jenkins,
Below Wilmington, N. C., Feb 13.

Dear Enquirer:—On the evening of the 7th instant, we bade, perhaps, a final adieu to the ancient town of Kinston, and took the cars to Goldsboro. Many sanguine hopes were indulged, that this time, we should see our good old State; but we are again disappointed. We reached Wilmington on the morning of the 8th, where we met the crew of the Yankee Gunboat, "Isaac Smith," on their way to Richmond.[1] They appeared to be mostly, a gentlemanly set, and seem to think the war will not last much longer. Asserting, as their belief, the impossiblity of our subjugation, and that the great masses of the North are becoming more and more satisfied of the same fact. They were quite jovial, and say the greatest harm they have against us now, consists in our boys having broken into their supper on the evening they were taken. The bell having just rung, when our cannon opened on them. A monster cannon passed us on its way to Charleston while we were here. Its calibre was about a 15 inch, and carries a solid ball of 200 lbs weight. We hope to hear good news from it among the "iron-clads."

Wilmington is a pretty considerable town, and has been improving very much within the past few years. The various Rail Roads concentrating upon it, and in process of completion, will render it, no doubt, a place of importance at some future day. It is being enriched now very much by the salt works, and vessels running the blockade. I had the pleasure of passing through the splendid English steamer, "Cornubia,"[2] then loading with cotton at the wharf. This vessel has made a number of successful trips within the last six months, bringing Government Stores and other useful freight, (by the way, this vessel went to sea again last night).

We remained in town until Sunday evening, when we were ordered to our present position, by General Whiting, the Commandant of this post. We passed through the place, and I must say that there are some of the most beautiful private residences that I have seen in my wanderings. But the ravages of the Yellow Fever and the threatened condition of the city, have left the houses mostly tenantless. On our route, we found the approaches protected by fortification after fortification, and huge cannon already mounted, standing sentinel over the safety of the place. If the enemy ever attack us here, they will be welcomed, without doubt, with "bloody hands to hospitable graves." On our way, we passed the camps of some of our old companions in arms, on *our coast*, who have been "spoiling for a fight," all this time without getting into it. May they never be called upon to have the "wire edge" taken off as we have had it done.

We arrived at our present camp on the 9th, which our Colonel has called by the name of "Jenkins," in honor of the rising hero from York. By the way, I see the English correspondent of the *London Times*, pays our "Jenk," as the boys call him, a handsome compliment. May his star shine brighter and brighter. The situation of our camp is on "Topsil Sound," a branch, I suppose, of the Albemarle. I have had no opportunity yet, to learn anything of the Topography of the country, but will embrace the first opportunity to do so. Suffice it to say now, that we are some 14 miles North East of Wilmington.

Commissary department out of meat; but as there are mountains of oysters, and shoals of mullets, we are feeding better than one would imagine. We are not drilling but digging trenches and throwing up fortifications, with a vengeance. We are surrounded with salt works, which are turning out that indispensable, in quantities. The proprietors sell to our men at 10 cents per quart; but I learn they ask about $7 per bushel, by the quantity. The chief product of the soil here, is "pinders" or ground nuts, which are raised in astonishing quantities. Many wealthy planters being engaged wholly in their production, raising thousands of bushels, and, at the prices they are realizing now, they pay better than gold mines. There is a species of oil manufactured from them.

The York boys are all lively and enjoying good health. The same may be said of our boys in the 18th, who are camped near to us. The dread scourge, small pox, seems to have halted in its course for a while. May it never return. The names of Patrick, Smith, Wilkerson and others, have ceased to be heard at *our* roll calls. Away from their friends, obscurely laid, they await the calling of that *great roll* by the angel of the Most High, when we trust they will meet their friends where disease and war shall be felt and feared no more.

Yours, L.

Camp Benlow
Mar 3rd 1863

My Dear Wife:

I have received your letters very regularly since I came here. There is nothing new with us this morning. We are 4 miles from Town now in a

Pine barren, one of the poorest spots of earth I have ever seen. The health of the Regt is very good now. Scarcely any sickness at all. Small pox seems to have quit us altogether. Geo Menchouse got a letter from Lou McF which stated you had gone to Uncle Franks. I hope you have seen my Father & Mother. I still expect to get a Furlough when Lt Moore comes back (if we are not taken to Charleston). When I get home I want to see your letter from "Herbert" and I will then tell you if I know all about it. There are any quantity of vessels running the blockade here nearly every day. Dan Williams has come back. He left the Money with Dick Sadler.

You are mistaken of any meaning about "the Money." I meant this, that I wished the other heirs to be paid out of this money and if they call for their parts, and it is not on hand I will get it lent in order to save interest and risk of losing it. It would of course be better to invest in something by which it could be produced when called for. I wished your Father to write to the [Segatus ?] in the West that their Money is ready for them as the best way to dispose of it. I wish you to write me if it is really true that Capt Meacham has been reduced or cashiered. I am "acting Adjutant" in the Regt now. Have to preform on guard duty, and consequently get along finely.

Genl Evans has been acquitted of his Charge of Drunkeness but our opinion of him remains the same. He is a disgrace to the Service to So Ca and to all Christian people almost.[3]

Write soon and give all the news. We have had an election in our Company. O R Gunthorp was elected by a large vote. Dunovant & Happerfield were his opponents. My love to all the friends. I expect if Moore returns to be home about the 12th.

Your husband

D. J. Logan

Diary of David Jackson Logan

March 5, 1863: We are stationed now 3 miles from Masonboro Sound and the NC State Saltworks. We are also about 4 miles below Wilmington. The country is a pine barren and very sparsely inhabited. Our Camp is called "Benbow"[4] in honor of the Col of the 23rd SCV now in command of the Brigade. Genl Evans is absent on Furlough having been acquitted of the charges preferred against him, I believe by a partial Court.

I have been acting as Adjutant of the Regt for several days. We have received some recruits, Caldwell & Dover. The health of the men is better than I have ever known it before in Camp. I have taken dinner with a man called Bensly who lives near the sound. A number of vessels run the Blockade here almost every night.

———————

Wilmington N.C.
April 6th 1863

My Dear Wife:
    I wrote you yesterday and as Capt Avery is going home I shall write again.[5] I wish you to come near as you possibly can to Wilmington. I wish you to write me before you start and mention the day you intend starting so that I can meet you at the Depot or boat.
    We are in very comfortable quarters here and I know you would like to see more of the army & curiosities. Come prepared to stay some two weeks. You had perhaps better bring a servant with you. (Ceilla, if you can spare her from the children.) I can get boarding & a very nice room here at 1.50 per day. Money is worth so little. We had about as well enjoy some of it while we can. Be sure to come if you can and as soon as possible. You can put yourself under the care of the Conductors. You may have some little inconvenience at Kingsville but it is only a very small touch of war. When you get into the cars there you will not change until you see me. You had better ware your blk silk dress, and you can get shoes when you get here to suit. You be sure to write soon. Perhaps Uncle Henry would like to come after salt. He can get it at $11. by taking as many as 5 sacks. Come if you can. Love to all.
    Your husband
    D J Logan

*   *   *

Wilmington N C
April 7th 1863

My Dear Wife:

I am quite well this morning. I have written you by Capt Avery. I wish you to come as soon as you possibly can. We expect to remain here in the city for some time and I will have an excellent chance to stay with you here. You can come by Kingsville. Take the cars for the junction, then to Kingsville, and from there to Wilmington where I will meet you. Bob Caldwell's wife is here now and I expect to board at this same house. You can bring John if you think advisible & a servant. I would send you a pair shoes but you can get them here to suit you. I have written this for five. Capt Avery may request to deliver his. Come prepared to stay 2 or 3 weeks if you can. I may get a furlough to go home before a great while. We will if we stay here. Come as soon as you can for if we are moved from here I will hardly have a chance to see you soon. Salt is worth 11 to 12 Dollars. Love to all in haste.

Your husband
D J Logan

Write soon as you get this when you will start so I can meet you.

———————

Sallie Logan traveled to Wilmington in early April almost immediately after receiving the previous letter from her husband. Although neither knew it, developing military events were about to dictate a transfer of the Tramp Brigade yet again, this time back to its home state of South Carolina.

On the day Logan wrote his letter of April 7, 1863, to Sallie, nine Union ironclads steamed into Charleston's harbor and launched an attack against Fort Sumter. The noisy but unsuccessful barrage turned out to be the last major naval attempt to capture the important seaport. The vigorous effort, however, coupled with other Federal activities, prompted Richmond authorities to reinforce the critical logistical center, and within days the 17th South Carolina Regiment was ordered to Charleston.

———————

Wilmington N.C.
April 26th 1863

My Dear Wife:

    I am quite well this morning. The day you left here our Brigade was ordered to Charleston sure enough and on yesterday our Company left. I was just getting on the boat to leave with it, when I was summoned to remain behind as a witness in the trial of Col Goudlett. I know but very little about his conduct but cant get off. Maj Culp & Capt Edwards are with me. We are boarding at Mrs McCables. I wish you & the children were here with me.

    The Conductor told me you got away safely from Kingsville & said you were in charge of a Captain somebody. I hope you got along finely. Our Brigade is encamped 4 miles this side of Charleston. I feel very lonely here—like a fish out of water. I never want to hear Court Martial again. I may have to stay here 10 or 12 days yet. I shall endeavor to run the blockade for a day or two when I leave here. I shall come to Smiths T.O. and I shall risk getting a horse from Duff or McClenllock. If you see them tell them I expect to write one. The last Company of South Carolinians left here on yesterday. You must write, soon as you receive this. Direct to me without stating Regt or any thing as they will all be forwarded to Charleston & I cant get them. Give my best respects to all enquiring friends & kiss the children for me. I will write in a day or two again. Look out for me about next Sunday or Monday if nothing happens. I will come if they will let me. I will take passage by Goldsboro, Raleigh, Charlotte, &c to Charleston.

    Your Husband
    D J Logan

    The coming of spring and warm weather brought the beginning of another round of widespread warfare across the Confederacy. The Army of the Potomac, under its new commander Maj. Gen. Joseph Hooker, began moving on April 27 up the Rappahannock River in Virginia in its attempt to flank and defeat Lee's Army of Northern Virginia. The armies battled at and around Chancellorsville during several early May days before Hooker finally withdrew his divisions north of the river. Thomas J. "Stonewall" Jackson, the same general with whom Logan was so enamored during the previous summer, was mortally wounded at the height of a massive Confederate flanking operation.

Out west in Mississippi another Federal major general, Ulysses S. Grant, transferred his army to the east bank of the Mississippi River and began his overland campaign against the Southern stronghold of Vicksburg. A series of pitched battles sent Confederate forces under the command of Lt. Gen. John C. Pemberton scurrying into the confines of the city's defenses. With Pemberton unable to throw back Grant's legions, Richmond was pressured into piecing together a patchwork army under Gen. Joseph E. Johnston—dubbed "The Army of Relief"—to raise the siege of Vicksburg.

————

Secessionville
James Island, May 13th

My Dear Wife:

I wrote you a small note hurriedly after I had returned from an expedition to Seabrooks Isld.[6] I am pretty well rested now. I was almost broken down in the trip. My account of absence is all settled up now and I am still in command of the Company. Capt Avery, Guntharp being in town. Lt Moore is in the Hospital in Charleston. He is better to day as Dr Sandifer informs me. He & Dick Sadler are on a visit to our Camp to day. We are located in a very picturesque place here in full view of the yankee camps on Folly & Colles Islands and of their shipping in the river. They are very busy working away on their batteries & brestworks.

I understand we are ordered to Vicksburg, Miss. We are to leave tomorrow evening. We have been expecting this for some time, and have been ordered before but it was suspended for a time. The men are quite low in spirits about going. I have been unable to get any shoes mended and I fear these will be too frail for the trip. I am hardly well. My bowels have not acted once in three days, although my appetite is pretty good and I feel very little inconvenience. If I go West I want you to write to some of your friends and let them know that I may call on them as I shall be on the lookout for friends, especially if I should get sick. You can perhaps get out on a visit while we are there. I dont think our lines can be far away from where they are. Write to them and I may not surprise them. Uncle Jeff is in the City waiting for aunt Jane, but I learn she has not come yet. They will be disappointed I expect. There are almost as many women in the Regt now as ever. A number of the men's wives in my company are here.

If we go to Vicksburg I expect a number of the men will run the blockade.[7] I wish you would see about my taxes. I have asked Mr Wheeler to attend to so much that I dont wish to ask any more. I suppose I will have no taxes to pay on house & lot, & the other or store debts. I will let Meacham have attended to this year. I am afraid to hear from my brothers. I see their Brigade has been in the hardest of the fighting.[8] If you hear from them write me. I am a little loath to go to the West as it is so far away from home, but it is no use complaining. I will get to see a great chance of country if I am spared from Disease & the enemy. I shall not murmer at the trip.

We have some very formidable Forts here and if preparation can save Charleston I think all is right. The men talk like all intend to run the blockade. If so, I may have to go hunting them. Pray for my welfare & may God preserve and protect my Dear wife & children.

Your husband

D. J. Logan

Federal troops before Jackson, Mississippi. *Harper's Weekly*

CHAPTER 5

"War is horrible—horrible."

Vicksburg, Jackson, and The Army of Relief

May – July, 1863

W hen the threatened Union attacks at Charleston and other points along South Carolina's coastline failed to materialize, the 17th South Carolina, in conjunction with the rest of the Tramp Brigade's regiments, was ordered west in May of 1863 to bolster Gen. Joseph E. Johnston's effort to lift the Federal siege of Vicksburg, Mississippi. After a lengthy and often perilous journey by boat, train, and foot, Logan and what was left of the 17th Regiment arrived in Jackson, Mississippi, where the South Carolinians joined Johnston's growing "Army of Relief." The men went into camp on the banks of the Pearl River, attached to Maj. Gen. William W. Loring's wing.

It was during this western transfer that the earlier conduct of the Confederate authorities came back to haunt the Richmond officials. The shift to Mississippi was the second time Logan's outfit had been sent out of its home state to fight. The South Carolinians still harbored ill-feelings over the manner in which the Richmond War Department had earlier handled their transfer north to join Robert E. Lee's Virginia army. Most of these soldiers had already dedicated eighteen months of their young lives to drilling, marching and fighting in the Carolinas and Virginia, and the majority of them had not seen their families since the day of their enlistment. The transfer to distant Mississippi increased the likelihood that many would never see their families again, or at least not for a long while.

When the train carrying the Tramp Brigade from Charleston reached Branchville, South Carolina, "many of them left the train. . . and went home. It was the last time the soldiers of the brigade manifested a spirit of insubordination."[1] The mass exodus was discovered by a startled General Evans when he arrived at Jackson and found only about one-half of his brigade present for duty. Realizing there were too many men absent to effectively punish without destroying the brigade's morale, Evans implemented a unique plan for restoring his unit to fighting strength. The general ran notices in the local hometown newspapers during the last ten days of May designed to reach those who had taken a "flying visit home." The announcements stipulated that a pardon would be issued if those men absent reported to Capt. B. B. McCreary in Columbia, SC by the end of the month. In short, the men were being granted a short furlough with their friends and families without fear of retribution. By the time the window of opportunity expired on May 30, nearly every man in the 17th South Carolina had availed himself of the offer and was once again bound for Mississippi.[2]

Although David Logan did not take the opportunity to go AWOL, one of his mess mates, O. R. Guntharp, had no compunction about breaking ranks and spending extra time on the home front. While Guntharp was enjoying his family, Logan was recording with some excitement the trip to Mississippi and the accompanying sights and events experienced along the way. Once the men reached Jackson, they made camp west of the town. The regiment did little other than wait for the opportunity to engage U. S. Grant and the Federals surrounding the beleagured river port and the Confederates trapped within.

Unfortunately for Lt. Gen. John Pemberton and his embattled men, Joe Johnston spent weeks gathering an army he would never use. By the time Evans' regiments received their marching orders and began moving toward the Big Black River, Vicksburg was already a doomed city. Along the way Logan and his fellow Carolinians learned of the fortress' surrender and the rapid advance of the Federals upon the city of Jackson. A spirited defense of the important rail junction ensued, the Confederates fell back, and the Tramp Brigade once more returned to its home state.

Yorkville Enquirer
May 20, 1863

Arrival of Soldiers

The 17th and 18th Regiments, a part of Gen. Evan's brigade, having been ordered to "change their base," are fully represented in our District at this time. They determined to pay a flying visit home, and seem to be enjoying it; though we have strong suspicions that in their hurry, furloughs were <u>forgotten</u>. They will soon be on the track again, however, when the Yankees will hear from them, as usual. The 17th has missed but few battles since its organization, and the flashing of the guns always showed the 18th near by. The boys look as fat and saucy as pine smoke could make them.

*   *   *

Yorkville Enquirer
"From the West"
Jackson, Miss., May 25, 1863

Dear Enquirer:—Evan's "foot cavalry" are still "alive and kicking" on the banks of Pearl river this morning, or at least a part of them. It has always been too much the case, that a "good pulling horse is pulled to death," but as we are "toughened" and "seasoned" to hard times, it is perhaps better that we should submit to them, than expose our effeminate "pound-cake" brethren, who are enjoying themselves on our own Carolina coast, *especially* as I have understood the ladies have been very solicitous for some of them to remain where they are. May they prove their devotion to their State, and show that they appreciate the great privilege conferred upon them, by driving back the invader whenever he shall endeavor to pollute the soil of South Carolina.

The "old seventeenth," with considerable heart-burning, left Secessionville, James Island, on Saturday, the 16th ultimo, for Jackson, Mississippi, at which place it arrived on Saturday last, having been one week on the road. The diverging path from home was too strongly felt by a number, and the temptation and yearning for loved ones was so strong, that many who have heretofore been the most obedient soldiers, laid aside all military discipline, and went their way, regardless of consequences, but I am assured that their love of home and country are co-existent, and that they will be present with us in a few days, ready to do battle as bravely as ever, for Southern rights and liberty.

I should be pleased to give you an account of our trip in detail, but my opportunity will not allow. Our boys were perfectly delighted with Georgia, its crops—its lands—its houses, and especially its girls, who were thronging the road at every town and station, showering upon us their boquets of flowers, and dispensing refreshments of various kinds. Before reaching West Point[3] all the "young fellows" had decided to give the Georgia girls a call before they made a final selection, and the "old married fellows" were in extracies, almost, thinking they were boys again, in the struggle made for boquets, &c. On first entering Alabama the boys were prejiuced in favor of Georgia, and every cotton field and indifferent corn field were saluted with a huzza for the latter State, but this did not continue; before the train reached Montgomery the boys were undecided for which State to declare a preference. We reached Montgomery after dark, and about midnight were aboard the R. B. Taney, and winding our way down the Alabama river in the same steamer that carried out the Palmetto Regiment,[4] when on its way to Mexico. May the banner of the 17th come back as unspotted, but with ranks less thinned by battle and disease.

We reached Selma about 10 o'clock, A. M., Tuesday, the 18th, where we took the train for Demopolis, and here the Alabama crops, land and girls, took the palm from Georgia. Between Selma and Demopolis I have never seen such land or crops—corn large enough to lay by—wheat already cut and shocked. At Demopolis we took a boat and went 11 miles down the Tombigbee, then took cars and came to Meridian, there again, and here we are in Jackson, which the Yankees have left almost a smouldering heap of ruins. The streets are covered with burnt sugar and molasses, and every house, to use an expressive but not very refined word, is completely "gutted." We have had a number of severe fights here, in which we have generally been overpowered. The sound of cannon I hear distinctly, as I write, in the direction of Vicksburg.[5]

In reference to our troops and movements I can say nothing; but be assured, the Confederacy will soon achieve or sustain one of the greatest triumphs or defeats.

The boys of Company F, send their kindest wishes and regards for their sweethearts, and kind friends at home, and although the girls of Georgia and Alabama are hard to beat, still there is "no place like home." Old Mississippi is in tribulation and trial now, and where every one is fleeing from home and property, and fair ladies are lying in tents, and under trees by hundreds, we can't expect much help from them while in such adversity. Our people at home should rightly value their blessings, and be prepared to assist and lend a helping hand, as they would that others should do unto them.

I would gladly write more, but we were stripped for battle some 150 miles back, having left there our trunks and baggage of all kinds, and now await, at any moment, the order to "Forward and attack the enemy." More anon.

Yours, L

*   *   *

Yorkville Enquirer
May 27, 1863

Editorial Items

All absentees from Gen. Evans Brigade, who may be about these parts, are ordered to report to Capt. B. B. McCreery, at Columbia, on Saturday next, and a full pardon will be granted them for their late "raid" home. A good many of our boys are already on the way, the balance can be surely counted on. They will "get off" far better than we had any idea of.

Camp Sprawls May 28th
Near Jackson, Miss

My Dear Wife:

I received your welcome letter this morning mailed at Yorkville. I am quite well and in as good spirits as possible under the circumstances.

We arrived here at day light last Saturday morning and this is Thursday. We have been bivouacked right on the bank of Pearl river in the suburbs of the city. Jackson is about or was the size of Columbia, but the yankees have burned the greater part of the place. You have never seen such vandalism in your life. Hundreds & thousands of Hhds & barrels of sugar & molasses have been burned & destroyed. The streets in many places are several inches deep with sugar & molasses. Our men are gathering up quantities of the sugar, and live well as far as sweet things are concerned. The people many of them seem not to have been looking for the enemy until they came upon them. They are piled up in tents and in the woods in every direction around the city but are coming in daily now and making the city look somewhat inhabititable again.

Uncle Jeff is here having arrived some days ago. He is unwell from cold but not serious. There has been fighting almost every day at Vicksburg. The yankees are entirely between us and that place and have it entirely cut off. Genl Johnson reviewed us yesterday, and Genl Evans arrived. I expect we shall move from here in a few days. Our address will still be Jackson.[6] The impression is that the army in Vicksburg has provissions enough to last three months and if they can hold out until we get a sufficient force to attack the enemy in the rear we will have them in a fix. So it is strength.

Our baggage is all behind at Demopolis and I have taken a change on my back. Capt Avery was left at Meridian with chils and has not got with us yet. I am still alright. We have no field officer at all. My Company is much the largish in the regiment. I have 46 men. We have 15 still out who ran the blockade and I would not be surprised if Davis called for men up to 45 before Fall. They may look out at least. I have written to the Enquirer. You will see the piece soon.

If you can get Steve for 1500 Dollars I wish you would do so and put him into the Crops until I can get him or find I can do with out him. You can get the money from Wheeler or I can send a note and have it arranged that way. Find out whether you can get him and let me know, and I will arrange the money matters. I wish to hear from my brothers very badly. We have lost all of Miss pretty much now if Vicksburg goes. If we whip them then we will gain the whole state back pretty much. If they take it our next stand will be on the Ala river.

Give my love to all and be sure to send my shoes as I am next to barefooted. You can send by Capt Mills or others. Kiss the children for me. We are getting collected here a pretty large army.

Your husband
David J Logan

Write 2 or 3 times a week.

*   *   *

Suburbs of Jackson Miss
June 2nd 1863

My Dear Wife:

This is the third letter I have written since I heard from you. I have only received one letter directed to this place. We have crossed Pearl river since my last letter and are encamped in the precints of the city. To the North Troops still continue to poor in here from all directions. <u>When</u> the grand battle will be fought is altogether matters of conjecture. Fighting has been going on for over two weeks, at, and around Vicksburg and I hear distinctly the sound of cannon again to day. We have the most encouraging reports from our forces in Vicksburg. A number of yankee Generals and an estimated loss of 40,000 men Killed & wounded seems to be credited here.[7] The Official report of the effective men now in Vicksburg is upwards of 24,000, and provisions enough to last until 1st of September.

This country here I find much hotter than the Coast as you will see. It is much lower. I almost suffocate with heat, at times. We are camped in woods without our tents or trunks again. Capt Avery is at Meridian still and I hardly expect him with the company soon. Lieut Guntharp was arrested by Genl Evans as soon as he returned, and is confined to the Camp and not allowed any command. I am in sole charge & have been since we left Charleston. We have no field officer with us yet, dont know when we will have. We may stay at this place for some time yet. We cant leave it far before we run up with the enemy. Last Saturday I saw a number of persons with their slaves from Senatobia, one, Dr Bonner & others. The yankees are closing in on that place. Uncle John Jackson is entirely inside the yankee lines. I expect we shall be in Genl Breckenridge's Division. He is now over us.

This is about as poor a country as York District can be. Also no water except from cistern and that not good. How a man is to live if he gets wounded here is more than I can see about. Perhaps he may be cared for. Water will be the worst. There is beginning to be sickness amonst us. Two over in my company have taken sick in the last two days. Uncle Jeff is getting well now. If you can buy that negro for the price I mentioned, take him and I will arrange the money. I have never heard a word from my Brothers yet. Do try to hear from them and let me know how they came out. Have you seen Mr Whceler lately. Write in regard to every matter of interest and try to write at least three letters every ten days. I hope you have sent my shoes or boots by Capt Mills. Have you seen Lieut Moore — how is he? What do the people think about peace now? If Vicksburg falls I think I shall leave for Europe as soon as possible. If the yankees dont get me before. At least I shall feel very much like it. Write to my parents for me. I have no paper except what I beg & cant write to many. I sent you a "comic midly." Did you get it?

You have heard of the Baudonn case I suppose. Dr Peters had suspected his wife and went and obtained a pass from baudonn to cross the yankee lines. He pretended to start off and while he was gone the wife & baudonn engaged to meet each other at his house but Dr Peters returned before it was late at night and found his wife in her night clothes crying very bitterly. He asked her what was the matter and she gave him no satisfactory answer and while they were speaking some one knocked. Peters opened the Door and there was baudonn who broke & ran, Peters after him and caught him. Baudonn then stated he was there on God's business. Peters gave him until 10 oclock next day to make a proper explanation which he failed to do and Peters shot him. These seem to be the facts of the case. The Mrs. Peters was very handsome. Had been married 5 years. Was of wealthy & respectable parents.

I should like very much to be at home now to see what kind of crops are making &c. By the way, are you "caught or not." You have never said. It is just 930 miles from Yorkville to this place by the route we have to come. We pass Augusta, Atlanta, West Point, Montgomery Ala, take steam boat and pass Selma, then Demopolis, then Meridian, then to Jackson. Some go by Mobile. Give my love to all and kiss the children for me.[8]

Your husband

D J Logan

From the 17th Regt., S.C.V.

Picket Post on Caton Road
Near Jackson, Miss., June 20th, 1863

Dear Editor:—Much to our relief, but very unexpectedly, we have been kept from the "roar of battle and the clash of arms," up to this time, quietly resting upon our oars. How long we are to remain in our secure *status* deponent saith not; but from appearances, such as the completion of pontoon bridges, the equipment of commissary trains, &c, he thinks the day of tribulation will not be long delayed.

Gen. Johnston takes things easy—appears to be in no hurry; but is doing much in the way of organization and equipment, more than appeared possible under the circumstances. Quarter Master's stores are being distributed bountifully, and batteries are being equipped and furnished with the best "carriage horses" of the Mississippi planters.

We have any quantity of rumors in camp, among others, that our regiment and the Holcombe Legion are to be consolidated. This may be the case soon, but I hardly think it will take place until the fate of Vicksburg is decided. Some dissatisfaction will, no doubt, be occasioned for awhile, but as the thing is becoming frequent in the army, and good reasons exist for it, it will, no doubt, be submitted to with a better grace than we at first supposed. Different reports are current in regard to the amount of subsistence in the hands of the garrison at Vicksburg. I have settled down to the conclusion that there is about 40 days rations on hand from this date, and if such is the case, there will be ample time to mature arrangements for its relief.

The health of our regiment and company is good, such is the case with all the "old regiments" of the Brigade. The 26th S. C. V., I understand, is passing through its second acclimation to "mother earth," and is suffering some little from sickness, but not as seriously as might be expected.[9] We have in this army two splendid brigades from the Old Palmetto, and one from the Old North State. The inhabitants around seem to think we of the "Palmetto" are calculated to perform anything in the way of prowess and valor. Our company (F,) has been on picket for the past two weeks, and your correspondent has been enjoying himself hugely in the advantages offered by this duty to "forage;" he has, also, met up with some of the noble emigrants from old York; among whom we may mention Mrs. Taylor, the daughter of our old Ordinary, Benjamin Chambers, Esq. Carolinians still find a warm greeting wherever and whenever they meet their friends from the "Fader-land." I would like to write you a long letter, but paper is scarce here, and I think I will post all the interesting little episodes (that occur in camp life here) away in memory's book, and reproduce them under more favorable circumstances. You can tell all the girls about Buffalo, King's Creek, Bullock's Creek and Yorkville, that their sweethearts in Company F, are fat and hearty, and hope to prove Grant's grant of Vicksburg a humbug, and then expect the "muss" to be about over, when they wish to see the girls all looking their best.

Hurriedly,

Yours,

L.

*   *   *

On Pickett, Canton road
Near Jackson June 21st 1863

My Dear Wife

I am quite well this morning & still on Pickett. We have been out now over two weeks, and we consider ourselves favored by being allowed to remain as. We can live much better away from the Brigade. I have a house to sleep in too which is very pleasant. Capt Avery returned but is acting Major of the regiment and I am still in command. Guntharp is still under arrest. I fear they will be somewhat rough with him yet. There was a tremendeous fight at Vicksburg yesterday. We have heard nothing from it as it is entirely cut off the garrison. They are holding out nobly and if they have rations enough will perhaps come out with flying colors yet. We have been surprised that we have been kept back from the enemy so long. Johnson is a cautious man and will not risk his reputation on our uncertainty.

We have very little sickness in our Regt. I am glad to hear that wheat is turning out well. I hope you will make a good crop. I am needing a boy very badly yet. I am entirely too <u>dependent</u> or my notions are rather <u>aristocratic</u>. I can command the respect when I have to depend upon my men to cook my meals for me, and find no other officers do it scarcely in the regiment. I cant cook or wash my self as you can imagine. If you can get me a boy you can pawn or sell my bonds in pmt, and can get the balance of the money from Mr. Wheeler, although I hate to part with my bonds. Try which you can get a boy at. If you can buy Steve at 1500. take him. I wish you to preserve all my pieces in the Enquirer. We are getting very good water where we are now. My shoes fit me very well.

Conl McMaster acquitted.[10] Has arrived and the court has rebuked Genl Evans considerably. The Conl is not here yet. The yankees have been and are now this side of aunt Jane Rowells. She is cut off. A part of our army left Canton yesterday to meet them as it was expected. The enemy intended to come to Granada. I expect they have played havock with the country. Our column passed through Senatobia coming this way. We expect stirring times here soon. The fate of the Confederacy will soon be known. If Vicksburg fall, peace will be a long ways off. If we hold it the war will be near or closed. There is heavy firing at Vicksburg this morning.

Give my love to all the friends and kiss the children for me. Uncle Jeff is well, though I have not seen him for a day or two. Your letters come in six days. If you get a boy he will be entitled to transportation over here. Write me & I will write more fully.

Your husband

D J Logan

PS You will have to keep my parents posted as I have no paper except what I beg.

––––––––––

While the gallant defenders of Vicksburg marked time within their entrenchments, General Johnston sought another major general for his army. Richmond complied and transferred Maj. Gen. Samuel Gibbs French, who had been holding a backwater command in Southern Virginia. On June 21 French arrived in Jackson, Mississippi, and Joe Johnston promptly created a division for him.

This change in the army's organization aligned Evans' regiments under French's command. The new division consisted of three brigades: Evans' South Carolina Tramp Brigade, Samuel Maxey's mixed brigade of Louisianans, Tennesseeans and Texans, and Evander McNair's Arkansans and North Carolinians.

––––––––––

Near Vernon Miss
June 24th 1863

My Dear Wife:

We marched from Jackson Miss day before yesterday and we are now 20 miles from that place on Big Black river. We are massed here—coiled up ready to Strike. We have about 30,000 men here within a few miles. We are in the Division of Genl S G French. There are three Brigades in our Division—Texans, Louisianians, & Tennesseenians. You may look out for news now. A grand battle will perhaps be fought before this reaches you, and the fate of the South decided. Many will be the poor fellows whose dead bodies will be heaped upon this sunny soil. I shall trust in that God who is able to save from the shafts of the enemy for my deliverence.

My shoes are hurting my feet pretty badly. The soles are not bound enough. We will suffer I fear for water here. We are using out of mud holes now. I have not seen a branch or running stream since I left Pearl river. There are none in this country. Direct your letters as before, only state Genl French's Division. I have received your letters very promptly. Col McMaster will be with us tomorrow. We shall all be glad to see him. Uncle Jeff is quite well. I will write or telegraph as soon as possible if I survive the fight. The fight may not come off before next Sunday. Kiss my sweet children for me & give my love to all.

Your husband

D J Logan

The fortunes of war did not shine brightly for the Confederacy in early July. The advance of Lee's Army of North Virginia into Pennsylvania crested at Gettysburg, and Lee was decisively defeated on July 3. Before news of this reversal reached Richmond's ears, another army suffered an even more disastrous—and humilating—defeat the following afternoon. After a number of engagements and almost fifty days of siege, General Pemberton surrendered the city of Vicksburg and his army to U. S. Grant on July 4, 1863. Joe Johnston had held his army relatively immobile, refusing to make even a half-hearted effort to relieve Vicksburg's defenders. Thus the battle with the enemy besieging the city expected by Logan never materialized.

Jackson Miss
July 8th 1863

My Dear Wife:

I am back safe to this City having made one of the hardest marches yesterday in the annals of war. A tropical sun & no water was enough to kill a man almost. My company numbered 44 when started and only 6 got here with me. The others broke down. Capt Avery came to. The enemy's cavalry followed us at a respectful distance. We are in doubt whether we will remain here or retreat further. I rather think we will make a stand here, at least for awhile. We are all down in the mouth. Every body looks serious. I am as dirty as a hog and the wagons are gone so that I have no clothes to change.

I fear this horrid war will not end for years. It rained on us last night & we are wet this morning. Some think Grant will advance on us soon. Others think not. We hear of good news from Virginia.[11] I am in anxiety again for my brothers. My shoes are use to my feet now, as I have them broke. People are flying from the enemy again & cotton is being burned in every direction. War is horrible—horrible. I pray it may never touch our country. Secession has certainly brung a great many bitter fruits so far, but we will hope that the darkest hour is just before day. Bob McLean has been another. Pemberton & some 150 officers & men is camped across the river & were not taken prisoners.

Give my love to all & kiss the children. Direct your letters as heretofore. Two men died in our Regt last week. One Wm Dover from my company. We have only about 25000 men here in all our army. Write often.

Affectiontely, Your husband in tribulation

D J Logan

——————

When Joseph E. Johnston heard of the surrender of Vicksburg he immediately began retreating toward the rail center of Jackson. Grant responded by dispatching William T. Sherman's corps to pressure the Confederates. The resultant small engagements and skirmishes between July 5 and July 16 forced Johnston to abandon Jackson, which was the capital of Mississippi. Light skirmishing continued as the Confederates retreated fitfully towards Meridian, Mississippi.

——————

From the 17th Regt., S.C.V.

In the Woods
18 miles east of Brandon, Miss., July 19th, 1863

Dear Enquirer:—Since my last letter, we have been passing through the dreadful scenes of battle and retreat, and though we are almost worn out physically, and

SAVING THE BRIDGE ACROSS PEARL RIVER.

"Saving the bridge across Pearl River"

Harper's Weekly

badly depressed mentally, we have abundant reason to be thankful that so many of us are thus far, safe and sound. On the morning of the 4th of July we were within three miles of Big Black river, and on the morning of the 6th, would, no doubt, have crossed and assailed the rear of Grant's army, but on the evening of the 5th, the crushing news of "Vicksburg has fallen" smote our ears, and, with sad hearts, we were ordered to return in the direction of Jackson. The sound of cannon and musketry reaching us from the direction of the river, where our cavalry and the enemy were engaged; the latter having already commenced following up his success, through two long, sultry days, with no water, except from horse-ponds, and with perfect clouds of dust breasting us, we turned our backs to the enemy before reaching the Pearl River.

We rested there one night, and on the morning of the 9th our regiment entered the redoubts of Jackson, the cannon and musketry of the enemy coming closer and closer. All was quiet in the trenches for the first day; but on the 10th the ball was opened by a shell thrown by the enemy, up the Clinton road, after which a series of the heaviest skirmishing I have ever seen, took place. Had not the reserve force been so large, a considerable battle might have been reported each day. The first assault or attack of the enemy, was made on our left, when the enemy were driven back with considerable loss, by a portion of Gen. Breckenridge's Division. There was, afterwards, a charge of the enemy amounting, almost, to an assault, on our right, which was repulsed and followed up, our troops leaving their trenches and charging the enemy in turn. This occurred in Gen. Loring's command; considerable loss was inflicted upon the enemy here. An assault or charge was made upon our right centre, on Thursday, the 16th, in which our regiment had a small share, but the principal fighting was done by Walker's Division, which formed our right centre. Gen. French's Division, to which we belong, held the left centre, and upon the whole centre the heaviest cannonading and skirmishing was kept up all the while. In the charge referred to, the enemy suffered much more than our troops. The 46th Georgia, Col. Colquitt; and a Texan Regiment charging them, and driving them back a considerable distance.[12]

A little episode occurred on the 14th, a flag of truce, (we suppose for the purpose of burying the dead) was exchanged, and hostilities were suspended from one o'clock, p. m., until four o'clock, p. m., in which time the soldiers of both armies met by hundreds at half distance, and had a hilarious time. The subject of peace was discussed, when several of the Yankee privates remarked, that if the privates of both armies could meet "they could make peace in 24 hours and take a drink over it, into the bargain." Many regrets were expressed that they should be mingling "so socially now, and in a few minutes would be doing their best to cut each others throats." The officers and privates in the Yankee army here, seem to have a supreme contempt for the Eastern Yankees and Abolitionists. The expiration of the truce was announced by the report of cannon, blank first and then shotted. Upon which our boys all made for their "rat holes," but a solemn silence seemed to have succeeded. Each side seemed loth to begin. Our pickets and the enemy's rested upon their guns. After a long silence, a Yankee cannon belched forth, when very soon the skirmishers begun their work of death.

Late in the afternoon of the 16th, I began to suspect, from certain movements, for the first time, that we would evacuate the city. At dark the order came. We were to leave our works at 10 o'clock, the pickets to remain in front until 1 o'clock, a.m. When the hour of 10 o'clock came, we silently bade farewell to the spot where every man felt confident that he could drive back all force sent against him. The whole affair was concluded in the best possible style. All leaving at the designated hour, and with unexpected quietness. At one time I thought the "thing was out," at 9 o'clock, p. m., a shell was thrown into the city, but its long tail of fire, and infernal noise, was the last I have seen or heard of the Yankees up to this time.

Dr. D. F. Barnette has furnished me with the following list of casualties in our regiment:

Company A.—Wounded—Private J. J. Edwards, contusion.

Company B.—Wounded—W. H. Macon, hip, severe.

Company C.—Wounded—Sergt. W. H. Smith, hip, slight; J. C. Gilfillen, slight.

Company E.—Wounded—J.J. Faries, knee, severe; Jno. Meadows, head, severe.

Company F.—Wounded—Sergt. F. Happerfield, slight; Corp. I. M. Hope, severe; Private P. Seapock, slight.

Company H.—Wounded—J. S. Gillan, slight.

Company I.—Killed—R. Montgomery. Wounded—W. Fail, slightly.

A large amount of property was destroyed in Jackson, despite all efforts to save it. The fall of the place was unavoidable. A natural result of the fall of Vicksburg. How far we are yet to retreat is hard to state. We have walked hard, and almost fainting for the past two days, and yesterday we weathered a most dreadful storm of rain, which, with the sequence, mud, was supremely horrid. We have just halted to dry.

In great haste,

Yours, most drippingly,

L.

*   *   *

From the 17th Regt., S.C.V.

Bivouack near Forest Station, Scot County, Miss., July 29, 1863

Dear Enquirer:—After the enemy have shown no disposition to accompany us, but only indeavered to complete the destruction of Jackson, our Generals have concluded to rest us for a season, and, in order to find water, they have led us into a wilderness, from which, if I was at liberty, I could not extricate myself upon a cloudy day.

We are located on a place very hard to describe in such a manner as to make it accessible to a stranger, without difficulty. The nearest point on the Rail Road is Forest, 13 miles distant, and our camp, "Sprawls," is located on a range of sugar loaf hills, that line the banks of Caney Creek, in Scot County; the most home like stream I have seen in this State. We have been halted here about a week, in which time we have been recovering from our fatigue and disheartening misfortunes. I hope soon to be able to say that the "old seventeenth" is at the "top of her mettle again."

As to speculation or statement in regard to army movements, I can say nothing, but must content your readers with matters of a different kind. We have found a spring in this State, at last, *and a good one too*, and we are permitted to have as much water as we please. The hearts of all the soldiers in this Division were made to leap with joy as one spring after another was discovered near to us. How the poor fellows were beginning to think the State was not worth fighting for, no how; but if they are called upon here, they will battle gloriously around the springs. I understand the land around our camp is public, and was held by the Government at $150 per acre. The hills would be hard at the price, but the bottoms are magnificient. I have just returned from a walk with some friends, and as it may interest some of your readers, I will give you the result of our observations. We had been informed of a Beaver's dam upon the creek below us, and although we have creeks of that name in old Carolina, yet the Beaver's dams, like the Indians, have disappeared, and live only by name, or the recollection of "the oldest inhabitant."

We proceeded down the banks of the creek for some distance and were very much struck with the richness of the low lands. The well timbered hills and enourmous Magnolias that grow upon the banks of the stream, together with all the varied undergrowth. One Magnolia tree measured 12 feet in circumference, the largest I have ever seen, and bearing the richest foliage. We soon came to the head of our dam, and upon looking around us, discovered the toil of that sagacious animal, the Beaver, as manifested by the numerous stumps cut in a peculiar manner, which attracted our attention. The trees cut down are usually from 1 1/2 to 5 inches in diameter, and are invarible cut in such a way as to leave the sharp point up. When the tree is large, it seems a number of them have been cutting together, or else one carries on the operation in a number of places at the same time. They seem to make little or no distinction between the different trees, if any is favored, it is the Magnolia. I have sent home a stick, cut and trimmed by a Beaver, which is

Holly, I also find a number of the ironwood, or Beech trees cut down. The construction of the dam was the next point of interest, and in that they have exhibited wonderful sagacity indeed, every small bush has the top turned upstream, the large ones to the contrary, and so compactly is the whole structure placed together, and cemented with leaves and mud that the water can scarcely "seep through," but pours in a steady stream over the top, like the stone or plank dams of our mills in Carolina. When a boy I once thought I was "capital" on a "dam," but I must knock under to an animal, one time. They can beat me. I find a number of trees recently cut by them and learn that they work mostly at night. The approach of civilization is fast driving them from existence, together with the red man in this county, who still linger in a broken* tribe, hunting the scanty game and keeping company with those doomed Beavers of Mississippi.

Our boys have suffered dreadful privations in their retreats from Big Black and Jackson, but I think are fast recovering from their fatigue and suffering. They think often of home, and from their inmost hearts desire to be there among their friends and loved ones. A little incident will make known the intensity of the affection entertained by the soldiers for home, more than anything I could say. During their retreat from Big Black river, when the enemy were pushing us closely, and the sun was shining with all its power, and water was not to be had except from horse ponds, and then at long distances from each other, I have seen several soldiers throw away their blankets, coats, and other clothing, but upon being asked "why not throw away your knapsack," they replied: "I have my paper, envelopes and ink in that, and if it was not for them, I would, but I must stick to them as long as I can." The soldiers ruling passion strong in death, in the army here, is "home, sweet home."

Yours, L

*a reminate of a tribe of Cherokee Indians still located in this county and Rankin.

––––––––––

Camp French July 30th 1863
Scott County Miss

My Dear Wife:

I am quite well this morning and have had the pleasure of eating a green water melon for which I paid $5.00 but unless they are reduced in price I dont think I shall repeat again soon. Our army is receiving furloughs now, and if Avery & Guntharp had been here I should probably have got one myself. However, I shall hope I may get one yet when one of them returns. Our army is resting here now and recovering from its late Campaign. Where we will operate next I cannot imagine. Our troops have been polluted with lice in this trip but are cleaning up alittle now. I have had a small supply but am getting clear of them. I sent to Gutheriesville by Jim Clark $120.00 which I hope you will receive. I also wish you to pay over to L M Grist $19.00 for subscription to paper which I was afraid to send by mail. I have received a letter from Pa & hear that Bro Ben prospd unhurt through the battles in Pa, and was at Hagerstown.[13]

You wish my opinion in regard to the war. I must say that I am at sea all together now. The yankees have the whip hand of us badly now, and in the language of Old Abe "we must keep pizzing away" or submit which I hardly think will be done. I have no doubt the Feds will offer terms of peace since their recent successes, but I feel they will be rejected. I anticipate more hard fighting around Charleston soon. The enemy will be very hard to drive from Morris Island. I fear Bonds, Confed money &c will be awfully depreciated now. Dispose of my bonds if you can favorably for a negro, land or any thing. If you can buy house & lot or land in NC you & Pa may pitch in and buy me a free hold there so that if SC is conquered NC may be a refuge. Pa has received the appointment of Collector of war tax for Cleveland.[14] So you see he has made something by being in the Legislature at last. It will pay quite handsomely.

I shall need a suite of winter clothing before late Fall but I hope I may be able to come for them. The worst is about Furloughs. It takes all our Officers pay to settle his fare home now. It is so far. I intend to send you a walking stick cut & trimmed by a Beaver if I can. You may not believe it was [not] cut by me but I pledge my word it is so. I guess the old fellows are trying to be over 45 now. If our country does not exhibit a little more bravery & willingness to defend itself I will certainly think Abe Lincoln will master the whole of it yet. I will write more this evening.

Evening: I am still quite well. Lieut Moore & Capt Crawford have been foraging & have returned with some peaches. Uncle Jeff is here, and we have been eating them. They got nothing else. However, we are all in pretty good health here, and improving in spirits.

I hope I may see you all before long. Tell John I will get him something yet. I hope your scholars are improving rapidly. Write often. Direct to Meridian P M Forward.

Your husband

David J Logan

CHAPTER 6

"The prospect of a future return to the homes of the loved and cherished, will sweeten the bitter cup, and nerve every Southern soldier to bear his yoke with patience and submission."

Charleston, Again

August 1863 – March 1864

The Tramp Brigade's exhausting and frustrating episode in Mississippi was followed by seven months of relatively stationary service in Charleston, South Carolina and Savannah, Georgia. David Logan and his fellow Carolinians welcomed this change of pace—especially after the grueling weeks they had spent in the sweltering Magnolia State. It was Logan's third visit to the historic city of Charleston. His months along the south Atlantic seaboard were both eventful and difficult.

Logan diligently continued his correspondence home, both to Sallie and the local newspaper. His writings during this change of station, however, are no longer the light and optimistic fare of earlier times. The correspondence assumes a more serious, ominous tone, with hints of personal exhaustion. Indeed, his words seem to bespeak the onset of depression. Although Logan mentions various events taking place around him—such as the arrival of blockade runners into the city—little of military affairs occupy his pen. For example, he barely mentions the Federal attacks on Battery Wagner and Fort Sumter, two critical events in Charleston's 1863 war. Likewise, the heavy bombardments he experienced on an almost daily basis go virtually unrecorded. He may have been trying to spare Sallie's feelings by not discussing the horrors that accompanied the steady skirmishing and tenacious shelling. The extent of the fighting in this theater, however, was routinely reported in the area's newspapers.

After some finagling Logan procured a furlough of about four weeks from the middle of September to the middle of October, 1863. During his absence he missed the six-day bombardment of Fort Sumter, carried out by Federal forces on Morris Island, from September 28 to October 3. He was also absent when a torpedo boat attack by the Confederate *David* was launched against the much more formidable Federal warship *USS Ironsides*.[1]

Logan's lengthy absence from home and family inspired him to dedicate a substantial amount of ink to various family and related financial issues and economic advice.

Charleston S C
Aug 27th 1863

Dear Wife:

We are in this city. You will direct your letters to this place. The enemy are quiet this morning; only firing every minute or so. A desperate fight occurred Tuesday & last night.[2] The enemy have possession of our rifle pits on Morris Island. We expect to be sent to that or James Island. My love to all.

Your husband
D J Logan

*   *   *

Mount Pleasant SC
Christ's Church Parish Aug 30th/63

My Dear Wife:

On this anniversary of the 2nd battle of Manassas I am found after many vicisitudes upon the main land at Mount Pleasant. It is a very pretty place for the coasts 8 miles from Charleston opposite Sullivans Island to which it is connected by a bridge. This place is the "Headstalls point" of The Revolution of 76. A monument of brick & granite in the Annuals of this village perpituates the names of some of the patriots who fell in defense of our liberties during our first revolution.

We arrived in Charleston Thursday morning last remained one day & night upon our old Camp Lee, on Ashly river, then marched thro the City to an Eastern wharf & took boats for this place. The enemy & our batteries have been keeping up a regular bombardment until this morning when as I write it is becoming rapid & heavy.[3] The country around our Camp bears evidence of having been in a state of cultivation many years ago. Our Camp is near Lucas' Mill and near a family grave yard in which are buried a number of the Baileys. Fort Sumpter does not appear to be injured near so badly as reports would indicate. The Confederate flag floats about as proudly as ever from its battlements, but no guns are belching forth their iron hail from its embrasures, interregnum.

Esq Clawson came over to see me this morning and we concluded to visit Sullivans Island from which we have just returned. We have had a hard walk but have seen the ships & batteries at close range. The enemy send a ball thro Sumpter about every 5 minutes. She is badly damaged but no lives are being lost in the Fort of any account. One battery high up in the Island was firing at the enemy reguarly. I have talked with Clawson about his negro. He asks me $3000.00 in Confederate bonds for Steve or my Note for $1500. I am to let him know whether I take him or not in 3 weeks. If you could get Jeff or some other boy and pay for him in Confederate money then give my note to Clawson for Steve and send him to me the first chance. I am a fat man no more it seems & If I can have any thing to help me in my troubles I must have it if my money or credit will procure it. I am in the vale of darkness now. I very much fear we shall be injured and if so ruined & if such is the case I dont think my enemies shall trouble with me in this country if I am living.

We were exposed to the most dreadful rain Friday night last without any covering, not even a blanket. I keep in good health and seem to improve upon exposure. I feel thankful to God for pressing my health & strength. My Country its situation hurts me worst than any thing else now, but I feel that it is reaping its just reward. The cowardly scoundrels at home are ruining us as fast as they can. Their day I hope will not be far distant to weep & howl. Confederate money stands ill severely as with the paper they are printed upon. If they continue to depreciate as they have & are where they are going & the yankees driving over us, then the Palmetto State will be "victorious" & perhaps her destiny accomplished. Some interposition of Providence may save us. Nothing else will do it. We expect to remove soon to Morris Island to which place we have to go in flats, exchange at night and then in great danger.[4]

I have received the box & am much pleased with my shirt. The things came right. Lt Moore & myself get along very well. I would like very much to see you and the children but if I keep well I know of no chance possible soon. I received a letter from you the very evening I told uncle Jeff what to write you. I have been feeling low down in spirits now for a long time. There seems to be but little that is bright for me in this world. I left my knife & fork in Miss and have no Towel. Send, if you can get them. Can get none here. Write soon & often & all the news. Also write to my parents that I am here. Love to all.

D J Logan

I send you a blank note for Clawson if cant get any where else. I fear it may take all. Will be worth to pay this in specie funds when the war is over but if Confederate money is not good at home I am a soldier and must do the best I can. It is all they pay me.

From the 17th Regt., S.C.V.

Mount Pleasant, S.C.,
September 1st, 1863.

Dear Enquirer:—The "foot cavalry" have again been on the wing, and a long *flight* they have made since my last letter; which, I think, was composed of stuff about "Beaver dams" and "wildernesses." Well, we are *out of the woods* now, in one sense if not in another. When the "order" came to us in that, *may I never see again* land, to be "ready at once to leave for Savannah, Georgia, every heart, I will say, in the 17th gave a quick throb for joy, and many were the "shouts" that echoed and reverberated, for the *last time*, among those hills, in the far distant west. A morning march, with elastic steps, brought us to Forrest Station, on the 4th of August, when we were permitted to taste our first peaches and melons, at $2 per dozen for the former, and $5 each for the latter. That night we reached Meridian, the Tabernacle Capitol of Mississippi. Here our boys procured rations and melons,

I fear from appearances, at some thing *less than Government prices*. However, early in the morning, with no one in the guard-house, we were all aboard for Demopolis, Alabama, where we arrived early in the afternoon, having met with the sad misfortune to lose a worthy soldier from Chester District, by his falling from a platform car and being crushed to pieces by the wheels; a moment of sadness was visible, but soon the cloud passed away. Before reaching Demopolis, we have to take a steamboat down the Tombigbee river four miles. The scenery upon this river, its high banks of variegated Limestone, reminds us of the oft described beauties of the "Palisade rocks of the Hudson." At Demopolis, we find the camp of the paroled prisoners from Vicksburg, about 1400 were in camp who were unable to get to their homes and enjoy the furlough granted them. May God soon interpose in behalf of those noble men, who have left their loved homes and friends, in Kentucky and Missouri, to fight for the cause of the South.

A brief stop, and we are away again for Selma, at a speed of 20 miles an hour. We pass the glorious corn fields and prarie lands we mentioned in a letter before, and with barely time to waive our hats to the dear girls of Uniontown and other places, we are on the banks of the *Alabama*, with its Indian meaning of "here we rest" realized to our heartfelt satisfaction. By chance we met our same old steamer, the R. B. Taney, and Captain, waiting to take us a board. Thank God, the old 17th is again aboard, and, as I sincerely prayed before, with "ranks less thinned by battle and disease" than the "old Palmetto"; but some are gone, along Pearl river and Big Black their spirits left us to join those of the "Palmetto boys" of '46 and their own comrades of '61, Messrs Dover, Morris, Gibson, Farmer, Montgomery, Dye and others have fought their last fight on earth.

In the cabins, upon the upper and lower decks, the tired soldiers was wrapt in sleep, and all night long the "Taney" holds her steady but winding course up the "Here we rest" river, save about midnight the scream of a drowning man is heard, but the waters have devoured him, and a Tennessee soldier is no more. "It is a small matter, only a private gone out of the regiment," such is our present estimate of human life. In the afternoon of the 6th, we arrived in Montgomery, not finding transportation we camped for the night, and here we were well supplied with fruits at reasonable prices. This is a beautiful city, and appears to be a place of considerable manufacture. The population is much increased by refugees from New Orleans and other places. We left this city on the morning of the 7th and steamed away for Opelika, passing and bidding adieu to many of the sweet ladies of Alabama, who cheered us on, in our journey to Vicksburg, a few months before. May they never be subject to Abe Lincoln, nor lack the right kind of husbands.

At Opelika we changed enjines and took the road for Columbus, Georgia. We passed Selma and as they would not allow any one to sell fruit to soldiers, but gave everything gratis, I judge very few have passed this way. I was amused at some little boys who charged upon the stock of a negro who was trying to sell, and scattered it in every direction. If there were many, or enough possessed of the right kind of patriotism at home, as well as in other places, there would not be so much *distrust* and cowardly *submissive feeling* as there is prevading the country; the trifling scoundrels at home who are depreciating our currency, are doing more against our cause than all of Lincoln's fleets and armies.[5] Let every true patriot when he sees such men, pitch into them with the instinctive feelings that prompted the little urchins I mentioned above.

About sundown on the 7th we arrived at Columbus, the *Lowell*[6] of the South, and although I had believed that there was no city equal in beauty, to our own Columbia, I had my faith almost shaken. This is the greatest manufacturing city, if we except Richmond, that is in the South. We had to await transportation again here; but before the break of day on the 8th we were all aboard for Macon, another noble city in our empire State, here we rested and fed on fruit until evening came, when we took the train for Savannah, and all night long with a puff, puff, puff, we were making our way to the beleaguered Seaport of Georgia, at which we arrived on the morning of the 9th, and in front of the city park, with the fountain throwing its water in all its beautiful combinations; the shade and walks filled with the fair ladies of Savannah.

I leave your readers with the old 17th in all its Western rags and dirt, its young men too modest to raise their heads, but risking one eye at the park and asking if those things are angels in there?

More anon.

L.

*   *   *

For the Mercury

Mount Pleasant, S. C.
September 2, 1863

To the Editor of the Mercury: Allow me through your paper, to make a suggestion, which has occupied my thoughts for a length of time and in making it public I must assure you that nothing save the purest motives for the welfare of our beloved Confederacy and its army have actuated me. For nearly two years, I have been an officer of the line, and in constant intercourse with the men who compose our army; and on that account should certainly be allowed to have some acquaintance with the working of our military system. My suggestion is this(:) *That a regular system of furloughs be instituted, so that every private soldier may expect to see his home and friends, once in every year.* I venture the assertion, that if such a system was inaugurated, there would not be found on earth, a more cheerful and self-sacrificing body of men, than the army of the South.[7] Privation, hunger and fatigue, are trying to the spirits of men; but the prospect of a future return to the homes of the loved and cherished, will sweeten the bitter cup, and nerve every Southern soldier to bear his yoke with patience and submission.

In my company there are about fourteen men, who have not seen their families or homes within the past twelve to nineteen months. Upon one occasion a number of others, who had proved their fidelity to their country upon many a battle field, when about to be removed to a distant State, were overcome by the intensity of their natural ties, and despite the remonstrance and efforts of their officers to retain them, made away to their homes; but only remained for a few days, and then clasped their loved ones to their hearts, and with a sad farewell, returned to their command, and are now faithful and obedient soldiers. Had those men a *probable certainty* that they could have an honorable home re-union once a year, no such occurrance would ever be heard of. Every true soldier would frown it down. We must remember that the Confederate soldier is no mercenary, but is frequently of as high social position at home as the officer who commands him. And another thing we must remember, that the destruction of those ties and associations that cluster around every Southern home, are not only subversive of our moral and social existence, but strike at the base and support of our glorious cause itself.

Let a system be commenced and carried out, with *unerring regularity*, and when the day of battle comes *more men will be found at their guns*—more men will be *always ready for duty*. There will then be fewer "reports of desertions" and "running blockades," fewer nondescript diseases to puzzle the brains of the surgeons, to steal opportunities to get home from hospitals; no more eternal croaking and complaining; but every man can look forward to the hour when his own gleam of sunshine shall cross his pathway. Not as now, an uncertain period, a night with an uncertain hour for the coming of the morning. Let our President give his soldiers this system, and I care not what may be the expectations of battle, *let it be uninterrupted*, and my word for it, he will carry *more* stout hearts and strong arms into every future battle than has been done heretofore.

Yours,
A Line Officer Of Evans' Brigade.

*   *   *

From the 17th Regt., S.C.V.
Mount Pleasant, S.C.,

September 9th, 1863.

Dear Enquirer:— My last letter left the "boys" gazing in mute astonishment, at the fair ladies of Savannah promenading in the city park. Well, after enjoying that feast to the eyes, and a reasonable quantity of water-melons and "ginger-bread" for the stomach, we lay down upon the bosom of mother earth, and with the magnificent star-bespangled dome above us, passed the night as sweetly, as if in one of the majic-conjured palaces of Aladdin, brought into reality for our accommodation, although at times the "gallinippers," (permeating the "evil Genii") would disturb our dreams. On the 10th of August, before the "Goddess of morn," had displaced the darkness, we were all under arms and moving through the city, on our way to the Isle of Hope, some nine miles distant, we passed to the South-eastern part of the city, and took the "Skidaway Shell road," which passes through the fortifications defending the land approaches. I am not permitted to speak in regard to them, but will venture this much, that there is a "Fort Brown" which will be like the present Governor of this State, "hard to beat." The country along this road, abounds in the rankest kind of tropical growth, and the Palmetto is as popular as upon any of the islands of our coast. We reached our camping ground by noon, and were delighted with our situation, an arm of the sea stretched out at our feet, affording a splendid opportunity to enjoy the sea bath, to our heart's content, and the amusement of fishing, even to a profitable extent. The umbrageous arms of the live oak, formed an awning, and welcome retreat from the vertical rays of sun. A good well of water was found near at hand, as our camp was around the residence of a planter who had fled from the near approach of "Uncle Abe's Folks."

How we passed the time here, I could not tell you in a volume; but with eating, sleeping, talking, smoking, hearing from home, fighting mosquitoes and getting better clothes, two weeks soon rolled around, and, "just as we all expected" here came the order to move forthwith to Charleston, S.C. There was a time when such an order would have been greeted with thundering applause; but we were so sadly disappointed in May last, by not being allowed to remain, after we had been engaged in an active campaign all the previous winter, that going to Charleston now, seemed to bear no good tidings, more than present expediency.

On the evening of the 26th August, we dropped our tents, and it seemed almost like the fountains of the deep had broken up and were pouring down upon us, but a soldier soon learns how to take a good wetting. We took up line of march, and were soon passing through the streets of the venerable city of Savannah, beholding perhaps for the last time, its delightful parks and gardens and its grateful monument to the patriot Pulaski.[8] May no hostile foe ever tread upon its streets, or despoil its homes.

We can all say, we have been well treated here. The citizens have exhibited more concern and anxiety for the welfare of the soldier, than in most of the many cities it has been our lot to visit. Our regiment got aboard the cars, during a violent storm of rain, but the danger of "cobwebs" and "malaria" were both *treated* according to the most approved maxim, "an ounce of preventive is worth a pound of cure." All night long in the crowded boxes, we "steamed" for Charleston "bobbing for eels" as we went, a hard jolt waked us as the train reached Pocotaligo. I looked out again upon some of our old "tramping ground" of 18 months by-gone, when the alarm of war was sounding in its infancy. Again I slept, and was roused by the shout, "we are near old Camp Simons again." And sure enough, there were still the same old trees and with some of our old tables and arbors still lingering to mark the spot. What a change since we left that old camp for Virginia. One third of our number is gone. Two hundred men who were buoyant with life and health one year ago, are lying buried in distant graves, or mangled by the missiles of the enemy and unfit for the duties of camp. Another year, and the same story may be told. We reached Charleston, or old Camp Lee, our first camp, on the morning of the 27th August, and after resting a day, were ordered to Christ Church Parish, where we now are, with the hated guns of the enemy smiting our ears with their hated music.

The chills and fever are troubling the 17th worst at present, than Yankee bullets, although we have just returned this morning from a night long watch upon the Sullivan's Island bridge, around which the enemy have been throwing their huge shells in the greatest profusion. Our brigade has been kept busy every day since our arrival, digging and preparing for the defence of this city, if attacked by land. It must appear to me that very bad management has been the order of the day here, or else the planters have been very backward in sending their hands. The time which has been given us to prepare, the whole coast, it seems to me, might almost have been converted into bomb-proofs and batteries. But we will still hope and believe enough has and will be done, to hold our city yet. If the enemy have Morris' Island with its Forts and old Sumter almost a ruin, some Monsters[9] are here, that if successful, will flatten the Ironsides, and send the Monitors after their sister, the Keokuk.[10]

Hurriedly Yours

L.

On September 29, the brigade surgeon granted David a ten day leave of absence because of the lingering effects of "rheumatism." Predictably, he used his precious few days to visit his family in Yorkville, South Carolina.[11]

Bivouack on James Island
Oct 12th 1863

My Dear Wife:
    After the most miserable luck I have at last reached the regiment. I missed the connection at Columbia & staid all day there then at Charleston and did not get to Mt Pleasant until yesterday when I met the regiment moving to this Island. They were surprised to see me so soon. I might have stayed days longer had I known it. I have been mad at my self for leaving in such a hurry. We are halted in the woods here and expect to leave to day for Secessionville or Legares Point. My box & Jug are all right here and we have been helping ourselves to them. Our baggage was all left at Mt Pleasant when we came over & we had nothing with us and were nearly starved before it came last night. Not having ate any thing in nearly 36 hours, I will be disappaired. I fear about getting salt as we have left the works.[12]
    The impression is that we will remain at Charleston. Our Brigade has been scattered now at different points which is a pretty good sign I think.[13] Genl Evan's trial is going on now.[14] I dont suppose they will do much with him though. Uncle Henry was at T O and was telling me of a negro Bob Morrison had. I fear he will not be at any reasonable price. If you or your father go to [Sunluck ?] soon you can look at him. I will draw my money first chance and send it home. In the mean time you can get my shoes and can settle when the money comes in. I expect we shall have some picket duty here & probably camp at our old place before we went to Miss. I saw Uncle Henry as he is still here. Begins to want a furlough. The old fellows are pretty "tired ones" already. They have every one broken into fine dwelling houses in the city, and are living in style. They will ruin them, almost. The Officers let the men lead them instead of vice versa. I wish you would have a Hammock made of my leather if you can get it to Yorkville. Mine is about out. Maj

Culp has gone home again. I think I will get home in Feby next. Look out for me then. I am in Command of Company. Avery is acting Major.

All is quiet in the harbor here yet. Only occasional firing going on. Dr Logan is home on furlough. Guntharp is rather "low down," afraid he cant make the trip. Jefferys has not got off. He will soon perhaps. If they get lose about home & hire him, get him for me. I certainly cant so if he is to be hired. Why I would not have as good right to do so as any one. My shoulder is as bad as ever again here. I dont understand it. I can scarcely use it. However I dont make as much fuss about it now as I did before.

Write soon & give the news & excuse haste as we are lying in the woods here. Kiss my dear children for me & love to all.

> Yours
> D J Logan

We will be under Genl Talliafirro here I understand. There is no place for woman on this Island, now a perfect Desert. If things ever get quiet you can come to the city. I think we will stay here. Genl Anderson's Brigade has gone to Tenn. I will write to my father to day. Uncle Jeff is quite well also Lt Moore & all friends & neighbors. Direct letters as before only send to James Island. Our A is still Charleston.[15]

From the 17th Regt., S.C.V.
Secessionville, James Island,

October 21st, 1863

Dear Enquirer: — After a brief stay with my family and loved ones at home, I have rejoined my regiment, which, in accordance with its past occupation, I found "on the move again."

The boys were just beginning to realize an attachment to the country around Mount Pleasant, when the order came to "pack up" for James' Island. We have found out that complaining does no good however, and we always try to submit to our fate with the best grace possible.

We are located near the same spot which we occupied, previous to our Vicksburg flight, and the scene has somewhat changed since that period. We could then look in the direction of Morris' Island without the pain of beholding a forest of hostile masts or the myriads of Yankee tents that now whiten the spot where Fort Simpkins and Wagner then stood, with the Confederate ensign proudly flapping in the breeze.

We could then, turning to the left, discern in the distance, the grim outline of Fort Sumter unharmed, with her parapet guns frowning moodily towards the harbor entrance; now we behold her majesty seemingly dethrowned. With all these changes, however, we still find it in our hearts to believe, that the Disposer of human events, will say to our enemy, "Thus far shalt thou go, and no farther," and that he will permit a Phoenix to arise, from the ruins of our humbled Sumter, more terrible than the Sumter of the past to our foes.

Our health is unusually good; a few cases of chills only, to keep up "the Surgeon's call." We had a grand review here last week, by General Beauregard, accompanied by Generals Talliaferro and Pierre Soul. The latter General still persists in wearing a hat of the "old churn" style, costing many of the boys a hard effort to refrain from ordering him, to "come out of that hat" during the review.

In the appearance of the troops on review, I must confess, the "old Seventeenth" and "Eighteenth" were pre-eminent for rags and dirt. Their treatment has not been of the best, in the clothing line at least, or a better show could certainly be made.

Our regiment has considerable picket duty to perform now, our Yankee friends are generally very pacific towards us, proffering to exchange papers, or give us coffee for tobacco, or sweet potatoes; sometimes their wooden gun boats in the Stono, become wolfish (perhaps by the rising memories of the Isaac P. Smith[16]) and shell the woods and fields about us like wrath; but they have never hurt many as yet, for which we are thankful.

On last Monday, I beheld for the first time, with my eyes extended and mouth wide open, a real simon pure descendant, or relative of the French Emperor Louis Napoleon, viz: Count De Marivaux, in command of the French ship of War, Tisiphone, now off this bar.[17]

The occasion of our fortunate "sight," was his desire to visit our Forts and batteries. While we were all lounging about, or preparing our scanty dinners, a military wagon drives up into our midst, and we were almost rendered insensible by the distinguished characters that alighted from it, *first* General Talliaferro, *then* the Hon. and Brigadier General Pierre Soul—then the Count De Marivaux, and last, the peerless Beauregard. They all passed familiarly through our streets, and I am *reliably informed*, that they *all*, actually lifted their hats and spoke *audible*, to the Captain of Company K of this regiment, and that since the occurence, he expresses the opinion, that he thinks he is in some way connected with royalty.

Beholding so much greatness and royalty in one day, has entirely unnerved me, and I must ask time to recuperate, so as the "Count" would say *au revoir.*

L.

＊   ＊   ＊

From the 17th Regt., S.C.V.
Secessionville, S.C.

November 5th, 1863

Dear Enquirer:—We are still flourishing—watching for Yankee barges, &c., at the same camp from which I wrote you before. Our *venemous* neighbors on the sand banks in front of us, attempted to interfer with our dress parade a few evenings since, but *bomb-proofs* are so *convenient* that a half dozen bomb-shells sent amongst us, *occassionally*, only turn out a very welcome and pleasant episode to relieve our monotony. The samples tossed over the other evening, weigh about forty pounds, and resemble, in shape, the top of our lamp-posts in Yorkville.

Two or three gun boats in Folly Creek, tried to kick up a stampede amongst our pickets on Battery Island, a few days ago. They expended several hundred dollars worth of "green backs",[18] raised a tremendous smoke, and kept up a dreadful noise for a while, but that was all. Our boys stood their ground and saw the thing out.

Gillmore's "big guns" keep up, day and night, their furious bombardment of Fort Sumter, but from appearances, they are not accomplishing much yet, and for the last day or two, their fire has perceptibly slackened.[19]

I have been "ciphering" a little in regard to operations in the harbor, and have come to the conclusion that if we have the right kind of bomb-proofs in Sumter, (and I believe that our General Gilmer has not been *so quiet* for nothing) that this is the very place where we shall break Abe's back-bone, (I mean his credit) and when that is done, there is *nuf ced*. Here are my figures: one thousand shots per day—300 pounds iron to the shot and 30 of powder—iron at 10 cents, powder at 50 cents—making for one shot a cost of $45.00; and for 1000 shots a cost of $45,000. The siege has been progressing nine days (according to my estimate) at a cost of $405,000. Thus you will see, that it is calculated to develop with *frightful rapidity*, a large addition to the family of "green-backs." In the above calculation I have said nothing of the enormous expense required to keep up and pay off the innumerable war vessels, transports, &c., and the hungry mercenaries (who are fighting for the paper promises of Lincoln as long as they can be made to swim). Neither have I taken into account the guns that are bursted occassionally, or rendered useless by excess of firing. Let us all keep a "stiff upper lip"—stand by *our own* Government and its credit, and ere long, we shall see the value of gold and "green-backs," shoot off in an opposite direction, and separate wider and wider, until the last convulsive throb of Lincoln's Government shall proclaim the independence of the Confederate States, and the return of our war-worn veterans to their happy homes. Down with all who deprecate our money in order to obtain starvation prices. May taxes disturb their dreams and worry their waking hours.

We have had the pleasure of looking upon our honored Chief Magistrate to-day. Accompanied by a host of Generals and other dignitaries, he visited our works here, passed twice round our old regiment in review, and halted several times, to enquir in regard to the barefooted men, who were in the ranks. By the way, there are a number of men in the regiment without a shoe—good soldiers—men who have closed in deadly conflict with the foe upon many a battle-field.[20] The President looks well, and appears to be in the best of spirits. I enjoyed the pleasure of being very near to him and hearing him, in an animated conversation with General Beauregard, in reference to the battle of Secessionville, while seated upon the ramparts of Fort Lamar.[21] He looks much more like *living*, than I expected to see him, and, as many of the boys say, he resembles the "postage stamp" not a little.

The health of our regiment is still good. We have a Chaplain once more, and can now decide much more easily, the return of the Sabbath. Rev. W.W. Carothers is a zealous man, and I believe will effect much good in our regiment.[22]

Very hurriedly, yours. L.

*   *   *

For the Yorkville Enquirer
Secessionville, S.C., Nov. 12, 1863.

Dear Enquirer:—In this our day of tribulation, it is natural to look around us for support and encouragement. It has been our *great error* to confide too much in the hope that foreign nations would interpose in our behalf. That hope, I trust and believe, has been pretty well "played out" by the intelligent and thinking of our country.

It now becomes our duty to lay aside all the uncertain reliance upon Kings and Emperors of the earth, and to bring into the field of actual conflict, *all* the muscle and strength of our land, unimpaired by disease or age—devoutly asking the blessings of Heaven upon our cause, go forth with the resolution calmly taken, to die or be free from the threatened dangers that surround us. Our heroic mothers and sisters, with our aged fathers, *maimed* and disabled brothers, will keep the agricultural and domestic machinery in motion, whilst we strike with terror and destruction, our ruthless invader. Let no man of Conscript age be relieved from his duty to his country and himself by the votes of our people at home, while men with hoary hairs can be found, fit and competent to preside in the councils of our State. Let the old Roman maxim of "young men for war, and old men for council," be felt and acted upon, by all the true, patriotic citizens of our District, who love the country and desire to see its independence established.

There is one man in our District, whose name I have repeatedly heard mentioned by the soldiers, with the highest admiration, around their camp fires. We remember seeing him, at the head of a noble regiment from our State, the morning we crossed the Rapidan river in Virginia, in pursuit of the braggart Pope. His snowy beard, and sunburnt visage, told of the hardships he had encountered. The smoke of battle had scarcely disappeared from Cedar Mountain when we saw him, yet with the re-kindled fires of youth, glowing in his countenance; he was pushing ahead with Stonewall Jackson, to strike the finishing blow to Pope's retreating vandals.

We parted at the Rapidan (as Longstreet's corps brought up the rear). The next we heard of him, was on the bloody field of the 2nd Manassas. After passing through a large number of our most important battles, with honor to himself and to his country, he has returned to his home for the rest his age demands. His sons are in the army. We know he can appreciate the soldiers denial and suffering, and in the opion of many of them, expressed spontaneously, he is the man to represent them in their Districts highest office.

SEVENTEENTH REGIMENT.

———

Secessionville SC
Nov 26th 1863

My Dear Wife:
    I received your kind letter last night after I had gone to bed—brought by Mr Knox Williams. I am glad to hear you are quite well & also the dear

James "Jim" Scott Logan

Courtesy of Historical Center of York County

children. I am very much pleased that you have succeeded in getting me a negro & I hope he will please me well. I was afraid you would find him unsound or so ugly that you would not have him. I dont care if he is not one of the stoutish kind of negroes as if I live he will be useful about a house or store, and will not be required to do any heavy work. I guess I can furnish him with a blanket, but I will have to get a comfort or quilt in the place of it. A comfort of half the size of a quilt would suit me as well. I have drawn a pair of shoes which I have paid $12.50 for. They would suit your Father very well as they are nice and soft. I think of sending them home. I have an old pair which I can let "Jim" have. I suppose he would not have the assurance to have a "less foot than mine."

In regard to the payment. I am perfectly willing to let your Pa have my house & lot in Shelby at the same I paid for it. I have no doubt it could be sold for more money now, but it is all in the family and if I could have got a negro when I was at home I should not have bought it.

Another thing you can do. My 8 per cents are worth more than your fathers 7 per cents. They are older & at a higher rate while the 7 per cents only bring part interest as yet, I believe or only a small premium. You can change them with him if mine cant be sold at a premium without difficulty, and you can use his in making payment. Make pmt & allow the interest on the 7 per cents at least any how. If you still lack a little in making payment you can perhaps get it from Bolivar or Mr Wheeler. I intend to try to save all my money now pretty much & if I can get into an Envelope speculation I can make some extra as they are selling here at $70. a thousand by wholesale. Write to Pa to take for me about 3000 nine. I will send more money home next week. I will also write to him myself. I think if we stay here I can save about $100. a month or near it. I dont go to Charleston any at all now as there are so many ways to spend money there. We have a good or pretty good stick of Bacon on hand yet & a <u>little</u> from home now & then will cause us to spend little for Commission. We get flour at 12 1/2 cents.

If Duff has any red flannel yet at 5 or 6 dollars better get some of it too as white flannel when I came thru Columbia was selling at from 17 to 20 dollars per yard & I will however get more of it too. We have just received bad news from Bragg.[23] I hope it may not turn out as bad as we fear, but he has to fight over powering numbers. The yanks are getting more quiet for the last few days here. Dont shoot near so fast, but they will perhaps open soon again.

I see negroes prchd in Richmond this morning at from 4 to 5000 Dollars for men. One man from our Company & 3 men from Crawfords will be at the York train about Tuesday coming down here. They will get on at Gutheries or McConnells. Their names are Ash, Lochart, Meek & Plexico. S N McElvee will go to Mt Pleasant which is a good ways from us. The 2 Femsters is not here & I cant get transportation. About 6 or 8 Dolls will bring the boy here or less. I sent a shirt & some things by Plexico & a hat by Mr Carothers which you have not acknoledged. Mr Wheeler has paid a pile for that old place. I think it is mightly pore, but our money unless something is done to save it, I fear will "go up." I will not have much to lose now, however (when I get every thing squared) if it does. Mr Corrthers has returned. I have sent another piece to the paper called a "Contrast with a Conclusion." I hope we may be moved to the rear soon so that I can get to see you but not wind of it yet. I will get home if nothing happens last of Feby or before. Capt Avery will come back in about two weeks now.

The yankees shell us here occasionally, yet, a telegraphic operator just out of Fort Sumpter here, says he had rather 40 times be in Fort Sumpter. He runs about here awfully scared when they open on us. He never had to go out of the bomb-proof in Sumpter though, when he was there. The boys who come out look blushed. We will not have to go next time. Our companies will go last. They are A F & D. I hope things may get quiet by the time they have to go.

The negroes who have been here last to work on fortifications have had to come down to their work. They have done more in the last 3 months than all that ever has been done before. It seems like we are as well fixed now as we could be. There are 5 Guns mounted in Fort Sumpter. Their bearing on the channel next to Moultrie. One 8 inch Blakely & 2 10 inch Columbiads. The other two are bearing towards Johnson. The inside of the Fort is being made into another Fort, & if the yankees get in the "old wall," they will find our boys inside of still another fort. My health is very good except I have a little touch of the "Exema." I think the Dr calls it a camp itch. He has it too. We nearly all have it alittle. I want to see you awfully. Gilfillins wife came here last week. She said she was only going to stay a day or two but "Gil" told her no.

The boys may think "she had gone to the expense to come here & now he was going to have to pay for it." As he has kept her over a week. I would like you to come to Charleston but this place is too rough.

A erunt shell killed a horse here the other evening. They have never hurt any man though yet which is a little strange as they have fallin nearly every where in our camp. If I was to [take] a little sick Dr Logan would work for me to get home. He thinks a great deal of me. I believe this day two years ago I first went into serve & left you in Yorkville. I hope & believe I am a better man & father. I love my wife better than ever & believe she grows better looking every day. I know she looks better now than she had before she was married as her ambrotypes prove.

My best pants have drawn so much I will have to get the him turned out. I think I drew a nice pair of pants. All I will need now is a cap or hat. I have been feeling "squamish" for several evenings. I may be taking your place in this way.

Your Old boy
Dave Logan

*　　*　　*

Sullivans Island SC
Dec 10th 1863

My Dear Wife:

I am quite well this evening, but have not received a word from you since the last of Nov—the mail must be wrong. Maj Pagan has arrived here from home, but no word from you—also Plexico & Ash.

I sent $375.00 by Geo Burris to J B McConnell for you. Also a letter by S Roberts who will leave Yorkville about today week. Every thing is comparatively quiet here. Dan Williams & J V McFadden expect to bring their wives down after Christmas if I do & I shall try soon to get a house at Mt Pleasant. I may not be able to get beds, but I suppose you could take soldiers fare for a few days by bringing another blanket with you. I will write you again in regard to it.

D F Barnette has just received a furlough to be married to a Miss Potts of Mecklenburg NC. I sent you a very valuable bundle by S Roberts & I forgot to send your bricks. I did it for fare, but it may be of use. There was a piece of good canvas in it, &c. I have a quantity of bottles on hand. What are they worth? What do the people think of the bad luck in Tenn?[24] I suppose Capt Beatty will be 2 M, Capt Avery major, & myself Capt of Co F, if every thing works as it is said be at present.

I would like for you to be with me where I was this evening, on the beach of the main ocean. As far as the eye could reach nothing but water, the waves breaking one after another in the wildest excitement. It is something that will impress a person with awe & wonder in spite of himself.

I would like for you to send down the boy as soon as convenient. We have but one, a very aged one. He cant do the washing. We are living high. Dunovant has a box of souse, sausages, spare-ribs & back bones &cc. We got good rations & you see our living well in a fine house. My love to all the friends. Kiss my babies. I have shoes &c for Jim when he comes that I can give him. Did you get a shirt I sent &c?

Your husband
D J Logan

*   *   *

Sullivans Island SC
Dec 19th 1863

My Dear Wife:

I am quite well this morning altho I was nearly frozen to death on picket last night. I was in command of the Beach pickets from "Moultrie" to "Beauregard."[25] I will send your last box by R. Mulholland. The large one he cant carry. "Jim" sends some "[?]" & "shells" for the children. I sent some bottles which I picked up here. If you run low on change you can speculate alittle on them. I have been over to Mount Pleasant and find I can get two rooms, one with a sofa in it, both with chairs & fire places. I have secured a good mattress & pillows for you & me if you come & the others will perhaps do as well. I have partially engaged rooms with beds (not certain). We can get the ones I mentioned certain. The only thing now in the way is our papers. I think there will be no doubt about them. I shall send up to see in advance & if cant get them will write you at once. You can prepare to come down. Uncle Jeff will meet you at the Depot on Tuesday morning or Monday night after New years. I will wait for you at Head Quarters at Mt Pleasant. You can have a "Christmas spree" any way. You had better only bring one Trunk between you & a blanket if you can. I want you to bring about $60.00 in money. I sent home perhaps alittle too much money. I can draw again at the end of this month. I would like to see John but it wont pay for him to come. The times will be too rough. Perhaps we can have a merry Christmas yet if every thing works right. I have not had a Christmas at home in several years.

I will give you a few of my ideas upon finance now. Congress will no doubt pass Memmingers proposition for a loan & a tax of 5 per cent on all property or something nearly akin to it,[26] and if so property of all kinds will depreciate for a short time. I see large sales of stocks of property of all kinds advertised in the Charleston papers & the idea is to have a large amount of currency on hand for speculation. I think it a good idea to sell off all supplies provided if the present high prices can be obtained for Congress will undoubtedly pass some act to contract the currence & bring down the price of property &c. If a person has money on hand it may be invested again at a better profit. I have wrote Jim Jefferies to sell my house & lot in Shelby for $3000.00 and if he does that to not sell my bonds. You will send these to him however, the first good chance.

You can send the papers and form an opinion also as regards the future and can advise your father in regard to my ideas of the state of the currency. If I was him I would sell about half my cotton if I could get 80 or 90 cts for it and my corn if I could get the highest price was selling for. No person will thank another for selling his grain below the market price. When the time comes to pay taxes he will have to pay as heavy ones as any one else. The only fair way is to sell for the most you can get & when you wish to bestow a favor or a charity bestow N "gratis."

I received your box and was highly pleased with it. The honey was praised very highly by the whole mess. Capt. Avery brot another very nice box. I also received boots & every thing I have heard of your sending me. I would like to see you & aunt Jane down here enjoying camp life. I think it would please you for a short time. I cant help but think about how "Banks M" will feel when he hears of the increase of his family.[27] Mt Pleasant is a larger place than Yorkville and a very aristocrable people reside in it. All Irish & German. Mostly decent people I believe but wupt.

I shall perhaps write you several times before you start here and you will then get the news or any of the new developments that may take place.

"Jim" suits me very well. I think if he keeps well he will do finely. He is very attentive to my wants at present & I am pretty stern at inch with him.

I shall send up to get our papers several days before you come down so if I fail to get them I can write you to Guthries or Smiths[28] to whichever place you take the cars at. Furloughs are getting along very briskly now & if anything happens I will get home in Feby some time. My love to all.

Yours
D J L

*   *   *

Dec 20th 1863

Dear Wife, I received yours of the 16th yesterday. I will look for you here the morning of New years instead of after. Uncle Jeff and myself will be in Charleston at the Cars to meet you. I have sent up our "Pass" to Genl Ripley this morning. When it comes back I will write you. I think some one should put Jim Erwin in the army. If your Pa has any beeves he had better kill them & sell them himself if he wishes to be sure of the hides. I wish you to let all those agents know that my wife & children have to be supported and that if Mr Rowell is not in the army, <u>I am</u>, and consider the matter all the same. If they go to pressing provisons from Soldiers families &c before touching it from others who have none in the army, they will find the army laying down its arms. I have sent your box to Smiths T.O. by Mr McFadden, to be left in care of Mr Duff.

 I will write soon again. A merry Christmas to you & a still more merry New Years.

 Your hus

 D J Logan

I received your letter writen 16th since. I wrote after enclosed letter.

———————

 There is a lenghthy gap in Logan's correspondence with Sallie from December 20, 1863 to February 6, 1864. During this time David was attempting to make arrangements for Sallie's visit to the city, while at the same time requesting a furlough for himself (Logan's request is reprinted below in full). The application was apparently denied.

 Although no actions of substance took place during this timeframe, the Federals continued to make their presence felt. While the navy conducted occassional bombardments of Confederate troops on Johns' and James' Islands, and on Fort Sumter, Southern infantry scouted and skirmished as Federals prodded Confederates defenses for weak points.

———————

Sullivan's Island, S.C.

Dec 24th 1863.

Maj. Jas R Culp Comdy 17th Regt S.C.V.

 Dear Sir, I would respectfully solicit through you, a leave of absence for twenty (20) days to visit my home in York Dist S C & my parents in Shelby N. C. for the following reason. Before the war, I was engaged in the mercantile business in Yorkville S.C. (My partners and clerks are all in the service, and are now in the armies of Northern Virginia & Tenn.) My business is in a very neglected condition as I am without any authorized agent to attend to it, in regard to the payment of Taxes &c.

I have only received one well furlough of Ten days at home, since I entered service. All four of the Commissioned Officers of my Company are present for duty.

Very Respectfully

D.J. Logan 1st Lieut
Comdy Co F 17th Regt S.C.V.

From the 17th Regt., S.C.V.
Sullivan's Island, S.C.,

January 27, 1863 [1864]

Dear Enquirer: — After a long silence, but one which has been undisturbed by anything of unusual interest, I again desire to trouble your readers with an account of our situation.

Our Regiment, after a stay of seven weeks on James' Island, (during which time it held the post of honor at Fort Sumter, Secessionville and the lines in front of Fort Lamar) was transferred to Sullivan's Island on the night of the 30th day of November, 1863, the bombardment of Sumter and the surrounding Forts being then at its *acme*,[29] necessitated our removal at night, we reached our present camp about 2 o'clock, a. m., December 1st, 1863. We are situated in that part of the Island most widely known as the "myrtles," where the shifting sands, like the snows of far northern climes, encroaches upon the works of civilization and calls up the remembrance of ancient Nineyeh. Our health has been unusually good here, first rate water, and the "dieting system" established by our Commissaries has placed the Surgeon in pretty much the same condition with "Othello" as to occupation. The morale of our Regiment was never in better condition — augmenting in numbers every day, they never betray by their looks, the evil treatment they receive from those who have been appointed to provide for them. Day after day passes without a "meat ration," but on the soil of their native State, no murmur will escape their lips, although they are well satisfied that the Commissaries are every day enjoying a sumptuous repast of the finest potatoes, choicest beef and bacon, and not sparing altogether, that which has been drawn for them for "the Hospital," but which seldom reaches it, such as the best Rio coffee, sugar tea, &c. Like "angle visits," we get a little beef now and then. The boys account for its failure to come in this way. "At the slaughter-pen, the butchers have a pole raised eight inches from the ground, all beeves able to cross that pole without falling, are reserved for the future, but any unable to cross without falling, are immediately killed and sent over, those that cross safely are driven over the pole each succeding day until unable to cross, when they are forwarded forthwith, to us."

As to the defences of this Island, I can say nothing, only come and see for yourselves; but if too much trouble, take my word for it, that other Moultries and Marions[30] are here to make it doubly glorious in coming years. We have a situation as romantic as a poet or novelist could desire. The mighty comes with a hostile fleet upon its bosom in front of us. The enormous flag of the Yankees floating upon Morris' Island, surrounded with new and increasing earth works. The numberless Forts and batteries of our own, with the *coveted city* in the distance, bearing itself to the invader's malice and hate, and uniting with Beauregard in the reply, "Do your worst—we never surrender."

There is one other spot on this Island which will long be remembered, the tears—the anguish of soul—the almost breaking of hearts which is the daily scene, will imprint it forever upon the soldiers heart. I have reference to this end of the "Island bridge." It is as far as the soldier is allowed to go, with the wife, the mother, or the sister, who may visit him around his camp fire. I have seen aged mothers clinging around the necks of their sons, invoking heavens protection and care. I have seen the tender wife, time after time and again, part with the "soldier left behind;" it is an affecting post for the guard that keeps it, and might well be called the "post of the soldiers parting."

In haste, yours

L.

P. S.—The 17th Regiment has more men for duty to day than at any period of its history, and over 200 dead and discharged.

Sullivans Island S. C.
Feby 6th 1864

My Dear Wife:

I am quite well this evening altho exceedingly tired.We have had one of the liveliest times on this Island during the past week that I have ever seen. A large steamer the "Presto" with a heavy cargo after running past all danger from the enemy ran aground off Fort Moultrie and was then exposed to the fire of the enemy to such a degree that it was almost impossible to save her cargo. However the soldiers went aboard and are about to get off the entire cargo almost now.[31] The Gov has got from the wreck 5000 prs shoes, 1 or 2000 blankets, 100 lbs Pork & many other things while about the same amount has been "passed in" by the soldiers to gether with nearly all the Apl cargo. We have had some two men killed & 15 or 20 wounded during the operation in all. I will state what I have got by the wreck, viz 1 pr shoes No 10 $12.00, 1 pr shoes No 8 $20.00, 1 pr shoes No 6 $15.00 & Jim has got a pair. I will send them home soon. They are excellent. Also 4 bottles Champaign which I shall send you to keep until I come. Also one large excellent blanket for which I paid $12.50. And last night I got for nothing out of the wreck my self about 30 or 35 quires of paper which I will send home. I am writing on a very inferior kind that I got. Send.

Jno Rainey has sent me a very valuable box of provisions. I have sent for them to day to Charleston. I tried very hard to get hold of some calico for you but as yet I have found none. If you have as much money on hand as $113.00 you can leave it with J A Carroll of Yorkville for Jno L Rainey. I intended sending home $100. but I have bought so much blockade stuff &c and loaned some that I will not be able to send any before the 20th of this month unless I make some sales.

Lt Moore has arrived in the City. Will be over here to night when I expect to get a letter from you. You can send those bonds up to Mr Wheeler. Let him send his receipt back for them. I have sold them to Rev Mr Anderson and he is to pay the money over to Mr Wheeler.

Furloughs for officers have been stopped for awhile again. I dont think they will remain so long. Capt Avery has sent up a special one. I hope he will get it. I wish you had gone to see Capt Meacham. I will try to write you a full account of this shipreck again.

I will try to send Jim home soon if I cant get off. I want you to kill that—and I will try to not do so any more (I mean the disease). We are faring pretty well now. I am a member of another Genl Court Martial & have no guard duty to do. If cant get a furlough I must see you before the summer if we both keep well. My love to all. I expect a letter tonight by Lt Moore. Kiss my children for me.

>   Your husband
>   D J Logan

*   *   *

Sullivan Island S C
Feby 9th 1864

My Dear Wife:

I am quite well this morning. Every thing is very quiet & still. I received a letter from Ma & Pink yesterday. Pa is slowly improving and the boys have all re volunteered for the war. Nearly all the N C troops have volunteered for the war. Furloughs to officers are stopped here. Capt Avery had an application disapproved yesterday & Guntharp cant send any up. So I fear I shall not get home soon. Uncle Jeff has received his certificate from Withers and will get a 20 days furlough in a few days. If I see you soon, you will have to come down. I received the box that Jno Rainey sent me. It has 2 large hams, spare ribs, 1 side, 50 lbs. of flour, 6 wax candles, sweet cakes & 1 bottle honey &c.

I will not be able to send any of my blockade articles home yet. I have not been able to get any cloths except a blanket. I may send Jim home when Uncle Jeff goes. I wrote you to send my bonds to Mr Wheeler. I have sold them to Mr Anderson. I wish you at the same time to send to J A Carroll $113.00 for Jno L Rainey. Give my love to all & write often. We are living pretty well now. If all the fellows would bring boxes. Guntharp has brot no box since we have been here. Larry Massey &c bring big ones.

>   Your old fellow

>   Dave Logan

From the 17th Regt., S.C.V.
Sullivan's Island, S. C.,

February 12, 1864

Dear Enquirer:—Since my last letter, we have had one of the most "rollicking" and jovial seasons it has been our lot to meet with since entering the service. It is impossible to describe the scene which was ushered in upon us by the wrecking of the steamer Presto upon the breakwater extending out from Fort Moultrie. The vessel had passed the entire blockading squadron safely, and with one lucky push of the helm would have made her way triumphantly into the Cooper river; but it has been said, "there's many a slip between the cup and the lip," and so it was proved in this case. However, there may have been something of a "God send" in it after all. Hitherto, the poor and self-denying soldier has found but a small chance to gratify his palate with the luxuries of other climes, and in this case he was not altogether ignored. The Presto grounded some time after midnight, and with the certainty of discovery by the enemy in the morning, no objections were made by the officers to the soldiers (who are always on hand) "pitching into" the cargo, and saving what they could for themselves and the Governmant; so in they all went, and with them some of the fair daughters of Erin's green Isle. I would fain describe the process of unloading which then took place, the ejaculations, and the beatific expressions of the human countenance, as this mass of human beings stumbled against piles of oranges, bananas, shoes, champagne, brandy, whiskey, blankets, silks, teas, coffee, cheese, sugar, &c., picking up one thing, then throwing it down and seizing something else. Your readers may picture in their imagination a small mountain of the articles here enumerated. Then, by fancying the command given "pitch in and help yourselves," they will arrive at something as near the reality as I can describe it.

Sure enough, when morning came, the Yankee guns on Morris Island opened their iron throats, and the monitors moved up to add their share to the hellish chorus. All day long, and through the night, and again the next day, the hugh missles of the enemy exploded upon and around the wreck, until at last, machinery and hull were riddled and ruined.

Every night some daring soldiers, despite the shells, were fishing for the shoes, pork, and "Old Bourbon" that still remained aboard. To-day I learned that almost the entire cargo belonging to the Governmant has been saved—the greatest losers being those who were trying to bring in a supply of the "water of Chickamauga."

A number of casualties have taken place among the troops here during the past week, three or four killed, a number wounded, and among these are several women. The Yankees have pretty much relapsed into quietude to-day, our guns being the most active. To-day a friend of mine, while sitting with a glass, watching a working party on Morris Island, saw a Yankee tumble over as one of our shells exploded above the party, the balance of the crowd made for shelter and then a few came back and carried off their comrade. I doubt not that in this way, every day, some of Lincoln's crew obtain their "southern homes" and "bounty land."

I hear quite a spirited affair took place on John's Island, the other day,[32] in which our forces under Maj. John Jenkins were pressed back for a time, but finally compelled the Yanks to retire, our forces getting much the best of the whole affair.

Our boys are discussing the question of re-enlisting for the war, but as our time is nearly ten months off, it may suffice to end it any way. When called upon, there will be no hesitation among the soldiers of this Regiment. They have suffered too much "to give it up so."

We are all very agreeably situated, and our ration department—all honor to the Presto—has improved a little. We have heard that the boys of Company F, in this regiment, are not forgotten by the dear ladies of Yorkville. There is many a ragged soldier in the company who drops his mouth open, and smiles complacently, when he hears of a box that the last boys on furlough did not get to the Yorkville depot in time. When it arrives it will be received with a shout, and the kind donors will ever be remembered.

Mess No. 1, has already received and appreciated, in the most improved style, a valuable offering in the shape of a box of provisions, from one of the staunch farmers of Bullock's Creek, made to your humble correspondent. May no drought ever overtake him, but it may be *Rainey* when he wishes it.

In haste, yours,

L.

————

As the winter months edged toward spring, David tried once more to obtain a furlough to visit his family. The request (reprinted below) would once again bring disappointment. Unable to visit his home, David attempted to get Sallie to visit him near Charleston. Such a trip was frought with perils and weighed heavily on his mind.

————

Camp near Green Pond, S.C.
March 14th 1864
Capt Jno Maley, A A Genl

Dear Sir, I would respectfully solicit a leave of abscence of fifteen days to visit my family in York District S.C.

Four of the Commissioned officers of my regiment are present for duty and have received leaves of abscence since I have. I received a furlough of fifteen days to visit my father in Shelby N. Carolina in December 1863, who was then being very low with fever. My own family being sick, I was only with them a short time, in going and returning from my father's. In the commencement of the war, I left my home and business, and placed my family in the care of my friends. I desire this "leave" to arrange my business preparatory to the 1st of April next and to attend to the wants of my family.

With the exception of the leave above referred to, I have not been away from duty through sickness or other causes, exceeding three weeks since March 1863.

Very Respectfully
David J. Logan
Company F 17th Regt

Approved & respectfully forwarded
J W Avery Capt , Comdg Compy (F) 17th S.C.V.

———

Burnets Farm
March 22nd 1864

My Dear Wife:

I wrote you yesterday by Shearer that I had failed in my furlough.

I am still feeling very badly. We are having a dreadful spell of weather here. Rain & the coldest wind I almost ever felt. I suppose you would all be looking for me home but you are calculating too serously as I have been. I am feeling most dreadfully "seedy." My old boots & pants are almost ready to fall off. My shoes & other pants I have left at Green Pond. I wish your father to invest all the money he has on hand except it be 5 cents in bonds. Jno A Brooks is the funding agent at Yorkville & unless he gets his in pretty soon, he may be too late. I wish Mr Wheeler to attend to my taxes if there are any to pay. I wrote for you to come down if you wished & bring Jim if you concluded to do so. You had better start on the night train from home, as there is no train on the Charleston road at night now and the Savannah road which we are on, the cars do not start until about 7 1/4 oclock from the city so the night before will have to be spent in Charleston where there is no fit place for a woman to get to unless I could be there when you should arrive. You had better send Jim by Capt Mills or some other person coming down if you have no good chance to come yourself. I fear you would have a rough time in the City unless some person was with you. Capt Crawford will be here I guess tomarrow when he comes & some others. I may send up my papers again, if Evans does not take charge of us before that time. Col McMaster left here yesterday for Richmond to make an effort to get away from Evan's Brigade. I fear he will not succeed. It would certainly be very hard to place McMaster under him again after being challenged by him. If we have to go under Evans we may expect to take the "front of battle" every time. I sometimes think I will resign, rather than go, but I dont know whether I would feel any better to do so or not. I trust McMaster will be able to have a hearing by the President. If I dont get home be sure to let Mr Wheeler have the bonds on my note at 108 & interest & explain to him how you thought the error in counting the money was commited. Meacham is at home now & I should like very much to see him but suppose I will not be able. If I cant get home I wish you to come down with some person when you can. Well as I am very anxious to see you before this summer campaign opens again. We will be very likely to get into some fighting before it is over & it may be pretty heavy. Capt Avery took Jims basket & all the shells set it down some where & for got it.

Capt Avery is now in command of the regiment & Maj Culp acting Brig Genl. We are lying out now in old fly tents & have to work very hard. I feel we will not get into our good quarters soon again. If I send up my application again I may get home about the 5th of April or some later. If it is approved which is very doubtful. I will keep trying if I can have a showing. Give my love to all & kiss our children for me. I am as black as you please with pine-smoke sitting over the fires.

Your unfortunate Husband

D J Logan

CHAPTER 7

"We have been fortunate to escape the fighting so far but I fear we will have our share yet, as Grant is determined to keep on fighting."

Side Trip to Wilmington

May 1 – May 16, 1864

The spring of 1864 approached with some promise for Southern arms. Robert E. Lee's Army of Northern Virginia, reorganized and rested after a relatively uneventful winter, lay south of the Rapidan River. The reorganized Confederate army was confident it could meet and throw back the expected advance by the Federal Army of the Potomac. In North Georgia, the Army of Tennessee's new commander, Joseph E. Johnston—the same Johnston under whom the Tramp Brigade had idly served in Mississippi during the Siege of Vicksburg—occupied the mountainous terrain below Chattanooga in the hopes of repelling William T. Sherman's three combined armies (Army of the Tennessee, Army of the Cumberland, and Army of the Ohio).

Despite the need for additional men and resources in Virginia and Georgia, the next change of venue for David Logan and his fellow soldiers of the Tramp Brigade involved another visit to the coast of North Carolina. Their two week stint in Wilmington consisted primarily of relentless marching from one point to another, and then back again. In some respects the soldiers seemed to be reprising their difficult marches in Mississippi. Two important events during this time, as far as Logan was concerned, included the loss of his hat on the journey

to Wilmington, and the subsequent procurement of a new straw head-
piece. Although the loss and acquisition of a hat may at first glance
appear to be trivial issues, proper head gear was most assuredly a
necessity for any soldier involved in constant marching under an early
summer sun in coastal North Carolina.

Logan's writings during this period are characterized by somewhat
less despair than his previous Charleston-based correspondence. But
even with his lighter tone, one can still sense a growing desperation as
to whether or not the cause to which he and his fellow Confederates
had committed themselves would be successful.

Wilmington NC
May 1st 1864

My Dear Wife:

We have just returned from the City of Charleston where we took the
yankee prisoners captured at Plymouth N.C. We have over 2500 of the boys on
our exchange list now. We are all nearly broken down, having been out 8 days
and being under the necessity of keeping awake nearly all the time as there
were 8 yankees to one of our men. They made no effort whatever to escape the
coming campaign. They were generally a very fine looking set of fellows — all
handsomely dressed, but I feel encouraged, aside from our victory to hope for
the triumph of our cause, from these grounds.[1] They are most generally the
most wicked, vulgar, & profane crowd of men I ever had any thing to do with.
Many of them seem to have high hopes of subjugating us yet while others seem
very tired of the war and admit that they believe it impossible to whip us.

Our regiment has been bountifully supplied with oil cloths, canteens,
pocket knifes & yankee notes. The yankees when they reached Tarboro were
severely starved & offered watches & some as high as one hundred Dollars for
something to eat. I will give you a list of my acquicitions. 1 fine Gutta Percha
pipe, 1 superior India rubber oil cloth, 2 excellent prs of Buckskin Gauntlets, 2
pocket books, one pocket Knife with spoon & Fork attached, also one very fine
cap to make up for the loss of one hat of which I wrote you from Tarboro. I
wore very new pants on this expedition & got them smartly soiled. I received a
letter from Bro Pink this morning. They are all well & still at Taylorsville but

expect to move every day. He has declined the idea of a Transfer for the present. They all seem to be in high spirits about whipping Grant when the fight comes on.[2]

We are certainly going to have a grand time in this state from the appearance of things. Genl Beauregard is at Weldon & we have in this department or near have, 40 or 50 thousand men. I am inclined to think that our forces will attack Newbern very soon. Washington in this state will be attacked also unless the enemy evacuate the place. The intention is to rid NC of the yankees & beat back Burnsides if he tries to take Richmond by way of Blackwater of James River. I do most seriously hope "this cruel war" will end this summer & with less blood shed than we all anticipate. God is all powerful & can grant us victorys like that at Plymouth, without great loss of life if we are surely true & faithful to him.

I left Uncle Jeffery unwell at Tarboro. Have not heard from him since. Only a part of our regiment has returned from guarding prisoners. I will learn some about him. He had cold I think. Capt Mills will be home again soon. I received several bequests from the ladies on the way from Charleston here. A great crowd was at all the stations looking for Hagood's Brigade which has been ordered here at last.

They will have a share of the war as yet in all probility. I have just learned to sing "when this cruel war is over." It is a beautiful song. Very touching, especially to us. I have not seen "Eloise." Her sister is at Raleigh at School. Miss Flora is looking well & entertains with music & conservation her friends or us real. I have only been in Wilmington a few hours. We have been away until to day & I fear they will keep us trotting again soon as we all get back here & rest a day or two. If we stay here, I should be very hopeful to see you. I miss my "old gal" most dreadfully & furloughs have played out now. I have a pretty sunset.

I will have to have a pair of boots or shoes made before long & must have them made larger than these shoes. Kiss my dear babies for me & dont you & Aunt Jane mis lead some young chaps like Bob Mitchell. When you are "flying round" if you come to that you can come to the army where your Liege Lord will be very happy to welcome you.

Write soon & give all the news. What do you hear about all the people being all so mean &c. Have you heard any thing farther from your bacon thieves? Are you a "Gentleman" yet or not?

D J Logan

From the 17th Regt., S.C.V.
Wilmington, N. C.,

May 2nd, 1864.

Dear Enquirer:—The "comet" is revisiting its old track. The "foot cavalry"[3] have again turned the head of column to the North East. After skirmishing, for the second time, the shores of our own State, the shrill voice of the war-whoop is heard in its highest key, echoing through Virginia and the shores of the Old North State, the command comes, "forward to the rescue."[4]

On the 15th ultimo, we bade adieu to the Cypress, the Mossey Oak, the deserted rice fields and the impenetrable marshes of the Combahec and the Ashepoo, and took the cars for Wilmington, N. C., at which place we arrived right side up, notwithstanding a smash-up near Florence, and a most annoying hindrance in waiting for "schedules."

Upon reaching the river, we crowded into the Ferry boat under a most pelting rain, and were soon landed under the spacious roof of the Wilmington and Weldon Depot, having in our passage regaled ourselves with the inspection of the neat building and superior finish of a number of Ocean Steamers of a suspicious color,[5] which were reposing quietly upon the bosom of the Cape Fear, or lying at the wharves loading with the great staple of our Southern land, or else disgorging the missles of warfare and the smiling barrels of "Old Ned" for the efficiency and support of our armies. After some delay, our regiment was assigned to a camp some two miles from town, said camp having the lowering heavens for the roof of our tents and the most exceedingly moist earth for the flooring. Next day ordered to Weldon, N. C., sent our baggage to the Rail Road when the order was countermanded. Next day ordered again, marched to town, reached the town, then ordered back to camp to await further orders. Next day ditto, except we returned this time to the good quarters of the 17th N. C. Troops, who had gone to Taraboro; but that night were roused in the dead of night, by the, "long roll" with all its hurly-burly of looking after haversacks, canteens, &c., which can only be described to home folks, by saying it is more waking up and finding their houses on fire over their heads, with the exception, that in one way, we never have much to lose, but in another, we always have a prospect of loosing what is still more valuable. The 50th N. C. Troops marched off and we remained nodding until day light, when we learned that Yankees had landed on barges and burned the State salt-works[6] and carried off some citizens, our pickets falling back before the superior force of the enemy. On the evening of the day after this alarm, we were ordered to Tarboro, N. C., to escort a very large assembledge of Black Republicans in an excursion "away down South in Dixie," a mass meeting, which Gen. Bob Hoke had succeeded in gobbling up, at Plymouth, N. C. This time we were soon all aboard, and on the way; about sun-rise we passed the scene of our old fight at Goldsboro, the din of war was hushed, however, and the plowshare had made ready the same fields (over which our columns charged the enemy) for the production of the staff of life. How long, O Lord! how long, before all the battle-fields of this war shall be made ready for the peaceful avocations of the plowman! A little further on we were passing the town of Railroads and pretty women, and just before we reached Wilson, your correspondent's hat was lifted from his head by a whirlwind, and like the boy's kite away it went never to be recovered by its proper owner again. He has realized by its loss, however, the true signification of what "chawed" means when expressed by a soldier. At Wilson, he sallied out with a large red bandana tied round his head, after the mode of our old African Mamas, for the yells of the men at his appearance prevented all earnest enquiry whatever. Every citizen almost seeming to consider him a perfect hoax. So, unable to procure anything in the shape of a hat, he was compelled, in disgust, to resume his seat, and muse over the depravity of his fellow soldiers, who would, rather than forego the least amusement at his expense, heap insult to injury upon him.

We reached Tarboro in the forenoon of the 23d of April, and found the Holcomb Legion and a host of "Tar heels" preparing to strike another blow to the Yankees in N. C. I was here fortunate enough to get an old straw hat for five dollars, and save myself from being the object of amusement for the army. We stacked arms near the Depot, and after a frugal dinner, took a promenade down town in our "new hat." This place I have mentioned before, in a previous letter, the Yankees have paid it a visit since then; but unlike their usual visits they have left but few marks of their displeasure behind, the Depot, Government Shops, Gun boat and Bridge are all their great minister, fire, has been successful in dissipating, and they are being replaced. This is a lovely place. Many old citizens from the country were in town and every one in the highest humor imaginable. Many refugees from Plymouth and Washington almost in extacies with the prospect of returning to their old homestead without the necessity of crouching to the cruel invader. The people here, I believe, are all as true as steel to our cause. This is the home of the lamented Pender,[7] whose life was opening with so much brilliancy for himself and country; but alas, whose youthful form now lies resting in his native soil, but mangled by the missles of the enemy. It is, also, the land of McNair[8] and others, who are shedding glory upon our cause, in deeds of daring and bravery.

Edgecombe county produces, in times of peace, 30,000 bales of cotton annually. Much land has been uncultivated for fear of the raids of the enemy, but with present prospects, we may well hope to see Eastern Carolina redeemed and disen-thralled before the coming winter, adding a section of country more valuable than East Tennessee. I will give my observations upon Black Republicans in my next, as I have been pretty closely associated with them for the last eight days.

In haste,

L.

———————

The campaign season opened in early May with an unprecedented and unrelenting fury. Major General George G. Meade's Army of the Potomac, to which Lt. Gen. U. S. Grant, the Federal commander-in-chief, had attached himself, crossed the Rapidan River on May 4 and engaged Lee's army in the Wilderness. The bloody and furiously-fought two-day affair was followed by an even bloodier series of battles around Spotsylvania Court House the following week. Viewing Lee's army as his objective instead of the Southern capital, Grant planned to utilize protracted combat to bleed the Army of Northern Virginia through steady attrition.

Another thrust into Virginia from below Richmond was also un-derway, this one aimed at Petersburg, a logistically valuable rail junc-tion. Headed by Maj. Gen. Benjamin Butler, the Army of the James moved steadily inland against Lee's rear. The duel pincer movement, supported by a third Federal army in the Shenandoah Valley under Maj. Gen. David Hunter, simultaneously threatened Lee's army, the Southern capital, Petersburg, and the always vital Weldon Railroad.

Logan and his comrades received news of the bitter fighting in Virginia and elsewhere and counted themselves fortunate to have es-caped the bloodbath that was sweeping toward Richmond. Veteran that he was, Logan also knew it was only a matter of time before the South Carolinians would be called up for service in Virginia.

———————

Wilmington N C
May 12th 1864

My Dear Wife:

I received a short letter from you yesterday embracing several days. We are still in this place. My health is tolerable good. I have some Diarhea. We are without any news here for several days. The lines are down in almost every direction. Many fear that our forces are being crowded into Richmond. Grant I hear no doubt has a very heavy force and will fight with desperation.

I sent a bundle to you yesterday by McClelland who goes home on sick furlough. I sent my old gloves & a yankee pocket book for you & a pair of yankee gloves which with a little soap applied to them will look very well. I have kept two prs of Gloves. You see I am well supplied in that way. I have not been able to draw a cent of money yet. They are determined to put the soldiers off until the last. Your Cousin Hutchinson is not benefitting the people much I dont think by his cloth. I consider this about the hardest place I ever saw for prices & the best Granitesville shirting I priced there at 3.75 per yard in new issue. I cant see how he asks more than it sells for here from the same Mills. There were four more ships came in here yesterday and three others besides since I wrote you before. They are laden with Bacon, shoes, & Apl merchandise. The wharves are lined with them. Some of them are almost covered with flags. 70 yankees passed through here last night, captured at Newberne. Genl Hoke says he could have taken the place in 4 hours if he had not been ordered to Richmond.[9]

We have been fortunate to escape the fighting so far but I fear we will have our share yet, as Grant is determined to keep on fighting. I am very anxious to hear from my brothers & I fear it will be a long time before I can do so. I wish you to communicate with my folks and when you hear from them write to me at once. I trust they have escaped. I suppose Yorkville is in gloom, Genl Jenkins & Col Miller both killed, it seems like taking all the officers from York.[10] Write me all particulars you may hear as to the killed & wounded as I will get no papers here.

Speaking of them, the Enquirer has failed to reach us. The mail North are all deranged. Can hear but little. Lt Moore tells me that Richwood has written to Mrs Moore that he cant get the peas shipped & will take the money. The salt was worth $14.00 per Bushel when we bought it. Salt is worth here 30 Dollars per bushel & peas retail at $80. per bushel. I wish I could get the peas here. If it could be done we might afford to pay high prices, cotton $2.50 per lb, Eggs $5.00 per Dozzen, Bacon 4 to 5 Dollars. Such things are declining alittle. If we did not draw rations I think Officers would be bound to steal or starve. I do hope our money will improve or be abolished altogether. I wrote a short letter to Pa the other day. Have not received one from them in some time. I hope the weather has got so that planting can be done. It is quiet enough here I tell you. We had rain to day.

I believe I wrote you about seeing Belle Boyd.[11] I also saw Elvira Wilson. When she saw me she ran to me as hard as she could & kissed me. She wishes to see you very much. Talks a great chance about you. I am beginning to want a pair of Drawers but I will want boots some of these months worse than any thing else. Troops are still passing on the Rail Road. We will have a tremendeous army at Petersburg or Richmond one. Some body will be hurt there is no mistake. Uncle Jeff I hear has been quite sick. I have not been to the regiment since we came here. Preserve all the papers that come during this crisis as I will wish to see them & can see but few here as the price is 50 cts per paper. I wish this cruel war would end before the sun shines in its verticle rays. Many have seen its beams for the last time & many more will see them for the last time before the days of August.

Write me long letters and all the items of news. Tell John & Lula they must be good children & try to learn something. I will send my wages home as soon as I can draw them but it makes me feel bad to know how little they would buy. I could only board here 3 days for a months wages & then find my own lodging. You have not answered all my questions again. You are growing reticent. I have that awful humor worse than ever. I fear I will not get clear of it soon. We all have it. Some have never been well. We have a bad chance for curing it in Camp. I scratch sometimes awfully.

Your husband

D. J. Logan

Write me all the persons killed & wounded from York that you hear from. If any news comes I will write more later this evening. Give my love to all.

Two more vessels have just come in. I hear that 100 vessels have sailed from Nassau for this Point. There is more Bacon, Coffee & Dry goods than ever was here before by a long ways. There is any quantity of Goods here. Our money is trash. There seems to be people with bushels of it every where. No chance for soldiers to get any thing.

Hold on to the Cloth. We will arrange to pay it off some way & we will need it badly as uniforms costs here out & out $1800.00.

———————

The fighting and manuevering continued almost unabated in Virginia. As the carnage unfolded both north and south of Richmond, it became necessary to reinforce the embattled armies by stripping the Atlantic coastline of some of its defending units. Logan's premonition that the 17th South Carolina would eventually have to join the relentless fighting in Virginia ("We have been fortunate to escape the fighting so far but I fear we will have our share yet, as Grant is determined to keep on fighting,"), became a reality when his unit received orders to transfer to Petersburg.

———————

May 16th 1864
Wilmington N.C.

My Dear Wife:
      We will leave this evening for Weldon or Petersburg. My health is tolerable good. I feel better to day than yesterday. I suppose we will see the enemy at last. I hear a grand fight is expected to day at Petersburg & that Lee has given Grant a severe drubbing.[12] Pray for my safety. I hope I shall be permitted to see you all again. There are several sick in the company. Direct your letters to Weldon or Petersburg. Care Conl McMaster 17th Regt SCV. Our Brigade is now under Genl Walker.[13]
      Kiss my Dear children for me & give my love to all.
      Your husband
      D J Logan

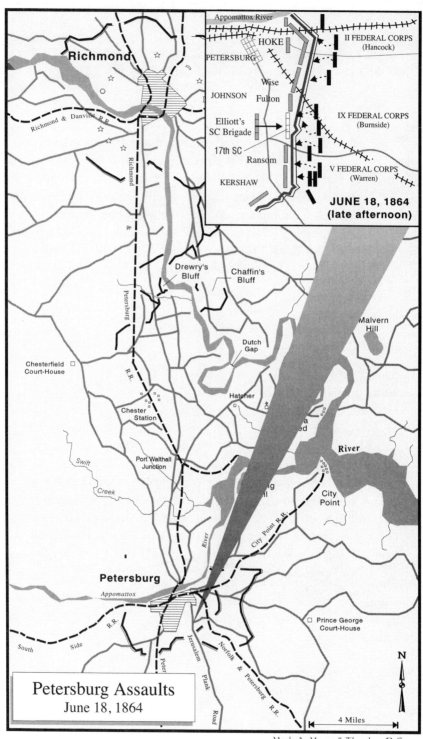

Appomattox River

II FEDERAL CORPS
(Hancock)

HOKE

PETERSBURG

Wise

JOHNSON   Fulton

IX FEDERAL CORPS
(Burnside)

Elliott's
SC Brigade

17th SC

Ransom

V FEDERAL CORPS
(Warren)

KERSHAW

JUNE 18, 1864
(late afternoon)

Richmond

Richmond & Danville R.R.

Richmond

&

Petersburg

Drewry's
Bluff

Chaffin's
Bluff

Malvern
Hill

Dutch
Gap

Chesterfield
Court-House

R.R.

Hatcher

Chester
Station

River

Swift

City
Point

Creek

Port Walthall
Junction

River

City Point R.R.

Petersburg

Appomattox

Prince George
Court-House

South   Side   R.R.

Peter

Jerusalem
Plank
Road

Norfolk & Petersburg R.R.

N

Petersburg Assaults
June 18, 1864

4 Miles

Mark A. Moore & Theodore P. Savas

CHAPTER 8

"I am all cramped up, in a hole in the ground & I fear you can hardly read this. . .Pray for my safety."

Petersburg

May 16 – June 18, 1864

After a brief furlough home, during which David Logan seemed to be preparing everyone for the worst, he rejoined the 17th South Carolina and the forever-wandering Tramp Brigade on its move to Virginia. Logan's previous trip to Virginia had been made under more auspicious circumstances. During the summer of 1862, the South Carolinians had ventured north to assist Lee's army on its march to meet and defeat John Pope on the plains of Manassas. This time the move was to confront the menacing threat from Ben Butler's advancing Federals at Bermuda Hundred, just a handful of miles below Petersburg. Instead of dictating the course of events, the Confederacy was reacting to them. The war had clearly reached a crisis point.

Immediately upon its arrival at Petersburg, the 17th South Carolina was sent directly into the trenches—and straight into battle. Before long the armies settled into a stalemate characterized by miles of trenches and redoubts extending across a relatively static front. The opposing lines would eventually stretch from north of the James River around Richmond south past Bermuda Hundred before wrapping south and west around Petersburg. The advent of trench warfare would characterize military conflicts for the next sixty years.

Life in the hot and deadly trenches was always difficult and danger-
ous, and as Logan recorded, casualties mounted from the steady sharpshooting and skirmishing. The stagnant nature of the Tramp Brigade's
current assignment was not the only change in store for the unit. The
brigade's new commander, Brig. Gen. William Stephen Walker, was
wounded and captured during the fight at Hewlett's Farm on May 22,
1864.[1] A fellow South Carolinian, Brig. Gen. Stephen Elliott, took over
command of the brigade and remained in that position until he was
badly wounded in the "great blow-up," better known as the Battle of the
Crater, on July 30, 1864.[2]

From the trenches that held him, Logan requested Sallie to "Pray
for [his] safety."

17th Regiment S.C.V.
Hewlett's Farm

In the Rifle Pits, May 22, 1864.

Dear Enquirer:—On the night of the 16th instant, we left Wilmington, N. C.,
passed the night and the next at Weldon and Petersburg, and on the night of the
18th were ordered to our present position. We reached the vicinity of this place
some time after midnight, or not far from day light on the 19th. We were told to lie
down ready to spring to arms at a moment's warning, and we knew, from the sharp
conflict raging at the time, between our pickets, that the bloody work was near at
hand.

At daylight we were ordered to proceed to the front. General Colquit's brigade[3] was relieved by ours in the trenches, having an excess of the 17th and 26th
S.C.V., who were ordered to be in reserve, but as usual, the reserve never makes
much by being so called. Gen. Hoke, our Division commander, very soon ordered
the 17th to follow and support a line of skirmishers, who were to charge the first
line of the enemy's works. We got into position in advance of our entrenchments,
the enemy keeping up a continual fire of small arms upon us. Our regiment and
skirmishers then lay down until every arrangement was completed, the line properly formed and adjusted. We had to charge a distance of nearly 3/4 of a mile, up
an ascent, and across a number of fences, but the command was given, and with a
yell that was enough to frighten almost anything, the old seventeenth pressed

forward at the quick and double quick time in the face of grape, canister and minnie balls, and had reached a distance of some 30 yards from the enemy's works, when they gave way before us, leaving their dead, wounded, &c., in our hands; our boys did not stop at the works, but pressed forward in advance of them, and captured a number of prisoners.

Having captured the outworks of the enemy, in order to hold them it was necessary to change their construction as rapidly as possible. We had captured any quantity of the best arms, spades, and shovels, and to throwing dirt we went in a hurry. The enemy made four assaults upon our front, after being driven by us from their works, every one of which was repulsed with ease and much loss to the enemy. Gen. Walker, in placing the other regiments of our brigade into position, told them to "emulate the example of the 17th, whose actions to-day had been an honor to their State." Gen. Hoke, I learn, also, spoke very highly of our conduct in the charge. I should like to give you a full account of all the incidents which have occurred, but will try to do so again.

We are still in the face of the enemy, we had it hot and heavy for an hour last night, and both sides this morning are at work with all their might. We have captured, up to this time, a great number of prisoners. I believe Brig. Gen. Walker is the only prisoner lost in our brigade during the fight. We were attached to our new Brigadier, and for the time he was in command of us, he was having our most enthusiastic support, but he was unlike many other Generals, he was always present to place his regiments in position, and in passing down our lines on foot fell into a gap and was gobbled up when least expecting it. The Yankees may endeavor to claim a victory at Hewlett's Farm, by producing a Brig. General captured, but the facts are that they were driven from their works, leaving their dead and wounded behind, and also a number of prisoners. The great anxiety for obtaining a good position for his brigade was the cause of our General exposing himself so much, and then a gap having been left in the lines, he fell into that and was taken.

During yesterday and this morning the enemy have been quiet, our "ball" last night making us feel somewhat disposed to keep "aisy." I will give you an account of our losses to this morning, and if I survive the fight, will give you a fuller account of the battle of Hewlett's Farm, again. The scene of this battle ground is about 3 miles from Drewry's Bluff, and 2 miles from Chester Station, our line of battle extending some four miles. Our Colonel has endeared himself to us again; while standing beside him the other morning, he was struck in the breast by a ball, tearing his clothes and bruising the skin, but it was, fortunately, too far spent to inflict much damage. Lt. W.S. Moore, of my company, was seriously wounded at nearly the same time, when standing together.

I will only give the losses in the York companies. Casualties in 17th Regiment S.C.V., in the battle of Hewlett's Farm, up to May 21st, 1864:

COMPANY E.—Lt. Neely commanding.—Killed—Corporal Minor Poag.

COMPANY F.—Lieut. D.J. Logan commanding (Capt. Avery acting Major)—Killed—Private Wm Martin—Wounded—Lieut. W.S. Moore, seriously; privates Wm Dixon and R.S. Randall, slightly.

COMPANY K.—Capt. Crawford commanding—Wounded—Private John Whisonant, slightly.

COMPANY C.—Lieut. J.C. Sanders commanding—Wounded—Michael Dover, leg amputated, J. Childers, slightly in hand.

Our York companies have fared well, the wounded are being well cared for, and rapidly sent home when disabled from service. We are all in fine spirits, and believe we can whip the enemy any time they come.

In dreadful haste.

Yours &c.

L.

*   *   *

17th Regiment, S.C.V.
Near Ware Bottom Church, Va.

May 27, 1864.

Dear Enquirer:—After the battle of the 20th instant, I sent you a hasty note from the trenches. We are still in the rifle pits confronting the enemy, at not more than 250 yards distance, but as we have grown somewhat more pacific, more time is allowed for reflection and retrospect. A large number of accounts of the fight here have appeared in the various papers, written mostly by camp followers, and thus are almost entirely erroneous; by some means the Petersburg *Express* and the *Richmond Dispatch*, struck upon a jet of truth; but other accounts of the operations here have been altogether *exparte*. I shall proceed in as short a manner as possible, to give you the facts as they occurred, and as I shall be confined to my own observation, I shall be responsible for their truth.

After dark on the 19th of May, our regiment then, just removed to the line of works, south of the Appomattox river, was ordered to return to Petersburg, cross the Pocahontas bridge and join Gen. Beauregard as soon as possible. We immediately got under way, and after a march of about 14 miles, were halted sometime after midnight, near Chester Station, on the Petersburg and Richmond Railroad.

Our situation was partly defined by the ferocious discharges of fire arms then going on, but a short distance from our bivouack. We occupied the remainder of the night in sleep, notwithstanding it was apparent to every one, that hot work was in store for us on the morrow. Sure enough, at daylight the order was "to fall in," and under Gen. Walker, we were led to relieve Colquitt's Brigade, but it was found that two of our regiments were sufficient to fill up the trenches. We were then ordered in reserve, but had not settled down well, nor finished our congratulations upon our good fortune, when we were again ordered to the front. This time we passed our friends of the other part of our brigade, and near the skirt of a dense wood, in front of the residence of Mrs. Clay, we formed upon the right of the 8th N. C. Troops. Very soon the word came along our line, that Gen. Hoke was on our left and wished to see Col. McMaster. A short conference took place, when our regiment moved by the left flank to the front, across a deep ravine, tangled underwood and gullies, crossing into a field, we formed into column of companies, then deployed into line of battle and began our advance across an open field; here the enemy's bullets first began to whistle over us, we moved steadily forward in a small run, some half mile, where we lay down, and found two companies from the 42nd N.C. Troops and two companies from the 34th Va. Troops, in a skirmish line behind a fence, we remained here but a few minutes, when, by order of Col. McMaster, the skirmishers rushed forward across the fence, our regiment following with a yell.

The enemy was strongly posted behind another work, some half mile in front of us, the ground being under cultivation, was entirely free from any screen to the angry missiles of the enemy, but the determine expressed in the faces of all was to reach their works and to drive them from them, so at a quick, and double quick, the boys pressed onward shouting as only rebels shout, until we reached to within 30 paces of the works, when the Yanks probably having a vision of Fort Pillow cross their minds, ingloriously fled, leaving behind, their overcoats, blankets, oil cloths, shovels, spades, haversacks, &c., to our tender mercies. Our skirmishers leaped their works and followed them for some distance, and our boys, in a perfect glee of excitement, were halted, and poured into their retiring ranks a destructive fire. A number of the enemy were here captured. We had the outside of the enemy's works for our protection now, and with bayonets, tins, &c., the dirt was shoveled in a hurry, the enemy very soon had a regiment pouring down upon us, to the assistance of their retreating commrades. We allowed them to come in good range, when we opened a fire upon them, which sent the few left, living, to the rear at the double quick. They essayed three times again, to repossess their works, but were driven back with heavy loss.

Their first attempts were made on our right, but we held them at bay until Martin's and Wise's Brigades[4] were brought up and completed the advance of our line in that direction, the 8th N.C. came in very handsomely on our left, soon after we captured the works in front, and after some delay, our lines on the left were brought up, the enemy contesting the advance in that direction with much spirit and determination, here the other regiments of our brigade were brought in, their severe loss attesting the enemy's reluctance to yield that part of their line, and in this struggle was lost our gallant Gen. Walker, a man we were just beginning to look upon with pride and hope. He is severely wounded and a prisoner. The 17th Regiment was the first with the skirmishers, that charged, occupied and held the enemy's works in the fight of the 20th May, in front of Hewlett's house, and these works were silenced in as open a country as can be found in any plain in Europe, the approbation of General Hoke, and the commendation of Gen. Walker has already been received. We are grateful to the Author of our being for His gracious protection and care.

The whole loss of regiment was only 28 killed and wounded. Lieut. Moore fell by my side, amid a storm of bullets, and until borne from the field, exhorted the men to stand their ground. Wm Martin, of my company was killed instantly by a shell, while near me, a noble soldier. "He has for his country fallen." Some others were wounded but mostly slight. We are still in the trenches, have moved from our old position to the ground where the 26th regiment fought last Friday. We are working night and day, and hope to make this place too hot for Butler soon. We listened for stirring news from Lee and Johnston, and rather think the seat of war moving towards us here. We are all full of sorrow, to hear from home, the sad news of the death of so many of the brave and honored sons of old York, in the late battles in Virginia.[5] Send our papers to Petersburg, we have not received but one in six weeks.

Au revoir,

L.

June 2nd 1864
In Rifle Pits on James River

My Dear Wife:

I am still alive & well this evening. We have had another severe battle here to day,[6] mostly on our left. I was in command of two companies of skirmishers and advanced near 1 1/2 miles in front of our position but fortunately did not encounter the enemy. I passed almost to the rear but behind their works. Our line was separated and useless. The order to fall back had arrived. As soon as it did we stood a good chance to have been cut off. The left of our regiment was engaged. Crawfords company list two men severely wounded. Black Davidson, brother of Bill and another. This was the only loss. The 22nd SCV on our left suffered more. They charged the enemys works & Colonel Dantzler was killed and I hear cant be brought off. He was a good Colonel. Was senator from Orangeburg District. I hear that Ransoms NC Brigade captured the yankee Rifle Pits & some two hundred prisoners.[7]

They have had heavy fighting on our left ever since 7 oclock this morning. The yankees have charged a time or two but have been driven back. There is still some heavy picket firing going on. I cant get the correct news altogether. Our Regt killed 5 men & took two prisoners this morning. We are in hearing of the guns of Lee & Grant. They have been fighting there for several days.

We have had a severe fight here to day. The 22nd SCV has lost 23 men prisoner, its Col killed. The enemy have sent a large part of their forces here to Grant I believe. We have been feeling them to day to learn their strength. I am thankful to God for any preservation to day. We have been formed in our present position. I advanced further to day inside the enemys lines than any other troops but found no enemy in our front.

Write soon & often. My love to all friends. My dear children, remember me to them. I cant write much now as I am in haste.

Jack Floyd was wounded & taken prisoner on the 20th. I cant get any home papers. Give all the news. I will write a full account of my days work again.

Pray for my safety.

Your husband
D J Logan

17th Regiment S. C. V
South Side. June 3d, 1864

Dear Enquirer:—Our regiment is in the trenches its fifteenth day, to-day. We have changed our position three times since we came here, and we are now on the right wing, next to Appomattox river. We had a quiet time until the 1st instant, when our truce was broken up by a heavy cannonading from our batteries, responded to by those of the enemy.

On the night of the day mentioned, the enemy ceased to reply to our cannonade, and we rather suspected that most of their force had been sent to Grant, so at day light on the morning of the 2nd, our entire picket line in front, was ordered forward, to charge the enemy's works, occupy and hold them, if possible. At a given signal, our advance took place, and very soon, on our extreme left, the rapid firing of musketry told us our line had struck the enemy in that direction. We still moved forward, not yet meeting the enemy, but the firing gradually neared us, until the left of our regiment was engaged, it met the enemy's pickets, and after a sharpe and rapid fight, they were driven in, with a loss of 5 killed and two prisoners.

Our loss, two men severley wounded, as follows: in Co. K, Capt. Crawford, Black Davidson and J. A. Lockhart, none killed. In the meantime, the pickets of our regiment making a very extended line, and having to pass through a densely covered swamp, became separated, and the works of the enemy bending off towards the river, in our front, the right, with which was your correspondent, passed beyond the line of works in front, and to a distance of some 1 1/2 miles from our own works; finding that our left was uncovered, we changed our front and sent a courier for orders who returned with an order to fall back, as our left had already returned to the rifle pits. We returned in good order, with the right wing unhurt. Our advance had accomplished the design in one particular, in ascertaining the position of the enemy's works, although fortunate in not striking the enemy. Our entire line was under command of Capt. J. T. Steele; the pickets of the regiment, under Capt. Wm. Dunovant.

The operations of the troops upon our left was of a more sanguinary character. The 22d S. C. V., led by their Colonel, charged the works of the enemy, capturing some 60 prisoners; but were repulsed from the enemy's main works, with some loss. Among the killed was their brave leader, O. M. Dantzler, whose body was inst sent into our lines this morning. He was brave perhaps almost to rashness. I learn he used a gun, and by example urged his men forward, leading and firing as he went, almost within the shadow of their huge fortifications. His regiment will sadly miss him. The whole number of killed, wounded and missing in the 22d S. C. V., I learn is only about 25.

Still to the left of that brigade, the contest waxed warmer, Ransom's North Carolinians, Wise's Virginians, and Johnson's Tennesseeans,[8] occupied the rifle pits of the enemy's pickets, capturing in all some two to four hundred prisoners, and inflicting nothing definite, this morning, as to our casualties in those brigades. Rumors are as rife along a line of battle, as in a crowded city, and many of them entirely unworthy of credence. During last night, although the rain was pelting down on our uncovered heads, the din of battle was heard on our left. Commencing slowly at first, it would increase, until the mind can conceive of nothing as a comparison, except a fire ranging in a dozen cane brakes, when dry, and a stiff breeze stirring. I can assure you there is nothing romantic in the sound of it, to a man who has made the bottom of a ditch his bed, for fifteen nights, though to the Yankee bugler, who stood inside the ramparts of his fort, and sounded the charge which was taken up by a drummer along the line, it may have been. Our boys almost understand their signals. In their night attacks, an artillery bugle, generally, is first heard, then some later, a drum, and then comes the "tug of war." I have received no correct account of the result of the firing last night, but rumor says they assaulted our lines four times and were repulsed. One thing I know, we still hold our lines and a portion of the Yankee line captured on yesterday.

Our men are beginning to feel the privations to which they are exposed; a good many are sick, but many are coming in daily, which keeps us up to a considerable extent. Our men have labored hard here. It would appear almost incredible if I could describe the amount of work they have performed, together with the skirmish and picket duty, which is exceedingly heavy. We had some accidents along the lines last night, Hugh Sherrer, of Co. F, and one man of Co. E, were wounded, the first in the arm, the last in the foot, by the discharge of their own guns.

We are now commanded by Brig. Gen. Stephen Elliott, the hero of Fort Sumter.[9] We are very favorably impressed with him so far. The loss of Gen. Walker is universally regretted by all. Just before he fell into the hands of the enemy, he was in advance of the 17th S. C. V., waving his sword, and calling out to them, "brave Carolinians follow me," while the balls were then flying thickly around him.

We are in hearing of the cannon of Lee and Grant, and wait with confidence of success, the issue of the struggle.[10] We are commanded now by Gen. Bushrod Johnson, he is an elderly man, has the appearance of a stern old veteran.[11]

We shall endeavor to keep the Beast[12] from interfering with the Railroad here, and if he ever moves far from his forts and gunboats, upon a stealing expedition, he will lose more in oil cloths, &c., than he will make; besides, somebody will get hurt. Our boys have a passion for "Spencer rifles" now, oil cloths was the "rage" for a while, but the "seven shooters" are sought after now with a will. About 200 have been captured along the line. It is the most complete gun I have ever seen.

Yours,

L.

Penciled below this entry was the statement, "The last communication he ever wrote for the Enquirer."

In The Trenches, South Side James
June 5th 1864
Sabbath Morning

My Dear Wife:

I am feeling as well this morning as circumstances will admit It has been raining ever since yesterday and the ditches are running with water & slipping with mud. Jim has been sick for the last two days and I have been compelled to shift for my self. He complains of a pain in his head & side. I have not heard from him since yesterday morning. He is back at the wagon yard some two miles from here. I fear he will get in the lift here and if he does I have no chance in the world to see him & besides he has my clothes &c. He is some trouble to me now. We had a fight on the 2nd of which I wrote you. We had some dreadful firing that night but no person hurt much that I can hear. Two men shot Thursday by accident on the night of the 3rd, one in my company & one in Mills. Neither seriously.

I received your letter by Mr Sandifer. Am glad to hear you got the news from one fight here as correctly as you did. Uncle Jeff arrived here yesterday morning from Wilmington. He appears to have recovered pretty well. Phil Sandifer looks rather lost shivering in a wet trench. I have no doubt he thinks of home with many a sigh. We have sent off another Brigade from here yesterday. I dont know where they went. It was Ransoms.

We are under marching orders. There seems to be an impression that we will be sent to the Black Water but it is hard to tell. Lee & Grant have had some desperate fighting. You will hear the news from there sooner than I can write you. I fear we shall have a long and desperate campaign here. Grant seems determined to wear out our men by exhausting them. I hope we shall be endowed with powers of endurance sufficient to cope with him. Lee's army is certainly very strong yet. He has received a great many reenforcements. You will have heard of the death of Col Keitt & Col Dantzler.[13] Col Dantzlers body was brought over to us the other morning. He was a brave man but I think rather too rash.

I have not heard a word from my brothers since Pinks letter. They have had a great chance more of hard fighting since & I fear have met with misfortune again. Sam Lowry received a letter yesterday stating that Capt Meacham was only slightly wounded and a prisoner. It is a sad thing if Mrs Meacham's death was caused in part by the news of his death. Capt Avery is sick and at his uncle's near Petersburg. Lieut Moore is staying in Petersburg at Mr Lyons who married a Springs. Col McMaster is sick in Richmond. A great many of the men are sick & almost broken down. This is the 17th day we have been in line of battle in the trenches, sometimes at hard work, then fighting alittle & the men on guard every night. I cant see through our work here. It may last for months. I believe the great trial of strength is now being made. If we are successful I believe the people of the North will let us alone, but they are determined on a desperate effort to crush us first.

If Genl Lee can prevoke Grant to charge him in his works he can soon demoralize the yankee army but I fear Grant will now go to entrenching & perhaps force Lee to attack him, or perhaps Lee can move on Washington & draw him out in that way, if he can procure an army large enough to leave Richmond with safety. I feel very lonely these nights. Dunnevant is Captain of Co C now & has left us. Avery & Nunn gone. Guntharp generally on Pickett when I am not. A man has rather perculiar feelings when he lies down at night and about the time he gets partly to sleep a heavy fire of small arms commences on the line, and grows louder and nearer, he springs into his place & every man seizes his gun expecting the mortal combat every minute, but pressently it turns out only a fight between our pickets. The yankees keep up a continual playing of bands & beating of drums & blowing of bugles. They have sent away most of their troops from here I believe & we have done the same. I should not be surprised if we were not moved from here to night. Continue to direct your letters just as before. They will come right. Capt Beatty & Lt Stevenson have had their boots made so they dont wish any now.

I fear so much wet weather will be bad on the wheat. I fear it will take rust. I hope your corn is all planted. My health is pretty good now. I always seem to improve upon hard living. Our regiment is still strong in numbers. Give my love to all friends, to your father & mother and my sweet little ones. I would like so much to see you all. Pray for these dark days soon to pass away. If I hear from Jim before the mail comes I will send a note.

Write soon & often. I am all cramped up, in a hole in the ground & I fear you can hardly read this. Give all the news.

Your husband

D J Logan

*   *   *

In Rifle pits, South Side
June 8th 1864

My Dear Wife:

My health is very good this morning, with the exception of that "itch." Lying on the ground has aggreviated it and made it much worst & I fear if it dont get better I will not stand it here. I tear my flesh up smartly.

We have had a quiet time since my last. Very little firing at each other. Several flags of truce & exchange of papers. This is the 19th day in the ditches and I cant see any prospect for us to leave here soon again. Lt Nunnery & Sergt Collins of Co A are retired from service & going home. I will send this letter by them. I am in dreadful situation about underclothes. One of my drawers has gone entirely to pieces & I have been going with my breetches next the skin & that has irritated the hurnea & made it worse. Jim has been sick & my clothes have not been washed properly. As he is better now perhaps I will fare better. I wish you to send me a pair of Drawers the 1st opportunity. A good many have come on here lately Samy Duff, Perry Martin & others. There will still be others coming occasionally. If you can send my boots with safety let them come. If not hold on to them until I write again but send the Drawers. There is rather a lull in the storm here now. There was worse firing on yesterday towards Lee but dont know with what result. The test of war is yet to come. I find they are both in large force yet, and Grant will have to accomplish something or go under. I have heard nothing from brothers since I wrote before.

I am getting awfully warm here. I thought Jackson Miss was partly bad. 8 days in the works but this probably be 2 months. The men are getting full of lice. Cant wash their clothes. I fear we will have all the plagues almost before we get clean of Grant & Butler.

I want something in the shape of vegatables most badly. Continental Bacon & corn bread would go down so well. There are a crowd of negroes from Petersburg here every day with things to sell.

They have butter milk $1.00 for tea cup full, molasses bread $1.00 for a piece size of a walnut, cherry pie $5.00 &c. We cant draw a cent of money here. Every thing is in a disordered condition almost. I hope wheat & corn will all prosper at home this year. We are in the dark shadows here. No cheerful sights to greet the eye or cheer the heart. We have to look away from our position for joy & pleasantness. My Genl health is very good. I am as hungry as I can be this morning. I am waiting for the boys to bring me breakfast from Camp. If it does not come I will have to do without until evening. Your letters come here right away in two or 3 days. I suppose they must send mine to Charleston. You ought to get them in 2 1/2 days.

I am about to run out of paper & envelopes. Every thing having been left at Petersburg. I hope this cruel campaign will soon close & give us peace without more blood shed. I suppose it hardly will but let us all pray that it will end without any more horrid carnage. Write often & all the news. My love to all. Kiss my babies.

Your husband

D J Logan

*   *   *

June 8th 1864

Dear Sallie:

I am now in charge of a fatique party building a 5 Gun battery. We have been very quiet for the last two days. Our yankee friends are all in good speaking distance of us, but we continue on good terms. They wish to exchange papers coffee &c with us, but our orders forbid any communication. I wrote you a hurried note this morning. Jim is better but any thing to eat is dreadful Scarce. I wish I could get one peck of peas. I have got very fond of peas & bacon. Corn bread & bacon has become rough without any change. If you can see a good chance send me a little butter & something of that sort. It can be brought here with very little difficulty in small boxes or packages. Bill Wylie & Uncle Jeff are quite well also all the neighbors here. I suppose Lieut. Moore will get home as this letter goes. I am reduced to one pr of drawers & I fear these will go up soon.

I have not heard from you since the 31st or 1st of June. Your letters come in good time. They send all ours by way of Charleston which causes the delay. We have had no rest in 19 days. You can imagine we are pretty well broken down. I can buy butter milk here at $1 per cup-full. I have bought several but my money is running low. I dont know when we will draw. I suppose they are going to compel us to save our money any way.

Kiss our babies for me. Pray for my safe return & give my love to all the friends.

Amour

D J Logan

I suppose you have seen Dr. Logans pills in the Guardian. I wish you to preserve them for me. I must close. Good night.

On June 18, 1864, David Jackson Logan was ordering his men to keep their heads down in order to avoid the deadly fire of enemy sharp-shooters. In his zeal he accidently exposed himself and was killed in-stantly when a bullet struck him in the forehead.

David's death weighed heavily on those who had lived and fought by his side. His loss was a keen blow to Company F's Lt. Samuel Cosmo Lowry, who discussed Logan's passing in his own diary on June 18, 1864:

This evening at about five o'clock the enemy commenced massing in our front. At first they threw out a skirmish line, but our line, under Major Betgil of 18th, charged them and ran them back. They displayed a line a little to our right and drove in our pickets. Shortly after this they threw a line of battle in the edge of a piece of woods, and making them lie down massed four lines behind them. They deployed another skirmish line and advanced it forward. It was at this juncture that we lost our much lamented company commander, Lieut. David J. Logan. He ordered the men to keep down their heads for the enemy were sharpshooting fast, and in his zeal for his men, exposed himself when a stray ball struck him square in the forehead killing him instantly. He never groaned, but was dead in a minute. It threw a gloom over every countenance and cast a damper over the whole company. His bloody corpse was borne away by our ambulance men, which was the last of our lamented Lieutenant.

He was an officer and a gentleman, a man of brillant intellect, who by his kind heart and gentle ways, had attached himself to every one of us. I can say no more, but his death was a shock so unexpected as to almost overcome my discretion. He is gone, and I trust is with his God in Heaven.[14]

The cover of the "Funeral Discourse" delivered for both
David Jackson and his brother, Pinckney.

CHAPTER 9

"Fully appreciating the many beautiful traits which adorned the character of your husband, and rendered him an object of admiration amongst his friends and acquaintances, and feeling for him more than the ordinary attachment which binds comrades in arms, I cannot refrain from expressing to you my sorrow at his death, and my sincere condolence with you in the affliction which now oppresses you."

— Col. Fitz W. McMaster, 17th South Carolina Infantry

Postscript

Unfortunately, no account has been found on how Sallie Logan received the tragic news that her beloved husband was no more. Her own reaction to his death and the family's response has gone unrecorded. While the measure of the man can be taken from his copious public and private correspondence, several surviving examples of how the news was received by friends at home and comrades in the field, however, shed considerable insight into how others viewed David Jackson Logan.

One of the fullest accounts of both Logan's death and his depth of character comes from his commanding officer, Col. Fitz. W. McMaster. In a letter of condolence to Sallie, McMaster tried to convey the sorrow he felt in Logan's passing and the respect in which he held him:

Trenches, Petersburg, Va.
June 26th, 1864.

Dear Madam:

Before this time you have heard of the great calamity which has befallen you and your household, in the death of your noble husband, Lieut. Logan, who fell the 18th instant from a ball in the forehead, just as he was about to give a command to his company to fire on the enemy.

I know all human sympathy is cold where alone the comfort must come from the Fountain of all blessing. God alone can pour the balm into your wounded heart and sustain you and your little ones under his bereavement, which now seems to you to render the world void and desolate. But fully appreciating the many beautiful traits which adorned the character of your husband, and rendered him an object of admiration amongst his friends and acquaintances, and feeling for him more than the ordinary attachment which binds comrades in arms, I cannot refrain from expressing to you my sorrow at his death, and my sincere condolence with you in the affliction which now oppresses you.

Many noble men have fallen in this struggle for freedom, and tears of sympathy flow in a continuous stream for the brave who perish; but while individual losses and individual distresses are great, your misfortune should and does excite more grief than that of his kindred, for I look upon it as a public calamity when such a man is cut off; society loses an ornament and the commonwealth should grieve over the grave of a useful man who seemed created for a high sphere of good to his country. In the death of Lieut. Logan, not only yourself and friends suffer, but York District and the State of South Carolina have lost one of its most promising young men, who possessed qualities of head and heart which undoubtedly would have rendered him an extremely useful and popular citizen.

The evening before he was killed, I ordered him to take charge of a line of pickets in advance of the Regiment. He came to my quarters and in that bland and polite manner which never forsook him, stated he had not slept in two days and was nearly exhausted. I stated to him the duty was arduous and all of us were jaded and I wanted him to take charge of the pickets, as I had faith in his skill and discretion. Without a murmur, but on the contrary with that cheerful manner for which he was conspicuous he went off. My Adjutant that day remarked to me, he was the best soldier he ever saw—he was always so cheerful in danger and privations. Often has his bright and cheerful countenance gladdened my heart when there were trials enough around us to make the stoutest heart sad. I soon relieved him Friday night, and the next morning had a short conversation with him, when he suggested getting wire to stretch before our line, and asked permission to detail men for the purpose. In a few hours afterwards, it came along the line, "Lieut. Logan is killed." I ran to the right and found the noble fellow weltering in his blood. The noble and handsome Logan slain by the cruel foe! As I stood over his manly form and reflected on so much worth and youth buried, my heart bled at the sight! The whole Regiment laments with you over his untimely end. It may be some consolation for you to know that he has left an unspotted name—as a patriot and soldier—and greater than either as an humble and God fearing christian, as a heritage to his bereaved widow and loved little ones at home to point them to paths of virtue and honor.

To the God of all mercy—to Him who has promised He will be a Father to the fatherless, and a husband to the widow, I commend you and your little children and his noble father in whom he took so much pride. May that good God support you all in your sad bereavement, and bring light out of the darkness which now overhangs you, and comfort out of your sorrow.

With sincere sympathy, I subscribe myself the admirer and friend of your departed husband.

F. W. McMaster

———————

Within a few weeks of David's death, his brother Pinckney ("Pink") wrote a letter to Sallie. His words eloquently speak to the depth of sorrow generated by his older sibling's fate. The letter is even more poignant when read with the knowledge that "Pink" followed his beloved brother in death just seven months later when he fell at the Battle of Hatcher's Run. "Pink" was killed just two months before Robert E. Lee surrendered his army at Appomattox Courthouse:

Shelby NC
July 4th 1864

My Dear Sister

I do not know how to begin to write to you. I have been thinking I would have a Chance to come down and see you but Pa has so much to do that he cant spare a horse without giving up his crops to these weeds and grass. It seems like I cant go back without seeing you but under the circumstances I know I will have to do it unless you can come up. Nothing would rejoice me more than to see you come up before I go back. I will have to start back about the 14th inst. I have no idea where I will find my command as I hear they have gone through the Valley.

I had been flatering my self that my dear Brother was not Killed until we received the dispatch and letter from you but was only wounded but alas my hopes were blighted and I found the report too true. It is a sad afflication and seems like we cant give him up. I believe he was a true Christian and has gone home to reap his reward around God's throne in glory. May we be prepared to meet him there and join with him in singing songs of praise forever in Paradise.

It has been near two years since I saw him last and I had promised myself when I returned to go by Petersburg and see him but alas we know not what a day will bring forth.

The Confederacy has lost a true Patriot officer and the Country a useful and promising man in his death but our loss seems to be the greatest. May God help us to bear up under our sore afflication and when our course is run we may meet him in Heaven is my prayer.

We have not had a letter from Ben since the 12th June. We received a letter from Gaffney dated 26th instant. He was well and in fine spirits. We heard from Marion he is at Point Lookout, Maryland a prisoner.

I can think of no news to write at present. Come if you can and bring the children. Kiss John and Lula for me.

Write on the reception of this to
Your Affectionate Brother
Pink

P. S. Dont think hard of me not coming as Pa's chances for riding are so bad and he has so much to do it looks impossible for me to come.

––––––––

More than a year after Logan's passing a funeral discourse was delivered by the Rev. Tilman R. Gaines, editor of the Baptist Messenger and the first minister of the Baptist Church in Yorkville, on Sunday, August 12, 1866, in Shelby, North Carolina. Sadly for the Logan family, the memorial service included David's brother "Pink," who was killed south of Petersburg at Hatcher's Run in early February 1865.

"Of the myriads of our friends, who fell in the late bloody struggle," began Rev. Gaines' discourse,

> we can think of none more worthy of praise than the two noble sons whose memory we would this day perpetuate. It is not necessary to dwell at length on the characters and deeds of these brave young men. The elder, Lieut. D. J. Logan, was a rising star of promise in his adopted District. Many eyes were turned upon him. He shared the affections and confidence of the people. His short life was one of activity and usefulness. His public and private communications breathe a desire to do good. But his devotion to his country proved his spirit. When his loving companion and tender babes, his home, his aged parents, his country and his liberties were endangered, he flew to the post of honor and of danger, and after years of privation and suffering, he laid down his life for his friends.[1]

Shortly thereafter, the *Yorkville Enquirer* likewise wrote fondly of their former correspondent:

> David J. Logan was about 27 years of age, and was born in Cleveland County, N. C., but married in this District, and was doing business here as a merchant, when he voluntarily gave it up, with home and all its fond endearments, to battle for his country. At the formation of the 17th Regiment he was elected 2nd Lieutenant of Company F, but at the time of his death was in command (Capt. Avery acting as Major). In one of the severe battles of Virginia, Lieut. Logan was shot through the breast, but his ardent patriotism kept him home no longer than was actually necessary—since then he never missed sharing with his men all their dangers, cheering them with kind words and deeds, and dying at last in their arms. Lieut. Logan was calculated to adorn the walks of private life from an amiable disposition, almost effeminate; all his actions were marked by probity and honor, and if ever he had an enemy, such could not have been worthy to be called a friend.

This is no fulsome eulogy of ours—our gifted correspondent is dead and gone—we miss him from our columns when away, and the genial smile that announced his short sojourn when among us; but there are other circles where his loss will be sincerely felt, whose privacy it is not our priviledge or disposition to invade—South Carolina adds another link to the chain which binds her to the noble dead.[2]

"David was not only a Confederate soldier," wrote "A Friend" in a short testimonial in the paper,

but had in early life enlisted as a soldier of the cross; having been baptised into the fellowship of the Baptist church in the year 1851. He was of course like other frail, imperfect, mortal men, not without sin; but few indeed walked more circumspectly and worthily of the vocation where-with he was called. He was ever concientious and true to the principles of his profession. His last letters breathe the spirit of the humble christian devoutly interceeding with his Heavenly Master for protection from the missles of the enemy, and the termination of the cruel war.[3]

*   *   *

David Jackson Logan was laid to rest in the Bethesda Presbyterian Church Cemetery in York County, South Carolina. Sallie would not follow her "beloved Davy" until many years later, in 1904.

Appendix

Biographical Roster of the Individuals Mentioned in the Correspondence of David Jackson Logan

The following individuals are listed as they appear in Logan's writings. Corrections, dates of birth, death and pertinent regimental information are provided, whenever available.

Aiken, William

William Aiken (1806-1887) served in the State House of Representatives from 1838-1842, before becoming governor of South Carolina (1844-1846). Prior to the war, he developed one of the largest rice plantations in the state on Jehossee Island.

Adicks

Henning Frederick Adickes (1809-1881) was of German descent. He moved to Yorkville sometime around 1829 and clerked for merchant Robert Latta before moving out on his own. He eventually built a three-story brick structure on the corner of Congress and Liberty Streets in Yorkville and operated as a merchant there for nearly fifty years.

Anderson, Rev.

Rev. John Monroe Anderson (1821-1879) was originally from Ebenezerville. He graduated from South Carolina College in 1841 with a degree in law. Returning to York District after graduation, he began a law practice in Yorkville before turning to the ministry. Training under the famous Presbyterian Dr. James H. Thornwell, Anderson received his degree in theology in 1854, after which he became president of the Yorkville Female College. When the war began, he enlisted as a chaplain in the 12th South Carolina Volunteers. Following the war he returned to the Yorkville Female College. He remained there until 1866, when he became Professor of Logic and Bible Letters at Davidson College in North Carolina.

Anderson, General

Richard Heron Anderson (1821-1879), better known as "Fighting Dick" Anderson, was a West Pointer from South Carolina who served the entire war with the Army of Northern Virginia. He was relieved of command and sent home by Robert E. Lee one day before the surrender at Appomattox due to the disintegration of his corps at Sayler's Creek.

Ash

There were two members, both privates, from Company C, Broad River Light Infantry, 17th SCV by the name of Ashe: Andrew Francis Ashe (1836-1910) and John J. Ashe, Jr. (1843-1926).

Avery, J. W.

John William Avery (1831-1892) was from the Ebenezer section of York County. He originally enrolled in the 5th Regiment, but soon transferred to Co. E, Indian Land Tigers of the 17th SCV as its 3rd lieutenant. He then transferred to Co. F, Carolina Rifles of the same regiment as 1st lieutenant, rose to the rank of captain of Co. F, and finally to major in 1864. Avery returned to York County following the war, where he became embroiled in Ku Klux Klan troubles during the early years of Reconstruction. Arrested in 1871, Avery escaped while awaiting trial in Columbia, South Carolina, and fled to Canada. He returned to the United States at the end of Reconstruction and settled in Norfolk, Virginia, where he became a lawyer, land speculator and oyster farmer. Avery was one of the signers of the request for a Regimental Transfer in 1863 from Nathan G. Evan's Brigade.

Barnette, D. F.

David Frank Barnett (1839-1902) enlisted as a private in Co. E, Indian Land Tigers, 17th SCV in 1861. Barnett was a doctor prior to the war and became the surgeon for the 17th in 1863. That same year, Barnett married Lucinda Dorcas Potts of Mecklenburg County, NC.

Baudonn

Unidentified

Beatty, E. A.

E. A. Beatty, private, Co. F, Carolina Rifles, 17th SCV.

Beatty, E. G.

E. G. Beaty, private, Co. E, Turkey Creek Grays, 5th SCV.

Beatty, James C.

James Beaty of Chester became captain of Co. D, Beatty's Co., 17th SCV.

Beauregard, General

Pierre Gustave Toutant Beauregard (1818-1893) was a West Pointer from Louisiana. As the commander of South Carolina forces during the firing on Fort Sumter in 1861, Beauregard became known as the "Hero of Fort Sumter." He also led Southern troops, in conjunction with Gen. Joseph E. Johnston, at the victory at First Manassas on July 21, 1861. Although his star seemed to be ascending, he did not get along with President Jefferson Davis. After brief service in the Western Theater, he served from the summer of 1862 to the spring of 1864 as the commander of the Department of South Carolina, Georgia, and Florida, with his headquarters in Charleston. Beauregard considered the theater a backwater area (which in several respects it was) and chafed for an active field command. The job of defending Charleston and the surrounding coastline was a difficult one, although Beauregard proved up to the task. His efforts made it difficult for the Federals to follow up their advantages in the Hilton Head/Port Royal enclave. He later was ordered to Petersburg, where he assisted in the defense of that city during the Bermuda Hundred Campaign.

Benbow, Colonel

Henry Laurens Benbow (1829-1907) entered Confederate service as a private in Co. I, 23rd SCV. He soon rose to the rank of captain of the company and eventually became colonel of the regiment. During the summer and fall of 1863, Benbow was in temporary command of the Tramp Brigade due to the continued absence of General Evans. Benbow was severely wounded at Second Manassas in 1862 and again at Five Forks on April 1, 1865, where he was captured. Following his release from a Union prison in the summer of 1865, he returned to South Carolina.

Bensly

Unidentified.

Black

Although there are several possibilities for this soldier, the two most likely are Thomas Black, private, Co. G, Mountain Guards, 18th SCV, who died of measles in 1862, or Thomas Black, private, Co. D, 17th SCV, who was killed in action.

Black, James

James P. Black (1834-1862) first enrolled as a private in Co. I, Turkey Creek Grays, 5th SCV and later transferred to Co. B, Bethel Guards, 5th SCV as a lieutenant. Black died of wounds received during the Battle of Seven Pines in Virginia on May 31, 1862.

Boheler

Andrew Henry Boheler (1832-1920), private, Co. F, Carolina Rifles, 17th SCV.

Bolezn

Bolezn (?-1862), private, Co. C, Broad River Light Infantry, 17th SCV.

Bolivar

See Byers, William Bolivar.

Bonham, Milledge Lake

Brigadier General Milledge L. Bonham (1813-1890) served on the South Carolina coast for several months before participating in the Battle of First Manassas on July 21, 1861. After a short stint in the Confederate Congress he was elected governor of South

Carolina in December 1862. Following the war he became South Carolina's first railroad commissioner.

Bonner, Dr.
Unidentified.

Boyce, Captain
Robert Boyce was the first captain of the MacBeth Artillery Battery. Boyce and his battery fought through the majority of the first two years of the war on the South Carolina coast before being transferred to the Western Theater in May 1863.

Bragg, Braxton
General Braxton Bragg (1817-1876), a West Pointer from North Carolina, was one of President Jefferson Davis' favorite officers, largely because of Bragg's loyalty to Davis. Often engaged in bitter disputes with subordinates, Bragg enjoyed little respect from the common soldiers. His inability to get along with his generals severely limited his effectiveness as a field general.

Bratton, Dr.
Samuel Edward Bratton (1820-1893) was a grandson of Revolutionary War hero Col. William Bratton. He attended the Medical College of South Carolina in Charleston, receiving his degree in 1844. Dr. Bratton practiced in the community of Brattonsville in southern York County. He was a brother of N. B. Bratton.

Bratton, Gilliam
Robert Gilliam Bratton (1825-1887), private, Co. F, Carolina Rifles, 17th SCV.

Bratton, N. B.
Napoleon Bonaparte Bratton (1838-1918) was the grandson of Revolutionary War hero Col. William Bratton and the youngest of 15 children born to John Simpson and Harriet Bratton. In 1861 he joined Co. I, Turkey Creek Grays, 5th SCV. In 1862 he transferred to the 5th SC Cavalry of Matthew C. Butler's Brigade. Serving as 4th sergeant and wounded at Williamsburg, Bratton was captured and sent to Clifburn Hospital in Washington, DC. While recuperating in Washington, he was cared for by "Mrs. Mason." Exchanged in late 1862, he returned home, but not before marrying Minnie Mason, the daughter of the woman who had cared for him during his recuperation period. Once back in York County, Bratton joined the 4th South Carolina Cavalry. His unit took part in the last major battle of the war at Bentonville, North Carolina. Bratton returned to Washington after the close of the conflict to claim his bride. He was a brother of Dr. Samuel Bratton.

Breakes, Dr.
Little is known of Dr. Breakes other than he was a minister.

Breckenridge, General
General John Cabell Breckinridge (1821-1875) was a Democratic candidate for president in 1860 and former vice-president under James Buchanan. He was also the

commander of the Army of Tennessee's famed "Orphan Brigade." Although he did not have any pre-war military training, Breckinridge went on to lead a field army in May 1864 and defeated Maj. Gen. Franz Sigel at the Battle of New Market. From March 1864 to February 1865 he served in Virginia, and thereafter as the South's last (and best) secretary of war.

Brodie, Miss M. F.
Miss M. F. Brodie was from Charleston.

Brooks, Jonathan A.
Jonathan A. Brooks was an agent in Yorkville.

Brown, John Alonzo
J. A. Brown (1809-1876), private, Co. I, Turkey Creek Grays, 5th SCV.

Bryan
Henry Bryan was major, assistant adjutant general, Department of South Carolina, Georgia, and Florida. Bryan served a time on the staff of General Beauregard. In 1863 he served as quarter master during the actions around Charleston.

Buist, James F.
James F. Buist of Barnwell County served originally as orderly sergeant of Co. H, Rice's Co., 17th SCV, before becoming chaplain of the regiment upon its reorganization in 1862. He remained in this position until after Second Manassas, when he retired from the service.

Bunting, Captain
Samuel R. Bunting was the first captain of Co. A, 2nd North Carolina Artillery. This regiment was also known as the Wilmington Horse Artillery. Bunting was from New Hanover County and appointed captain of "Bunting's Battery" in 1861. Ordered to Kinston, North Carolina in 1862 to stem the Union advance westward from the coast, the battery lost two of its brass 6-pounders in the fighting at that city. Bunting resigned in July 1863 to resume his duties as clerk of court of Pleas and Quarter Sessions in New Hanover County.

Burnside
General Ambrose Everett Burnside (1824-1881) led the expedition that captured Roanoke Island, North Carolina, in 1861. Except for some months in Tennessee, he served thereafter with the Army of the Potomac. In late 1862 Burnside was promoted to command the army. He kept the appointment for only three months, largely because of his inept handling of the army at the December 1862 Battle of Fredericksburg. He served credibly in Tennessee during the Knoxville Campaign, and repulsed James Longstreet's attack against the city of Knoxville in the fighting at Fort Saunders. The fiasco of the Battle of the Crater at Petersburg the following July 30, 1864, was in part Burnside's fault, and eventually led to his being sent on permanent leave. Following the war, Burnside served as governor and senator for Rhode Island.

Burris, George W.
George W. Burris (1827-1902) began as a private and later rose to the rank of sergeant major of Co. K, Lacy Guards, 17th SCV.

Burris, J. P.
John P. Burris (1833-1862), private, Co. K, Lacy Guards, 17th SCV.

Burton, Major
Augustua W. Burton (1828-?), captain, Co. E, Cleveland Guards, 12th North Carolina. Burton rose to the rank of major of the regiment.

Butler
General Benjamin Franklin Butler (1818-1893) was one of the most hated men in the South, as demonstrated by his nickmame "Beast Butler," pinned to him for his infamous "Woman Order" while in command of Union occupation forces in New Orleans. A political general with no pre-war military experience, Butler used his political connections and wealth to obtain his position. In 1864 he arguably allowed his forces to be bottled-up at Bermuda Hundred while trying to cut the railroad between Richmond and Petersburg.

Byers, E. M.
Edward Meek Byers (1819-1864), private, Co. K, Lacy Guards, 17th SCV.

Byers, W. B.
William Bolivar Byers (1825-1884) served as a private in Co. F, Carolina Rifles, 17th SCV. Byers was the oldest man in Company F, the only one over the age of 35 to remain after reorganization and one of the few to survive the conflict. Upon reorganization, Byers became ordnance sergeant for the company.

C., Mollie
Mary or Martha Currence. Kin to David's Jackson family tree by marriage.

Caldwell
Hugh Gibson Caldwell (1842-1865) was a sergeant of Co. K, Lacy Guards, 17th SCV. Caldwell was captured at Five Forks, Virginia, in April 1865, and sent to Point Lookout, Maryland, where he died.

Caldwell, Bob
There are three possibilities: Robert Pinckney Caldwell (1844-1903), private, Co. F, Carolina Rifles, 17th SCV; Robert Newman Caldwell (1822-1864), private, Co. K, Lacy Guards, 17th SCV, killed at the Battle of the Crater; and Robert Allison Caldwell (1834-1916), private, Co. K, Lacy Guards, 17th SCV.

Carlisle
William H. Carlisle, originally from Union County, was a lieutenant in the 21st SCV, and served on the coast of South Carolina near Charleston, where he was wounded.

Carothers
There are three possibilities for this soldier: William Harper Carothers (1835-1863) and James Franklin Carothers (1823-1892), both privates in Co. E, Indian Land Tigers, 17th SCV, and William R. Carothers (?-1895), private, Co. H, Catawba Light Infantry, 18th SCV.

Carothers, W. W.
William Washington Carothers (1819-1886) was a Presbyterian minister educated at Princeton. Carothers became the new chaplain of the 17th SCV in 1863.

Carrie, Samuel
Samuel Carrie was a staff officer in Nathan Evan's Brigade.

Carroll, J. A.
James Alfred Carroll (1830-1892). Little is known of Carroll's military career other than that he served as a private in Confederate service.

Carroll, Joseph
Joseph Williams Carroll (1833-1904) was originally a private and later corporal of Co. I, Turkey Creek Grays, 5th SCV. He later transferred to Co. G of the Palmetto Sharpshooters, where he rose to the rank of lieutenant.

Carroll, Wash
Washington Carroll, private, Co. F, Carolina Rifles, 17th SCV.

Chambers, Benjamin
Benjamin Chambers was Ordinary (modern day Probate Judge) for York County.

Chapin, Mrs. L.
Unidentified.

Chapin, Miss S.
Unidentified.

Clark, Frank
Robert Franklin Clark (1826-1888), private, Co. I, Turkey Creek Grays, 5th SCV. He was the brother of James L. Clark.

Clark, Jim
James L. Clark (1822-1892), private, Co. K, Lacy Guards, 17th SCV. He was the brother of Franklin Clark.

Clawson
Thomas Williams Clawson (1845-1913) was a graduate of the Citadel and served as a private during the war (unit unknown). Clawson was a farmer and lawyer in Yorkville and owned a slave named "Steve."

Clay, Mrs.
Mrs. Clay is unidentified other than she resided on the battlefield of Hewlett's Farm (Clay's Farm) around Petersburg, VA.

Coleman
Martin Coleman, private, Co. A [or B], 17th SCV, drowned in the Stono River near Charleston in 1862. He was from Fairfield County.

Collins, J. D.
John D. Collins (1830-?) enrolled as a private in Co. A, 17th SCV. He later rose to the rank of sergeant.

Colquitt
Alfred H. Colquitt began his Confederate military career as colonel of the 46th Georgia. He rose to the rank of brigadier general and after a stint with the Army of Northern Virginia commanded the Western Division of James Island. He later commanded a brigade in the Department of North Carolina.

Connor, J. W.
J. W. Connor, adjutant of the 17th SCV.

Cox, General
William Ruffin Cox (1832-1919) was a native North Carolinian and lawyer prior to the war. Cox had the unfortunate luck of attracting enemy fire. He was wounded eleven times during the war, five times at Chancellorsville alone. Cox was involved in the fighting at Kinston, North Carolina, in 1862. He rose from the rank of major to colonel of the 2nd North Carolina, and was promoted to brigadier general in 1864. Cox surrendered with his men at Appomattox. Following the war he served three terms as a U.S. Congressman.

Craven, Dr.
Dr. Alfred Cravin (1822-1872) was an Englisman by birth who came to Yorkville from Pennsylvania in 1850. He was the first full-time dentist in the town and also ran a watch making business. He served as a private in the 34th South Carolina Militia.

Crawford, Lieutenant
Edward Alexander Crawford (1830-1907) orginally enrolled as 1st sergeant in Co. K, Lacy Guards, 17th SCV. Crawford, from Chester County, became lieutentant and then captain of the company upon the retirement of Lucien Sadler during the unit's reorganization. Crawford served with the 17th in all its battles and surrendered at Appomattox Courthouse. He was one of signers of the regimental transfer in 1863. In 1868 Crwford was elected president of the McConnell's Club of the Conservative Clubs in York County. That same year he served as Precinct Manager in his district. Crawford was instrumental in helping form a South Carolina Agricultural Society chapter in Bethesda Township of York County. He served eight years as Sheriff of York County, beginning in 1887. In 1896 he was defeated for the position by John R. Logan, David Jackson's son

(see Logan, Johnnie). Crawford was one of the organizers of the local camp of the United Confederate Veterans.

Culp, Captain
John Ripley Culp (1829-1907) was the first captain of Co. A, Culp's Co., 17th SCV. When F. W. McMaster became colonel of the 17th upon the death of J. H. Means at Second Manassas, Captain Culp was promoted to major, and later to lieutenant-colonel. He was wounded in the head and captured at the Battle of Five Forks on April 1, 1865, and interned on Johnson's Island. Culp was one of the signers of the Regimental Transfer in 1863.

Curtis, Dr.
Dr. Curtis was from the Rockville area near Charleston.

Curtis
West Point graduate Samuel Ryan Curtis (1805-1866) was commissioned a brigadier general early in the war and commanded Union forces in the victory at Pea Ridge, Arkansas. Promoted to major general in the spring of 1862, Curtis was given command of the Department of Missouri. He finished the war in the Northwest negotiating treaties with the numerous Indian tribes that populated the area.

Daniel, General
James Daniel (1828-1864) was a West Point graduate from North Carolina. Daniel entered Confederate service as a colonel of the 14th North Carolina in September 1861. He rose to brigadier general and led a North Carolina brigade composed of the 32nd, 43rd, 45th, 53rd Regiments and the 2nd Battalion. Daniel was killed while urging his men on in an attempt to recapture the "Bloody Angle" during the Battle of Spotsylvania on May 12, 1864.

Dantzler, Col.
Olin Miller Dantzler (1825-1864) was a state senator from Orangeburg, South Carolina. He began the war as a private, although he served primarily at the rank of lieutenant in the 25th and 1st SCV, as lieutenant colonel in the 20th SCV, and a full colonel in the 22nd SCV. His last commission was dated April 29, 1864. Dantzler was killed in action at Bermuda Hundred, during the early stages of the Petersburg Campaign, on June 2, 1864.

Davidson, Harvey Black
Black Davidson (1842-1924), private, Co. K, Lacy Guards, 17th SCV. He was one of four Davidson brothers to join Co. K; two were killed in action.

Davidson, William
William F. Davidson (1837-?), enlisted as private, Co. I, Turkey Creek Grays, 5th SCV. He later transferred to Co. K, Lacy Guards, 17th SCV. Davidson is said to be the first man from York wounded at First Manassas. He was a brother of Harvey Black Davidson.

De Marivaux, Count
Count De Marivaux was a relative of French Emperor Louis Napoleon.

DeSaussure, Wilmot Gibbs
Colonel Wilmont Gibbs DeSaussure was a prominant attorney from Charleston before the war. As a lieutenant colonel he served on the staff of Brig. Gen. R. G. M. Dunovant of the South Carolina Army, and commanded the artillery on Morris Island during the bombardment of Fort Sumter in April 1861. As a colonel of the 15th SCV, he and his regiment were sent from the Charleston theater to Virginia along with the 17th SCV. During the last days of the Confederacy he was promoted to brigadier general in command of the 4th Brigade, South Carolina Militia (a state command).

Donnelly, F. Olin
F. Olin Donnelly was a doctor.

Dover, William
Willliam M. Dover (1837-1863) a private in Co. F, Carolina Rifles, 17th SCV, was killed in the Battle of the Crater at Petersburg on July 30, 1864.

Duff, Sammy
Unidentified. This was probably Lawrence "Larry" Duffy (1838-?), who was born in Ireland. He was a sergeant in Co. A, Culp's Co., 17th SCV, and was wounded at Second Manassas and later discharged. Duffy lived at Smith's Turn Out.

Duffy, Captain
Little is known of Duffy other than that he was a captain in the 23rd SCV.

Dunovant, Captain
Alexander Quay Dunovant was the captain of Co. C, Broad River Light Infantry, 17th SCV, and later rose to the rank of colonel. He was the bother-in-law of William Blackburn Wilson, first commander of Co. F, Carolina Rifles, 17th SCV. Dunovant was a signer of South Carolina's Ordinance of Secession.

Dunovant, William
William Dunovant, sergeant, Co. F, Carolina Rifles, 17th SCV.

Durham, Captain
Cicero Durham, captain, Co. F, 49th North Carolina. Durham was the recruiter of the 49th. Following the war he became a state legislator. He was from Shelby, North Carolina.

Dye
Leroy Henderson Dye (1844-1919), private, Co. E, Indian Land Tigers, 17th SCV.

Eckles, Mrs.
Unidentified.

Edwards, W. H.

William H. Edwards (1833-1920), of Chester County, was formerly orderly sergeant of Co. A, 17th SCV. Elected 1st lieutenant at the army's reorganization in 1862, Edwards later became captain of the company and served throughout the remainder of the war in this capacity. Edwards later wrote an account of the history of the 17th SCV. This work remains the only published account of the 17th.

Elford, Colonel

Charles J. Elford was from Greenville District and the colonel of the 16th SCV.

Elliott, General Stephen

Stephen Elliott (1830-1866) took command of what was left of the Tramp Brigade at Petersburg, Virginia in May 1864. Elliott was originally colonel of the Holcombe Legion and served most of the war on the South Carolina coast. Promoted to brigadier general in 1864, Elliott commanded the brigade until it was decimated at the Battle of the Crater on July 30, 1864. Elliott was badly wounded during the contest while leading a counterattack to stem the Federal breakthrough. After a lengthy recovery he transferred to the Army of Tennessee and surrendered with that army in April 1865 in North Carolina. Unfortunately, the wounds he received before Petersburg never properly healed, and he died within a few months of the end of the war.

Eloise

Unidentified.

Erwin, Jim

James A. Erwin (1835-1891) private in the cavalry (unit unknown).

Eugene

Unidentified.

Evans, General

Nathan George "Shanks" Evans (1824-1868) was a native South Carolinian and a graduate of West Point. Known as the "Hero of Manassas" for his holding action on the Confederate flank during that battle, Evans was given command of a brigade on the South Carolina coast. While he arrived on the scene late, he was nevertheless given the distinction of being the commander at the June 16, 1862 Battle of Secessionville. While in command of troops in Kinston, North Carolina, Evans fell into a serious dispute with his regimental commanders which resulted in two court martial trials on charges of drunkenness. Although acquitted of the charges, he was never an effectual officer after that point. His brigade was nicknamed the "Tramp Brigade" because of its many and varied travels and commands.

Farmer

W. B. Farmer, enrolled as private, Co. B, Bethel Guards, 5th SCV. After the army's reorganization in 1862, Farmer transferred to Co. F, Carolina Rifles, 17th SCV.

Feemster, E. G.
Elijah Given Feemster (1822-1896), 4th Sergeant, Co. F, Carolina Rifles, 17th SCV. Feemster resigned from the company during reorganization in 1862. He later joined Co. C, Broad River Light Infantry, 17th SCV and rose to the rank of 2nd sergeant.

Fitchett, Captain
Jonathan Fitchett (1828-1862) began the war as a private and rose through the ranks to 1st lieutenant and then captain of Co. B, Kings Mountain Guards, 5th SCV. He died on July 12, 1862, of wounds received at Fraser's Farm and Gaines' Mill in the fighting around Richmond during the Seven Days Campaign.

Floria, Miss
Unidentified.

Floyd, Jack
Jack Floyd, private, 17th SCV.

Floyd, John
John Floyd (1836-?) was from Darlington County, SC. He enlisted as 3rd Sergeant Co. I, Darlinton Guards, 18th SCV. Floyd soon rose to the rank of captain in 1863. He participated in the battles of Second Manassas, Sharpsburg, Jackson, and Petersburg. Floyd surrendered at Appomattox in 1865.

Foster, General
John Gray Foster (1823-1874) was a West Point graduate and a veteran of the Mexican War. During the early days of the conflict in South Carolina, Foster, as an engineer, was in charge of operations in Charleston harbor and assisted in the removal of Federal forces from Fort Moultrie to Fort Sumter. He later succeeded Maj. Gen. Ambrose Burnside in command of the Union Department of North Carolina in July 1862, where he enjoyed an undistinguished career. Foster launched an expedition in 1862 in eastern North Carolina in an attempt to cut the railroad between Wilmington and Petersburg. He remained in service following the war.

Frank, Uncle
David Franklin Jackson (1811-1883) was David's uncle on his mother's side.

French, General S. G.
General Samuel Gibbs French (1818-1910) was a native of New Jersey and a West Point graduate. French served in the Mexican War, and from February 1862 to April 1863, he commanded a department in North Carolina and Southern Virginia. He later saw service in the Atlanta Campaign as both a division and corps commander.

Gadberry
James M. Gadberry was the first colonel of the 18th SCV.

Gibson
Gibson is unidentified other than he was a member of the 17th SCV.

Gilfillin, John Mc.
John McCully Gilfillin (1829-1908), private, Co. C, Broad River Light Infantry, 17th SCV was a POW at the end of the war.

Gilmer, General
Jeremy Francis Gilmer (1818-1883) began his Confederate service as a colonel of Engineers. A North Carolinian by birth and West Point graduate, Gilmer spent most of the war working on the defences of Richmond. Eventually he became Chief of the Engineer Bureau. One historian described Gilmer as "the premier engineer in the service of the Confederacy." Following the war, Gilmer became head of the Savannah Gaslight Company, a position he held for sixteen years until his death.

Girardeau, Rev.
Dr. John L. Girardeau (1825-1898) was a Presbyterian minister and chaplin of the 23rd SCV. Prior to the war he was a member of Charleston Presbytery and strong advocate of the doctrine of State's Rights. He also pushed for religious instruction for slaves along with ordaination of some slaves to administer to others. In 1861 he helped draw up the resolves creating the Presbyterian Church of the Confederate States of America. Girardeau served with the 23rd through all its campaigns until captured at Sayler's Creek on April 6, 1865. After his release from Johnson's Island he returned to South Carolina and taught at Columbia Theological Seminary.

Gist, States Rights
S. R. Gist (1831-1864) was a graduate of Harvard Law School. At the outbreak of war, Gist became Adjutant and Inspector General for the South Carolina Army and participated at First Manassas. He served most of 1862 on the South Carolina coast and commanded a brigade at Jackson, Mississippi in 1863. While serving with the Army of Tennessee, Gist was killed while leading his troops at the Battle of Franklin on November 30, 1864.

Godard, Dr.
Godard (?-1861) was a member of the Rutledge [S.C.] Riflemen, regiment unknown.

Goudlett, Col.
Spartan D. Goodlett rose from the ranks of lieutenant-colonel to colonel of the 22nd SCV.

Gregg, Maxey
General Gregg (1814-1862), from Columbia, was a lawyer prior to the war and served as a member of the South Carolina Secession Convention in 1860. He commanded a brigade made up of the 1st, Orr's Rifles, 12th, 13th and 14th Regiments of South Carolina Volunteers in A. P. Hill's famous "Light Division." At Second Manassas Gregg replied to a frantic message from Hill, "Tell General Hill that my ammunition is exhausted, but that I will hold my position with the bayonet." In December 1862, Gregg was killed at Fredericksburg when a Federal attack pierced the line in front of his prone brigade.

Grist, Lewis M.

L. M. Grist (1831-1903) was a printer by trade who became Editor of the *Yorkville Enquirer*. In 1861, he enrolled in Co. A, Palmer Guards, 12th SCV and later became captain of the company.

Guntharp, O. R.

Osborne R. Guntharp (1833-1919) began the war as a private in Co. F, Carolina Rifles, 17th SCV. At the reoganization in 1862, Guntharp was elected 1st sergeant, and was later promoted to 2nd Lieutenant. After providing testimony in 1870-1871during the infamous Klu Klux Klan trials in York County, Guntharp dropped from public view. He was a friend and mess mate of Logan's.

Gwinn, General

Walter Gwynn was a colonel in the Confederate Engineer Bureau. At the time of the Union advance on Kinston and Goldsborough in eastern North Carolina, Gwynn was brigadier-general (state service) in command of the coastal defenses of the Northern Department of North Carolina under General William H. C. Whiting.

Hall, Dr.

Dr. Hall is unidentified other than he was the assistant surgeon for the 17th SCV.

Hampton, Frank

Franklin Hampton (1829-1863) was a brother of Lt. Gen. Wade Hampton. Frank owned "Woodlands," a plantation near Columbia, SC, in Richland County. He was the colonel of the 2nd SC Cavalry and was killed on June 9, 1863, in fighting at Brandy Station, Virginia.

Happerfield, F.

Francis Happerfield (1831-1891), private, Co. I, Jasper Light Infantry, 5th SCV. Happerfield came to the United States in 1850 from England, eventually settling in Yorkville in 1852 ,where he ran the Yorkville Marble Yard. He transferred to Co. F, Carolina Rifles, 17th SCV early in the war and rose to the rank of sergeant. After service during the war, Happerfield reopened his yard in 1869. In 1880, he branched his operations out into merchandising, serving the town of Yorkville as town warden for a time, and as a member of the Board of Trustees of the Yorkville Graded School.

Henry, Uncle

There are two possibilities: Henry Erwin McFadden (1830-1882), an uncle of Sallie; or Henry Green Gaffney (1815-1900) who married Elizabeth S. Logan (David's aunt).

Herbert

Unidentified; but probably a local resident of Yorkville or a family relation.

Hetherington, J. G.

There are two possibilities for J. G. Hetherington: James Hethrington (1831-1862), private, Co. F, Carolina Rifles, 17th SCV; or Joseph Green Hetherington (1841-?), private, Co. E, Turkey Creek Grays, 5th SCV.

Hill, Ambrose Powell

Lieutenant General A. P. Hill (1825-1865) became famous for his red battle shirt and his lightening-fast, hard-hitting (and occasionally rash) attacks. Hill was a West Point graduate and the commander of the famous "Light Division." After brief service under Longstreet early in the war, Hill's Division served as part of Thomas J. "Stonewall" Jackson's Corps. He took part in nearly every battle in which the Army of Northern Virginia participated. After Jackson's death at Chancellorsville, Hill was given command of a the Third Corps. He was killed April 2, 1865, during the Federal breakthrough near Petersburg. Hill's effectivness as a field commander was hampered by a chronic illness.

Hilton, M.

Miel Hilton enlisted as Lieutenant, 22nd SCV, and eventually rose to the rank of major.

Hindman

Major General Thomas Carmichael Hindman (1828-1868), a Mexican War veteran, fought exclusively in the Trans-Mississippi and Western Theaters of the war. Hindman was murdered in 1868.

Hoey, Captain

Samuel A. Hoey enlisted as private in Co. E, Turkey Creek Grays, 5th SCV, and his expertise was put to use as the company's drillmaster. He rose to 1st lieutenant, and in August 1861 was appointed captain of Co. H, 34th NCT. He resigned from service in January 1863 as a 1st Lieutenant. Hoey may have later served in Hampton's Legion of South Carolina Cavalry.

Hoey, William

Unidentified.

Hogue, James A.

James Hogue (1841-1917), private, Co. E, Indian Land Tigers, 17th SCV.

Hoke, General Bob

Robert F. Hoke (1837-1912) entered Confederate service as 2nd lieutenant, Co. F, 1st NCT. During the reorganization of 1862, Hoke was promoted to lieutenant-colonel of the 33rd NCT and distinguished himself for gallantry at New Bern, North Carolina in 1862. He was promoted to colonel of the 21st NCT, and fought in many of the major battles in Virginia, including Second Manassas and Fredericksburg (where he was wounded). Promoted to brigadier-general, Hoke planned and carried out the attack on Union held Plymouth, North Carolina in 1864, forcing the surrender of the town. This exploit caused the Confederate Congress to vote him a resolution of thanks and earned Hoke a promotion to major-general. His performance at the head of a division, first with Lee's army around Petersburg and then later in the defense of Wilmington and at Bentonville, North Carolina, was distinguished primarily by his inability (or unwilling-ness) to coordinate movements and assaults with other division commanders.

Holly, J. C.
Captain Holly (1838-1863) of Yorkville was originally 1st Lieutenant of Co. E, Indian Land Tigers, 17th SCV. He became captain of the company at its reorganization, a position he held briefly until June 1862, when he was stricken with apoplexy [stroke] and forced to retire from the service.

Holmes, Professor
Professor Holmes is unidentified other then he is probably from Charleston.

Hood
General John Bell Hood (1831-1879) was a West Point graduate who rose through Confederate ranks from 1st lieutenant to command of the Army of Tennessee. He did not get along with the "Tramp Brigade's" Nathan G. Evans, who had Hood arrested after Second Manassas in a dispute over the fate of some captured ambulances. Hood lost the use of an arm at Gettysburg and suffered the amputation of his leg at Chickamauga. The quality of his generalship in the Atlanta Campaign is currently being reassesed by historians, but his actions at Franklin and Nashville will likely always be considered unwise and rash. Hood died during a yellow fever epidemic in New Orleans.

Hope, J. M.
J. Meek Hope (1840-1864), private, Co. F, Carolina Rifles, 17th SCV, died of disease.

Hope, J. W. P.
Hope (1833-?), was originally from western York County. Raised in the Sharon area, where he was later a farmer, Hope later moved to Yorkville and began a grocery business in the town in 1867. He eventually became one of the largest dealers in the area in supplies and cotton.

Hope, R. H.
R. H. Hope (1819-?) was a doctor in the Rock Hill area in the 1860s.

Hugh, Uncle
Hugh Gordon Jackson (1820-1887) was a doctor and an uncle of David on his mother's side. See Jackson, H. G.

Jackson, Andrew
Uncle Andy Jackson (1832-1887), was captain of Co. F, Kings Mountain Guards, 5th SCV. Jackson was severely wounded at the Battle of Gaines' Mill in June 1862. The injury resulted in the amputation of his arm and he was discharged from the service. Andrew was a half-brother of Hugh Gordon Jackson and the uncle of David Jackson Logan.

Jackson, Colonel
See Jackson, Andrew.

Jackson, Dr.
See Jackson, H. G.

Jackson, Genl "Stone Wall"

Thomas J. Jackson, whose performance on the plains of Manassas on July 21, 1861, earned him his undying nickname "Stonewall," was one of the premier generals of the war. Jackson went on to lead one of the unofficial "wings" of Lee's army until after the Maryland Campaign, when he was promoted, together with James Longstreet, to lieutenant general and given command of the II Corps (Longstreet led the I Corps). Jackson was mortally wounded at the hour of his greatest triumph at Chancellorsville on the evening of May 2, 1863, and died eight days later.

Jackson, H. G.

Hugh Gordon Jackson (1820-1887), enlisted as a private in Co. A, Palmer Guards, 12th SCV. He later became assistant surgeon in the regiment. Following the war Jackson returned to York County as a physician. He was a brother of Andrew Jackson and Uncle of David Jackson Logan.

Jackson, John

Uncle John Jackson is one of three: John Law Jackson (1842-1921), private, Co. H, Catawba Light Infantry, 18th SCV; John O. Jackson (1823-1864), private, Co. F, Kings Mountain Guards, 5th SCV; and John McClain Jackson (1829-1901), private, Co H, Catawba Light Infantry, 18th SCV.

James, Captain

Captain James is unidentified other than he was from Lauren District.

Jane, Aunt

See Rowell, Aunt Jane.

Jeff, Uncle

See McFadden, J. V.

Jefferies, A. S.

Anderson Smith Jefferys (1842-1865), private, Co. F, Carolina Rifles, 17th SCV. Jefferys was one of three brothers who fought in York County companies. On April 1, 1865, his left leg was shot away at the knee at Hatcher's Run near Petersburg. He was left on the battlefield and taken prisoner the next day. His wound was attended to by his captors and he was sent to prison at Fortress Monroe, Virginia, where he died July 9, 1865.

Jefferies, Jim

James Jefferys (1801-?) was an Englishman by birth. He moved to Yorkville and became a prominent merchant in the town. Jim Jefferys is the father of A. S. Jefferys above.

Jenkins

John Jenkins (1824-1905) was from Edisto Island, South Carolina, and a brother of Micah Jenkins of Edisto and Yorkville. In 1850, Jenkins was elected to the South Carolina Legislature, and ten years later was a delegate to the South Carolina Secession

Convention. During the first year of the war he joined the Calhoun Artillery and became the unit's 2nd lieutenant. He resigned from the artillery to organize a state company of mounted riflemen from Charleston District, and was elected captain. When the company was reorganized for Confederate service in 1862, Jenkins was elected major of Company I, Rebel Troop, 3rd South Carolina Cavalry. Jenkins and the Rebel Troop served on the South Carolina coast throughout the war.

Jenkins, Micah

Micah Jenkins, (1835-1864) was from Edisto Island, South Carolina and a brother of Maj. John Jenkins. He was a graduate of the South Carolina Military Academy (presently the Citadel). After graduation he moved to Yorkville and began the Kings Mountain Military Academy with former classmate Asbury Coward. In Yorkville Jenkins quickly became a prominent figure in local society. He was instrumental in the formation of the Church of the Good Shephard, and at 20 years of age in 1852, was elected secretary and treasurer of the first Vestry of the Church. Jenkins enlisted as a major in 1861 and served on the staff of P. G. T. Beauregard. He led a regiment at First Manassas and led a brigade during the Peninsula Campaign. Jenkins was promoted to brigadier general on July 22, 1862, and was wounded at Second Manassas and sent home to recuperate. After he recovered, he traveled west with two divisions of the First Corps for service in Tennessee under James Longstreet (Jenkins was one of Longstreet's favorite officers). The young and promising Jenkins was mortally wounded by Confederate rifle fire while riding alongside Longstreet, who was permanently crippled by the same discharge.

Jennifer

Walter Hanson Jenifer, an obscure colonel from Maryland, served with several Virginia organizations during the war. He was a groomsman at W. H. F. Lee's wedding.

Jim

See Logan, Jim.

Jist, S. R.

See Gist, S. R.

Johnson

Bushrod Rust Johnson (1817-1880) was a West Pointer and veteran of the Mexican and Seminole Wars. Johnson taught at military schools in Kentucky and Tennessee before the war and led Tennessee troops through most of the conflict. He led a division during the fighting at Petersburg, and commanded the section of line in which the 17th SCV was located in July 1864, when the Battle of the Crater took place. Following the war, Johnson returned to education.

Johnston, General

General Joseph Eggleston Johnston (1807-1891) was a West Point graduate from Virginia and veteran of the Mexican War and frontier service. Johnston's wounding at Seven Pines on May 31, 1862, opened the door for Robert E. Lee, who replaced him at the head of the Army of Northern Virginia. Despite the burning enmity between

Johnston and President Jefferson Davis, "Old Joe" was given the command of a crucial department in the West, as well as "The Army of Relief" at Jackson, Mississippi in 1863 (where the 17th SCV took part in the defense of the city). Thereafter he led the Army of Tennesse during the Atlanta Campaign, but his continual retreats caused Davis to relieve Johnston of command in July 1864. He was reinstated in the late winter of 1865 in North Carolina and ordered to slow down Federal advances through that state. Johnston waged his finest action at Bentonville on March 19-21, 1865, although by then there was little he could do to stop William Sherman's advance. Johnston surrendered his army late the following month.

Jones, Dunovant
Dunovant Jones is unidentified other than he was a colonel.

Jordan, Dr.
R. H. Jordan (1830-?) was a doctor in Rock Hill in 1860. When the war began, he enlisted as a private, Co. E, Indian Land Tigers, 17th SCV.

Keitt
Laurence Massillon Keitt, (1824-1864) was a member of the United States House of Representatives prior to the war. Commissioned a colonel of the 20th SCV, Keitt gained fame as the commander of Fort Wagner at Charleston Harbor in September 1863 during the last stages of the Union attack against that fortification. He oversaw the successful evacuation of the fort. Keitt was mortally wounded leading his troops from horseback at Cold Harbor on June 2, 1864, and died two days later. He is buried in the family cemetery, St. Matthews, South Carolina.

Lavaughn, Lieutenant-Colonel
Lavaughn, Lieutenant-Colonel, 61st NCT.

Lochart
Two brothers, both privates, represent the best possibilities for "Lockhart": Edmond M. Lockhart, (1842-1864), Co, E, Turkey Creek Grays, 5th SCV, died of disease in Virginia; or Robert A. Lockhart, (1836-1864), Co. A, Palmer Guards, 12th SCV.

Lockhart, J. A.
J. Alexander Lockhart (1835-?), private, Co. K, Lacy Guards, 17th SCV.

Logan, Ben
Benjamin Franklin Logan (1842-1899), was a brother of David Jackson Logan and the third oldest son of John Randolph and Sarah Patterson Jackson Logan. Ben clerked in David's grocery business for a short time. He joined the ranks of Co. E, Cleveland Guards, 12th NCT as a private and soon rose to the rank of 1st lieutenant. He surrendered with his regiment in April 1865 at Appomattox. Following the war, Ben became sheriff of Cleveland County, North Carolina.

Logan, Dr.
See H. G. Logan.

Logan, H. G.

Henry Gaffney Logan (1847-?) was David Jackson Logan's younger brother. In 1864 he enlisted in Co. D, 71st NCT (a company of 17-year-olds), and was soon elected as a 1st lieutenant. Like his brother, he also became sheriff of Cleveland County, North Carolina, and later moved to Arkansas.

Logan, Jim

James Scott Logan was David Jackson Logan's body servant. He was purchased by David's wife Sallie in November 1863. After David's death Jim took charge of his body and buried him in a temporary grave in a Petersburg cemetery. He later brought the body home to York District. After the war, Jim took an active part in local Confederate Veteran's activities in his home county.

Logan, John Randolph

John Randolph Logan (1811-1884), was David Jackson Logan's father and a son of John Black Logan and Lois Rainey. Born in York District, John Randolph moved to Cleveland County, North Carolina in 1836 and settled in what would become Shelby. In that same year, he married Sarah Patterson Jackson, a granddaughter of David Jackson, a Revolutionary War veteran of York County. John Randolph was by training a surveyor—he helped lay out the town of Shelby, NC—and became a prominant person in the piedmont region of the state. He was also a Justice of the Peace, deputy sheriff, lay Baptist minister (serving as Clerk of the Broad River Association), county commissioner, school teacher, county superintendent of public instruction, tax collector and state legislator. His role as a state legislator during the life of the Confederacy forced him to personally petition the Johnson Administration in November 1865 for a Presidential pardon, which was granted the following month. A staunch supporter of state's rights, John Randolph Logan was an ardent advocate of knowledge and independent thinking. He took great pride in his "well-stocked library,"[2] and passed the love of learning on to his oldest son, David Jackson. John Randolph Logan died of a stroke suffered while tending his garden in 1884.

Logan, Johnnie

John Rowell Logan (1858-1921), was the oldest child and only son of David Jackson and Sallie. He became a prominant figure in York County and the town of Yorkville, where he owned and operated the largest construction company in town and served as sheriff and probate judge for the county. Johnnie and his descendants helped to preserve the diary and some of the letters of David Jackson Logan.

Logan, Lula

Lula Meacham Logan (1861-1931), was the only daughter of David and Sallie. It was through her marriage to Claude Love Moore in 1885 that the bulk of David's letters were passed and preserved.

Logan, Marion

Leonidas Marion Logan (1844-1889), was David Jackson Logan's brother and the fourth son of John Randolph and Sarah Patterson Jackson Logan. Prior to the war, Marion clerked for his brother in the grocery store in Yorkville. Early in the war, he enlisted as a private in Co. E, 12th NCT. He was wounded in the right cheek at Malvern Hill in 1862 and captured in May 1864 at Spotsylvania Court House. Sent to the Union prison at Point Lookout, Maryland, Marion was later transferred to the infamous prison camp at Elmira, New York. After the war he returned to Cleveland County, North Carolina.

Logan, Pink

John Pinckney Logan (1840-1864), was David Jackson Logan's brother and the second oldest son of John Randolph and Sarah Patterson Jackson Logan. "Pink" worked with David at his grocery business in Yorkville. In 1861, he enrolled as a private in Co. I, Turkey Creek Grays, 5th SCV, and was wounded while serving in Virginia. During his recuperation he served as a nurse in the Manchester Hospital in Virginia from December 1862 until February 1863. The following month "Pink" transferred to Co. E, 12th NC, the same company in which his brother Ben was a member. He was killed in Virginia at the Battle of Hatcher's Run in February 1865.

Logan, Sallie

Sarah C. Rowell Logan (1836-1904) was the daughter of Benjamin Rowell and Elizabeth Catherine McFadden Rowell, and the wife of David Jackson Logan. Known as "Sallie," she took care of the family's myriad domestic and financial matters while David served the Confederacy. Following the war, Sallie worked to keep the memories of her husband and other Confederate veterans alive in York County.

Longstreet, General

James Longstreet (1821-1904), a native of South Carolina, was a graduate of West Point and a Mexican War veteran. Longstreet was one of the Civil War's most capable corps commanders. His massive counterstroke at Second Manassas was perhaps the most devastating Confederate offensive thrust delivered during the Civil War, and his defensive efforts at Sharpsburg and Fredericksburg were magnificent. Lee was extremely fond of Longstreet, who led the army's First Corps, and once referred to him as "my old war horse." Longstreet, or "Old Pete," as he was popularly called by his men, was critically wounded in the Wilderness by a volley fired from his own men. Following the war, Longstreet was assisted by his pre-war friend U.S. Grant, and became a member of the Republican Party. Although scorned by many in the South for his politics, Longstreet was still loved by the men who fought under him.

Loring, Dr.
Unidentified.

Loring, General

William Wing Loring (1818-1886) was a native of North Carolina and a veteran of the Seminole and Mexican Wars (he lost an arm in the latter conflict). Prior to the Civil War Loring was a lawyer and state legislator. He saw some service in Virginia early in the war and substantial service thereafter in the Western Theater. His men were cut off from Vicksburg at Champion Hill and joined with Joseph E. Johnston's gathering army in the defense of Jackson, Mississippi. Later in the war, with the Army of Tennessee, Loring took part in both the Campaign for Atlanta and the Carolinas Campaign. Following the war, Loring went to Egypt and served as a division commander in the Egyptian army before returning to the South in 1879 as "Pasha Loring."

Love, J. L.

Jacob Lemuel Love (1822-1892), private, Co. F, Carolina Rifles, 17th SCV, from Chester County, SC. Love resigned from service during reorganization in 1862.

Lowry, Dr.

Dr. James McLure Lowry (1817-1907) of Yorkville. Father of Samuel Cosmo Lowry.

Lowry, Sam

Samuel Cosmo Lowry (1845-1864), rose through the ranks of Co. F, Carolina Rifles, 17th SCV to the position of 2nd lieutenant. He was promoted 1st lieutenant upon the death of David Jackson Logan, and was himself killed shortly thereafter at the Battle of the Crater at Petersburg. He was the son of Dr. James McLure Lowry.

Lyons, Mr.

Unidentified other than he married a Springs.

Maley, Captain John

Assistant Adjutant General

Mallett, Colonel

Richardson Mallett, Jr. (?-1863) was appointed Adjutant of the 46th NCT in spring 1862. In August 1863 near Scottsville, Virginia, Mallett was killed while trying to arrest deserters from another North Carolina regiment. There are also two other lesser possibilities: Peter Mallett commanded a North Carolina battalion at Goldsborough, North Carolina; and Edward Mallett was Major-Lt. Colonel of the 61st NCT.

Martin, James G.

Confederate General James Green Martin (1819-1878) was a North Carolina native, West Point graduate and veteran of the Mexican War. In 1862 and 1863 he served as a Brigade commander in eastern North Carolina. In the early summer of 1864 he assisted in containing Butler at Bermuda Hundred during the early fighting around Petersburg. Martin is often credited with being the brilliant master mind behind North Carolina's supplying more troops to the Confederate cause during the early years of the war, and with them being the best equipped. He was a popular with the men who served under him. After the war, Martin pursued a law career in Asheville, North Carolina.

Martin, Perry

John Perry Martin (1832-1920), private to 3rd Sergeant, Co. F, Carolina Rifles, 17th SCV. Perry was a brother of Thomas Booker Martin of Spartanburg District, a member of Co. I, Holcombe Legion.

Martin, William

William Martin (?-1864), private, Co. F, Carolina Rifles, was Wagon Master for the company.

Massey, Larry

G. F. Larry Massey (?-1866), private, Co. F, Carolina Rifles, 17th SCV, joined the company after reorganization in 1862 and later became a member of David's mess.

McCables, Mrs.

Unidentified other than she lived in Charleston, SC.

McClellan

George Brenton McClellan, (1826-1885) was a West Point graduate and served in the Mexican War. As commanding general of the Army of the Potomac, McClellan earned the nickname "The Young Napoleon." Relieved of his command by President Lincoln following his poor showing at the Battle of Antietam, McClellan resurfaced as a prominent figure in national politics. He ran as the Democratic nominee for president in the 1864, but lost to Abraham Lincoln.

McClenllock

Probably McClintock but otherwise unidentified.

McConnell, J. B.

John B. McConnell (1833-?) rose in rank from private to 1st Lieutenant during his military career. McConnell was a prosperous farmer in York County. In 1861, he enrolled as a private in Co. I, Jasper Light Infantry, 5th SCV and took part in the battle of 1st Manassas. During the reorganization of the 5th in 1862, McConnell was elected 2nd Lieutenant of Co. E, Turkey Creek Grays, 5th SCV. He was seriously wounded at the battle of Seven Pines that same year. After the battle of Winchester in 1863, McConnell was promoted to 1st Lieutenant of the Company. He took part in 27 battles during the war and is listed at the surrender at Appomattox Court House in 1865 with his company. The town of McConnells in southern York County is named for his family.

McConnell, R.

Ruben McConnell (1836-?), 3rd Corporal, Co. F, Carolina Rifles, 17th SCV.

McCreery, B. B.

Unidentified other than he was a Captain in Columbia.

McElwee

McElwee has two possibilities: S.N. McElwee (see below); and William Wright McElwee (1833-1912), private, (company unknown), 17th SCV.

McElvee, S. N.

This is probably S. A. McElwee (1834-1903), Lieutenant, Co. E, Indian Land Tigers, 17th SCV.

McF., Lou

Probably Lou McFadden, but otherwise unidentified. The McFadden family was related to David Jackson's wife Sallie.

McFadden, J. V.
Jefferson Valdora McFadden (1833-1894), private, Co. H, Indian Land Guards, 12th SCV. An uncle of Sallie. Jefferson V. McFadden surrendered at Appomattox.

McFadden, T. P.
Thomas (Tom) Patton McFadden (1830-1862), private, Co. A, Chester Guards, 6th SCV, was discharged in 1861. He was an uncle of Sallie's and a brother of J. V. McFadden above. McFadden later transferred to a Mississippi regiment [42nd or 62nd], which also held several of the McFadden family members.

McFadden, W. P.
William Patton McFadden (1813-1899) was Sallie's cousin and ran a store in the southeastern section of York County near the present-day community of Catawba. In 1868, he and his second wife, with some of his children, left on the steamer *America* for Brazil and self-imposed exile where he settled with other "Confederate exiles" as part of the Gaston Colony. W. P. died in Brazil and is buried in the Campos Cemetery in Americanas, Brazil.

McLaws, General
Lafayette McLaws (1821-1897). This Georgia native and West Point graduate served in several regions of the war, including Virginia, East Tennessee, on the South Carolina coast and in North Carolina. In 1864, McLaws commanded the District of Georgia and the 3rd Military District of South Carolina, Department of South Carolina, Georgia and Florida.

McL., I. J. V.
I. James V. McLean, private, Co. F, Carolina Rifles, 17th SCV.

McLean, Jona
Jonathan McLean (?-1862), private, Co. F, Carolina Rifles, 17th SCV.

McLean, Bob
Robert M. McLean (1841-1863), private, Co. F, Carolina Rifles, 17th SCV.

McLure, R. F.
Robert F. McLure (1820-1868). McLure rose from the rank of private in the 34th SCM to Captain in the Senior Reserves.

McMaster, F. W.
Fitz William McMaster (1826-1899). F. W. McMaster was born in Winnsboro, South Carolina. He graduated from Mt. Zion College in Winnsboro and was a practicing attorney prior to the war. When the war began, McMaster volunteered as a private, but soon became the lieutenant colonel of the 17th SCV when it was formed. McMaster was wounded at Sharpsburg in 1862. He was promoted to colonel after Col. John H. Means was killed during the Second Manassas Campaign. In 1864, after the explosion and subsequent Battle of the Crater, McMaster took temporary command of Stephen Elliott's Brigade. During the 1863 controversies with Nathan Evans, McMaster was the highest

ranking officer to request a Regimental Transfer from Evans' command. As a result of this request, Evans charged McMaster with cowardice, a charge on which he was cleared. Captured at Fort Stedman during the siege of Petersburg, Virginia, in the waning days of the war, McMaster was imprisoned at Fort Delaware, Illinois. After the war, McMaster became a founder of the Columbia public school system, and served as mayor of Columbia from 1890 to 1892. From 1894 to 1890, McMaster served in both houses of the South Carolina Congress. He also was a founder and first Chairman of the Board of Trustees of Winthrop College when it was established in Columbia, South Carolina. The college, now known as Winthrop University, is located in Rock Hill, South Carolina.

McNair

Evander McNair (1820-1902) was born in North Carolina, but moved soon after to Mississippi. Prior to the war, he was a merchant in Jackson and in Washington, Arkansas. When the war began, McNair became Colonel of the 4th Arkansas Infantry, and fought at Wilson's Creek and Elkhorn Tavern. He took part in Joseph E. Johnston's efforts to relieve the siege of Vicksburg, Mississippi in 1863.

Meacham, Banks

Samuel Banks Meacham (1834-1891) rose from lieutenant to captain, Co. E, Turkey Creek Grays, 5th SCV. Meacham was David Logan's partner in the grocery business in Yorkville and the son-in-law of B. T. Wheeler. He was captured at the Battle of the Wilderness in Virginia on May 6, 1864. Banks Meacham was a Master Mason and a member of the Presbyterian Church in Yorkville.

Meacham, Captain

See Meacham, T. B.

Meacham, Mrs.

Mary Elizabeth Henley Meacham, wife of Banks Meacham above.

Meacham, S. B.

See Meacham, Banks.

Meacham, T. B.

Thomas Boyd Meacham (1836-1908), captain, Co. E, Indian Land Tigers, 17th SCV. Meacham graduated from the Medical College of South Carolina in 1860. When war began he became the first commander of Company E and remained in that position until its reorganization in 1862, when he resigned and returned to York District. Following the war, Meacham opened and operated the Fort Mill Drug Company until his death in 1908.

Means, J. H.

John H. Means (1812-1862) was the colonel of the 17th SCV. Born in Fairfield County, South Carolina, Means served one term as governor of South Carolina (1850-1852). He became the first colonel of the 17th SCV when it was organized in 1861, and was killed in action at Second Manassas in 1862. He was the father of R. S. Means (see below).

Means, R. S.

Robert S. Means, Major, 17th SCV, was the son of Col. John H. Means (see above). He defeated Julius Mills for major during the regiment's organization in late 1861, and eventually rose to the rank of lieutenant-colonel later in the war.

Meek

John S. Meek (1837-1917), private, Company K, Lacy Guards, 17th SCV.

Melton, G. W.

George W. Melton (1835-?), Lieutenant to Captain, [company unknown], Congaree Cavaliers, [regiment unknown].

Memminger

Christopher Gustavus Memminger (1803-1888) was a native of Germany, a signer of the South Carolina Ordinance of Secession and the Confederacy's first Secretary of the Treasury. Memminger resigned his cabinet post in 1864. Following the war, Memminger practiced law and advocated education for freedmen. He was pardoned by the Andrew Johnson Administration in 1867.

Metts, W. B.

Walter Boylston Metts (1837-1879), private to Orderly Sergeant, Co. F, Carolina Rifles, 17th SCV. After reorganization in 1862, Metts became the regiment's Commissory. Following the war, W.B. Metts became a prominant attorney and served as the Clerk of Equity Court of York County prior to Reconstruction.

Mills, Captain

Edward R. Mills, Captain, Co. E, Indian Land Tigers, SCV. Mills took over command of Company E after the death of J.C. Holly.

Mills, Julius

Julius Mills, Major, 17th SCV. Mills was from Chester County and was defeated by R. S. Means for the position of Major of the regiment during organization in late 1861.

Mitchell

William H. Mitchell, private to 1st Corporal, Co. F, Carolina Rifles, 17th SCV.

Mitchell, Bob

Unidentified.

Montgomery

There are three possibilities in Co. K, Lacy Guards, 17th SCV: John Montgomery (1838-?), private; Peter Montgomery, (?-1863), private, died of measles; and Richard F. Montgomery (1827-1862), corporal, died of disease.

Mood, Dr.

Dr. James R. Mood of Charleston was the chief surgeon of the Home Hospital, located downtown on Market Street.

Moore, Bill

William Shakespear Moore (1829-1918) rose from lieutenant to captain, Co. F, Carolina Rifles, 17th SCV. He transferred from the 5th SCV, and was severely wounded at Hewlett's Farm at Petersburg, Virginia in 1864.

Moore, Blanton

Blanton Moore (1838-1862), corporal, Co. F, Carolina Rifles, 17th SCV.

Moore, E. P.

Eli Patrick Moore (1837-1911) rose from lieutenant to captain, Co. F, Carolina Rifles, 17th SCV. Eli P. Moore is also referred to as "Pat."

Moore, G. M.

Unidentified other than being from Charleston.

Moore, Miss Georgia

Unidentified other than being from Charleston.

Moore, Mrs. W. S.

Margaret A. Lewis (1829-1894). She was the wife of William Shakespear Moore. (See Moore, Bill above.)

Moore, Pat

See Moore, E. P.

Moore, William

See Moore, Bill.

Morehouse, George

George Morehouse, private, Co. F, Carolina Rifles, 17th SCV.

Morguny, Col.

W. C. Moraigne, colonel, 19th SCV. Moraigne was one of only four colonels the 19th Regiment had during the entire war.

Morris

Alexander Morris (1828-1863), private, Co. C, Broad River Light Infantry, 17th SCV, died of disease.

Morrison, Bob

J. Robert Morrison (1824-?), private, Co. E, Indian Land Tigers, 17th SCV.

Morrison, Colonel

Unidentified.

Mulholland, R.

R. Mulholland, private, (company unknown), 17th SCV.

Mullinax, A.

Andrew Jackson Mullinax (1835-1864), private, Co. C, Broad River Light Infantry, 17th SCV. A. J. Mullinax was killed at the Battle of the Crater at Petersburg, Virginia in 1864.

Neely, Lieutenant

Willis Wherry Neely (1832-1869), Second Lieutenant, Co. A, Culp's Co., 17th SCV.

Neely, Mrs.

Mary Cornelia (Workman) Neely (1844-1928). She was first married to James Archibald Gill. Before her marriage to W. W. Neely, Second Lieutenant, Co. A, Culp's Co., 17th SCV, she was known as the "Widow Gill."

Nelson

There were two privates who served in the Tramp Brigade who present possibilities for Nelson: Andrew Meek Nelson (1834-1862), Co. G, Mountain Guards, 18th SCV died of disease in Charleston; and John J. Nelson, Co. E, Indian Land Tigers, 17th SCV.

Nunn

Illy Nunn (1843-?), private, Co. G, Palmetto Sharpshooters.

Nunnery, Lieutenant

Joseph Nunnery (1836-1909), Second Lieutenant, Co. A, Culp's Co., 17th SCV. Nunnery was wounded at Second Manassas and rendered "unfit" for active duty.

Pagan, Major

James Pagan served on the staff of Brigadier-General R.G.M. Dunovant of the South Carolina Army in 1861 and commanded state forces stationed between Fort Moultrie and Butler's Battery during the firing on Fort Sumter. Pagan later became Brigade Commissary of Evans' Brigade. Pagan was from Yorkville. It was his house which David Jackson purchased in 1861.

Patrick

Samuel T. B. Patrick (1833-1863), private, Co. K, Lacy Guards, 17th SCV. Patrick died of disease in Kinston, North Carolina during the winter of 1863.

Pemberton

John Clifford Pemberton (1814-1881) was born in Philadelphia, Pennsylvania. Pemberton was in command of the defenses of Vicksburg, Mississippi and surrendered that important post to Union forces under General Ulysses S. Grant. After his loss of Vicksburg, Pemberton offered to resigned his Lieutenant-General's commission and serve as a private. Instead, President Jefferson Davis recommissioned him a Lieutenant-Colonel of artillery and placed him in command of the artillery defenses of Richmond.

Peters, Dr.

Logan's story is likely in reference to the "Dr. Peters" who shot and killed Maj. Gen. Earl Van Dorn, who was having an affair with Peters' wife.

Pink
See Logan, Pink.

Plaxico
There are two brothers who are possibilities here; both served as privates in Co. F, Carolina Rifles, 17th SCV: Joseph Leander Plaxico (1839-1892) who surrendered with the company at Appomattox in 1865, and James Marion Plaxico (1836-1875) who was discharged before the company surrendered.

Poag, Sam
Samuel Givens Poag (1823-1865), private, Co. K, Lacy Guards, 17th SCV. Poag was from the Bethesda area of York County and died of wounds suffered at the Battle for the Crater. Poag died the same day the Army of Northern Virginia surrendered at Appomattox.

Pope, General
John Pope (1822-1892) was a West Point graduate. Called east in 1862 by Lincoln to take command of the newly formed Army of Virginia, Pope became Confederate General Stonewall Jackson's opponent throughout much of the Shanendoah Valley Campaign. Because of his dismal showing as a commander and in containing Jackson's badly outnumbered Confederates, Pope was recalled after only about six weeks.

Preston, John S.
John Smith Preston (1809-1881) was a brother-in-law of Wade Hampton and served as Lieutenant-Colonel and Adjutant General. He was on General Beauregard's staff at Fort Sumter and First Manassas. Preston then served in Columbia, South Carolina in 1861 mustering men into State service. For the last two years of the war, he served as superintendent of the Bureau of Conscription. Following the surrender of Confederate armies, Preston fled to England where he remained for three years before returning.

Price, General [Prince]
Logan is actually referring to Henry Prince (1811-1892), the Federal brigader general captured at Cedar Mountain on August 9, 1862. He was released that December, and went on to lead a division in the Army of the Potomac. His poor performance at Payne's Farm on November 27, 1863 during the Mine Run Campaign cost him his position with the army. He committed suicide in England because of his deteriorating health.

Radcliffe, Colonel
James D. Radcliffe enlisted as Colonel of the 18th NCT. Later he became Colonel of the 61st NCT.

Rainey, Jonathan L.
John Leonidas Rainey (1844-1924), private, Co. G, Palmetto Sharpshooters, surrendered at Appomattox.

Randal
Martin Luther Randal (1831-1922), 3rd Sergeant, Co. F, Carolina Rifles, 17th SCV.

Randolph
Randolph is unknown other than he was a member of the Palmettoes from Charleston.

Ransom
Matthew Whitaker Ransom (1826-1904) practiced law and served as a state legislator from his native state of North Carolina. At the outbreak of hostilities, Ransom enlisted as a private, but soon rose to the rank of Brigadier-General. He saw action in Virginia and eastern North Carolina. Ransom later served through some of the Petersburg Seige and in the Appomattox Campaign. Before the surrender at Appomattox, his force was shattered at Five Forks and Sayler's Creek. Following the war he resumed his law practice and interest in politics.

Richardson, Adjutant
Richardson was Adjutant, 23rd SCV.

Ripley, General
Roswell Sabine Ripley (1823-1887) was a West Pointer from Ohio. Ripley served the Confederacy in the defenses of Charleston and along the South Carolina coast for most of the war. Following the war, he went to France for a time before returning to Charleston where he engaged in business.

Roberts, S.
Samuel Roberts (1842-?), private, Co. F, Carolina Rifles, 17th SCV, from York Township, surrendered with the company at Appomattox in 1865.

Rowell, Aunt Jane
Jane Rowell was Sallie's Aunt. Aunt Jane married William Randolph Rowell, brother of Benjamin Rowell, Sallie's father. She was also a sister of Eliza McFadden, wife of Benjamin Rowell.

Rowell, Benjamin
Benjamin Rowell (1809-1868) was Sallie's father and married to Elizabeth "Eliza" Catherine McFadden.

Rowell, Randolph
William Randolph Rowell (1814-?) was a brother of Benjamin Rowell and uncle of Sallie. He and his wife Jane moved to Mississippi, where he died sometime prior to the war.

Sadler, Captain
Lucien Sadler (1817-1877), Captain, Co. K, Lacy Guards, 17th SCV. Sadler retired from the service in 1862 when the company was reorganized for the Confederate Army.

Sadler, Dick
Richard S. Sadler (1815-1890), 1st Corporal, (company unknown), 46th SCM, from Yorkville.

Sandifer, Phil
Phillip Randolph Sandifer (1826-1864), private, Co. K, Lacy Guards, 17th SCV who was a cousin of Dr. Calvin Philip Sandifer (see below) and was killed at Petersburg.

Sandifer, Dr.
Calvin Philip Sandifer (1811-1882) was a doctor who served with Co. K, Lacy Guards, 17th SCV. Dr. Sandifer was a cousin of Philip Randolph Sandifer. (see above)

Sapach, Phillip
Philip Sapach (1834-1915), private, Co. F, Carolina Rifles, 17th SCV, from Earl, North Carolina.

Shearer, Hugh
Hugh Hicklin Sherer (1846-1940), private, Co. F, Carolina Rifles, 17th SCV.

Shearer, W. B.
Walker B. Sherer (1830-1864), private, Co. F, Carolina Rifles, 17th SCV, died of disease at home.

Smith
Charles F. Smith (1845-1863), private, Co. F, Carolina Rifles, 17th SCV.

Smith, W. B.
William Beattie [Beaty] Smith (1840-1909) entered Confederate service as 3rd Sergeant, Co. I, Jasper Light Infantry, 5th SCV. Smith soon rose to the rank of 1st Sergeant. In 1862 when the 5th SCV was reorganized, Smith became 1st Lieutenant of Co. G, PSS and was later promoted to Captain after the battle of Seven Pines. Participating in most of the major battles of the war, he returned to Yorkville following the war settling in the northern part of York County in an area referred to as New Centre. W.B. Smith became a prominent merchant and one of the founding fathers of the town of Clover beginning the Clover Cotton Manufacturing Company in 1889.

Springs
Unidentified other than she married a Mr. Lyons.

Soul, Pierre
Pierre Soule (1801-1870) was an exile from France. Fleeing to Louisiana, Soule became a lawyer and legislator from that state prior to the war. During the war, he served as a civilian volunteer with the honorary rank of Brigadier-General on General Beauregard's staff.

Starr, Jonathan
Joseph B. Starr was the first commander of Co. B, 2nd North Carolina Artillery Regiment. Starr's Battery was involved in the fighting during the battles of Kinston and Goldsborough in 1862. Later the battery became Co. B, 13th NC Artillery Battalion. This battery spent the entire war in eastern North Carolina and southern Virginia.

Steele, Captain J. T.

James T. Steele, Captain, Co. I, Lancaster Tigers, 17th SCV. Steele was elected to the Captaincy of Company I upon reorganization of the Confederate military in May 1862 while the regiment was encamped on John's Island, South Carolina.

Steve

Steve was a slave of Thomas Williams Clawson (see Clawson) whom David Jackson tried to purchase in 1863.

Stevens, Captain

Peter F. Stevens (1830-?) was born in Florida and later moved to the Pendleton District of South Carolina. Prior to the war, in 1853, he was a professor of Mathematics at The Citadel and in 1859 became Superintendent of that institution. He commanded the "Iron Battery" in the firing on Fort Sumter in Charleston harbor in 1861. In late 1861, Stevens was given command of the Holcombe Legion with the rank of Colonel. Following the war, Stevens became a minister of the Reformed Episcopal Church.

Stevenson, Lieutenant

William Jackson Stevenson (1825-1902), Lieutenant to Captain, Co. D, 17th SCV. Stevenson was badly wounded in the encounter with Union cavalry on John's Island south of Charleston. He later became a member of the Senior Reserves.

Strait

There are three possibilities in Co. A, Culp's Co., 17th SCV: George W. Strait (1843-1865) was killed at Fort Stedman during the siege of Petersburg in the last days of the war; William Leonard Strait (1830-1865) died in prison in Washington, DC of wounds received at Petersburg; John R. Strait (1835-?) wounded at Second Manassas, but returned to duty. He surrendered with the company in 1865.

Stules, Capt.

Unidentified.

Talliafirro, General

William Booth Taliaferro (1822-1898), a graduate from William and Mary College, was a veteran of the Mexican War. When the Civil War broke out, Taliaferro served as a major general of Virginia militia before becoming colonel of the 23rd Virginia Infantry. He served under Stonewall Jackson through the Valley campaign. Wounded at Groveton, he was ordered to the Charleston, South Carolina theater, where he served for most of the remainder of the war. Taliaferro commanded the troops on Morris Island in 1863 and later the 7th Military District of South Carolina. His last field duty was at the Battle of Bentonville, North Carolina, in March 1865.

Taylor, Mrs.

Unidentified other than a daughter of Benjamin Chambers, Ordinary (Probate Judge) of Yorkville.

Tim, Uncle
Unidentified.

Vardelle, Captain
William G. Vardelle, Captain, Assistant Quartermaster to Major, Quartermaster, First Military District of South Carolina, on the staff of Brigadier General Roswell S. Ripley.

Walker
There are numerous candidates for Walker. The best possibilities seem to be two privates in Co. A, Culp's Co., 17th SCV: Andrew Jackson Walker (1833-1918), and W. F. Walker (?-1864). There is also a James Felix Walker (1824-1862), Captain [in a SC regiment], died of wounds at Second Manassas.

Walker, General
William Stephen Walker (1822-1899) served most of the war on the coast, commanding several military districts. In the spring of 1864 he was ordered to reinforce Beauregard in southern Virginia. Walker takes command of the 17th SCV in the spring of 1864. In Virginia, Walker was engaged in the defense of Petersburg and took an active part in the action at Hewlett's Farm where he was wounded and captured on May 19, 1864. Having his foot amputated, he was exchanged that fall.

Wallace, O. L.
Oscar Lee Wallace (1841-1862), private, Co. F, Carolina Rifles, 17th SCV, killed at Second Manassas.

Walpole, Captain
J. B. L. Walpole, Captain, Stono Scouts, a part of Johnson Hagood's Brigade in the 2nd Military District of South Carolina.

Wheeler, Mr.
Bennett Truman Wheeler (1813-1886) was a prominent businessman in Yorkville. He was instrumental in organizing the Church of the Good Shepherd in Yorkville in 1855. Wheeler ran a buggy factory in the town. He was the father-in-law of Samuel Banks Meacham, David Jackson Logan's partner.

Whisonant, R. H.
Rufus "Roso" Henderson Whisonant (1825-1864), private, Co. F, Carolina Rifles, 17th SCV, died of wounds suffered in the Battle for the Crater at Petersburg in July 1864.

Whiting, General
William Henry Chase Whiting (1824-1865) was a West Pointer and a native of Mississippi. His service in the engineers prior to the war made him the perfect choice for his most important assignment for the Confederacy—strengthening the defences around Wilmington, North Carolina. Early in the war, Whiting served in the Shenandoah Valley. After an extended illness, he was sent to the North Carolina coast. In January 1865, he

was mortally wounded and captured during the reduction battle for Fort Fisher at the mouth of the Cape Fear River. Taken to a Union prison, he died two months later.

Wilkerson
John S. Wilkerson (?-1863), private, Co. F, Carolina Rifles, 17th SCV, died of disease.

Williams, Dan
Daniel Cahusac Williams (1829-1890), Commissary Sergeant, 17th SCV, from Catawba Township of York County.

Williams, Knox
C. Knox Williams (?-1862), private, Co. I, Turkey Creek Grays, 5th SCV. Knox Williams transferred to the 17th SCV in 1863.

Wilson, Captain
William Blackburn Wilson (1827-1894) was a prominent lawyer in Yorkville prior to the war. Wilson was a member of the Episcopal Church and a signer of the South Carolina Ordinance of Secession. With the outbreak of war, Wilson was elected Captain of Co. F, Carolina Rifles, 17th SCV. When the company was reorganized for Confederate service in May 1862, he retired from active duty and returned to Yorkville where he resumed his law practice.

Winder, C. S.
Brigadier General Charles Sidney Winder (1829-1862) was a Maryland West Pointer who served as the first colonel of the 6th SCV. He became a brigade commander under Stonewall Jackson during the Shanendoah Valley Campaign. Winder, a firm disciplinarian, was mortally wounded by a direct shell hit at Cedar Mountain on August 9, 1862.

Wise
Henry Alexander Wise (1806-1876) was a lawyer and a pre-war governor of Virginia. Although he possessed no formal military training, Wise was appointed a brigadier general of Confederate troops in June 1861. He saw action in Virginia, North Carolina and South Carolina, and surrendered at Appomattox. At Petersburg, Wise commanded a district in the Petersburg lines. He practiced law in Richmond after the war and died the year Reconstruction officially ended in the South. Wise never accepted amnesty. He was Union Maj. Gen. George G. Meade's brother-in-law.

Withers, J. N.
J. N. Withers is Isaac Newton Withers (1833-1892) rose from the rank of 1st Lieutenant to Captain of Co. I, Turkey Creek Grays, 5th SCV. Following the war, Withers moved to Winnsboro, South Carolina.

Witherspoon, Captain
John Alfred Witherspoon (1841-1862), captain, Co. C, Broad River Light Infantry, 17th SCV. Witherspoon was killed while leading his company into battle in Warrenton, Virginia.

Wylie, Bill
William Wylie (1837-?) enlisted as a private, Co. E, Indian Land Tigers, 17th SCV. Wylie later became a Lieutenant in Co. K, Lacy Guards, 17th SCV.

Wylie, Dr. William
William Wylie (1819-1868) was a doctor from Chester County.

NOTES

Prologue

1. For more on the emergence of the Southern society of the Upper Pied-mont, see Clement Eaton, *A History of the Old South* (Prospect Heights, IL: Waveland Press, Inc., 1975) 1-15. Two other excellent sources are Lacy K. Ford, Jr., *Origins of Southern Radicalism: The South Carolina Upcountry, 1800-1860* (NY: Oxford University Press, 1988); and Carlton Jackson, *A Social History of the Scotch-Irish* (NY: Madison Books, 1993).

2. Joseph E. Hart Genealogical Collection, Historical Center of York County, York County Historical Commission, York, South Carolina.

3. David L. Moore Collection, Historical Center of York County, York County Historical Commission, York, South Carolina.

4. "Cleveland School Records," *Eswau Huppeday*, 5 (November 1985), 289.

5. David and Sallie were married in York District on February 9, 1858. Newspaper clipping in Logan Scrapbook. This same clipping notes Logan as being from "Epp's Springs about 4 miles south of Shelby [North Carolina] on the road leading to Yorkville." Epp's Springs was one of the numerous mineral springs that dot the Carolina Piedmont region west of the Catawba River.

6. Benjamin Rowell was a farmer from southeastern York County; 1850 U.S. Census, York District; Hart Collection, Historical Center of York County.

7. "Return of the Commissioners of Free Schools for York District for the Year 1859," photocopies, Historical Center of York County, York County His-torical Commission, York, South Carolina.

8. S. B. Meacham was B. T. Wheeler's son-in-law.

9. *Yorkville Enquirer*, 8 March 1860. The King's Mountain Railroad Depot was located on the southern end of the present-day town of York.

10. Logan Family Scrapbook in the possession of David L. Moore of York County, the great-grandson of David Jackson Logan.

11. For more on this region, see Lacy K. Ford, *Origins of Southern Radicalism*; p. 46 lists the counties of the upper Piedmont as Anderson, Greenville, Lancaster, Pickens, Spartanburg and York.

12. *1850 Census of the United States of America: York District, South Carolina.*

13. *1860 Census of the United States of America: York District, South Carolina.*

14. Arnold Shankman et al, *York County, South Carolina: Its People and Its Heritage* (Norfolk, VA: The Donning Company, 1983), 24; Ford, *Origins of Southern Radicalism*, 50.

15. Ford, *Origins of Southern Radicalism*, 48, 251.

16. Ibid., 48, 246.

17. Ibid., 260.

18. Ibid., 83.

19. *1850 U.S. Census, York District.*

20. Moore Collection, Historical Center of York County, York, SC.

21. *Yorkville Enquirer*, June 18, 1857.

22. Ford, *Origins of Southern Radicalism*, 205, holds that 67% of the electorate supported the "cooperation ticket."

23. *Yorkville Enquirer*, December 6, 1860.

24. York County Confederate Veteran Registration Project, conducted by the Historical Center of York County; Samuel N. Thomas, Jr. and Paul C. Whitesides; *Under the Leaves of the Palmetto*, vols. 1 and 2 (York, SC: York County Historical Commission, 1995, 1996).

25. For more on the contribution of York County, see Randolph W. Kirkland, *Broken Fortunes* (Charleston, SC: South Carolina Historical Society, 1995).

26. For more on the 17th Regiment, see W. H. Edwards, *A Condensed History of the Seventeenth Regiment, S.C.V., C.S.A.* (Private Printing, 1908).

Chapter One: Palmetto State Soldier

1. The *Yorkville Enquirer* was begun in Yorkville, now York, in 1855 by Lewis M. Grist. It was one of the few newspapers in the region to continue publishing throughout most of the war, and is still in circulation today.

2. While in command of the 4th South Carolina Infantry and 1st Louisiana Special Battalion, Evans fought against overwhelming odds to stem the

Federal advance long enough to allow Confederate forces to establish a second defensive line, which eventually broke the Union advance and won the battle. For a good overall account of the fighting, see William C. Davis, *The Battle of Bull Run* (NY: Doubleday, 1977). A more detailed tactical account may be found in John Hennessy, *The First Battle of Manassas: An End to Innocence, July 18-21, 1861* (Lynchburg, VA: H.E. Howard, 1989).

3. This first letter to Sallie was written while she was staying with her parents on the Rowell Homeplace awaiting the birth of the couple's second child, Lula Meacham Logan, who was born March 5, 1861.

4. This is probably a reference to Logan's brother, Benjamin, who was born in 1842.

5. Gutheries was a small community in southern York County between the county seat of Yorkville and the present-day town of McConnells. In 1861, Gutheries was a railroad stop on the Kings Mountain Railroad.

6. Port Royal was captured by Federal forces under Flag Officer Samuel F. Du Pont and Brig. Gen. Thomas W. Sherman on November 7, 1861. The capture of the port town and Hilton Head Island gave the Union a much-needed base of operations along the southeast Atlantic coast from which to launch attacks aimed at South Carolina's interior and/or the cities of Savannah and Charleston. Although the Federals never pressed their advantage in this theater, their presence and the threat of serious incursions tied up thousands of Confederate troops and posed a serious concern to the authorities in Richmond. The Confederate troops retained in this theater were often shuttled back and forth to intercept various raids and thrusts, especially between Hilton Head Island and the city of Charleston. For more on Port Royal see, generally, Willie Lee Rose, *Rehearsal For Reconstruction: The Port Royal Experiment* (Indianapolis: Bobbs-Merrill, 1964).

7. The vandals were a Germanic people who sacked and burned the city of Rome in 455 AD, thus giving the world another term for destructive activities.

8. "The great fire" occurred in mid-December 1861 in the city of Charleston and raged for two days. Volunteers were brought from as far away as Augusta, Georgia, to fight the conflagration. It destroyed more than 500 buildings and caused an estimated $350,000,000 damage, some of which could still be seen four years later.

9. For background on organizations such as this, see Barbara L. Bellows, *Benevolence Among Slaveholders: Assisting The Poor in Charleston, 1670-1860* (Baton Rouge: Louisiana State University Press, 1993).

10. The "long roll," which was simply one continuous drum roll, was a method of calling the men to arms.

11. The first national Conscription Act, which passed on April 16, 1862, called up all resident white males between the ages of 18 and 35 for three year terms of service and allowed military units with enlistment terms of twelve

months to reorganize as Confederate troops and elect their own officers. This Act had serious repercussions on the army. See, for example, Kevin Conley Ruffner, "Before the Seven Days: The Reorganzation of the Confederate Army in the Spring of 1862," in William J. Miller, ed., *The Peninsula Campaign of 1862: Yorktown to the Seven Days* (Campbell, CA: Savas Publishing Co., 1993 and ongoing), vol. 1, 47-69. To date, three volumes have been published in this series.

12. The action at the railroad occurred on May 29, 1862, and was nothing more than a light skirmish. For an interesting account of life at Camp Pocataligo, see Jason H. Silverman and Susan R. Murphy, "'Our Separation is Like Years': The Civil War Letters of Deopold Daniel Louis," *South Carolina Historical Magazine*, 87 (July 1986), 141-147.

13. This camp was located on the "college green" of South Carolina College in Columbia. The site today is known locally as the "Horseshoe" of the University of South Carolina.

14. Camp Hampton was located on the estate of Frank Hampton, the uncle of Wade Hampton III, on the southeastern outskirts of Columbia.

15. The Indian Land Tigers became Company E of the 17th Regiment. Its men were drawn primarily from the town of Rock Hill and Ebenezer Township of York District.

16. The Carolina Rifles were taken into state service "about the middle of December." The regiment officially entered Confederate service on May 22, 1862, while stationed on John's Island outside of Charleston. See W. H. Edwards, *A Condensed History of the Seventeenth Regiment, S.C.V., C. S. A.* (Privately Printed, 1908).

17. Those companies comprising the 17th Regiment were: Co. A, unnamed, Chester District; Co. B, Lyle's Rifles, Fairfield District; Co. C, Broad River Light Infantry, York District; Co. D, unnamed, Chester District; Co. E, Indian Land Tigers, York District; Co. F, Carolina Rifles, York District; Co. G, unnamed, Barnwell District; Co. H, unnamed, Barnwell District; Co. I, Lancaster Tigers, Lancaster District; Co. K, Lacy Guards, York District. For additional information, see U.S. War Department, *The War of the Rebellion: A Compilation of the Official Records of the Union and Confederate Armies*, 128 vols. (Washington, D. C., 1880-1901), Series 1, Volume 6, 359, 362. Hereinafter cited as *OR*. All references are to Series I.

18. The fever Logan is referring to was typhoid, a common ailment throughout both armies—particularly in the first year due to the close living conditions and low toleration to disease, contaminated food and unhealthy water. Logan's disability certificate, signed by Surgeon Jas R. Mood and dated "Charleston, January 1862, Home hospital Market Street," read as follows: "Lieutenant Logan of the 17th Regiment S.C.V. having applied for a certificate on which to ground an application for leave of absence I do hereby certify that I

have examined this officer and find that he has suffered from a severe time of continued fever and is greatly reduced in strength and in consequence there of is unfit for duty. I further declare my belief that he will not be able to resume his duties in a less period than 14 days." Moore Collection, Historical Center of York County.

19. States Right Gist. A brief biography of this officer is provided in the appendix.

20. These two regiments were part of Micah Jenkins' Brigade and included several companies composed of York County men, one of whom was David Logan's younger brother, John Pinckney "Pink" Logan, a private in the Turkey Creek Greys, Co. E, 5th Regiment, SCV. Jenkins was from Yorkville.

21. On March 23, a few miles south of Winchester, Thomas J. "Stonewall" Jackson's 3,500 Confederates, largely because of incorrect reconnaissance information, struck Brig. Gen. James Shields' Federals near the small village of Kernstown. Outnumbered by nearly three to one, Jackson was able to inflict heavy casualties on the Federals before being forced to retreat. This battle is often seen as the opening of Jackson's "1862 Valley Campaign." Robert Tanner, *Stonewall in the Valley* (Mechanicsburg: Stackpole Co., 1996).

22. Logan lists only three.

23. Logan is mistaken. Elements of the 2nd, 5th and 9th South Carolina regiments were combined in April 1862 to create a new regiment, the "Palmetto Regiment Sharpshooters," of which one company (G), was made up of men from York County. Joseph H. Crute, Jr., *Units of the Confederate States Army* (Midlothian, VA: Derwent, 1987), 270.

24. Whether Sallie ever received the "long letter" is not known, and such a letter has not been located.

25. Major General Sterling Price, a former governor of Missouri and leader of the Missouri State Guard Militia who had only recently joined the Confederacy, fought a series of skirmishes on April 8 and 9. The best biography of Price remains Albert Castel's *General Sterling Price and the Civil War in the West* (Baton Rouge: Louisiana State University Press, 1968).

26. W. C. Moraigne.

27. On April 16, 1862, President Abraham Lincoln signed a bill ending slavery in the District of Columbia.

28. For a detailed examination of the campaign to capture Charleston and the resultant Battle of Secessionville, see Patrick Brennan, *Secessionville: Assault on Charleston* (Campbell, CA: Savas Publishing Company, 1996).

29. "Chickahominy," as Logan called it, is better known as the Battle of Seven Pines (Fair Oaks). The battle was fought on the Chickahominy River a few miles east of Richmond on May 31 and June 1, 1862, between Gen. Joseph E. Johnston's Confederates and Maj. Gen. George B. McClellan's Federals. Johnston, in one of his few offensive actions of the war, was severely wounded

on the day's first battle and was replaced by Maj. Gen. Gustavus Smith, who promply suffered something approaching a nervous breakdown, and was in turn replaced by Robert E. Lee. The 5th, 6th, and 12th South Carolina regiments—made up of men mostly from York, Union, Lancaster, and Chester Counties—were involved in the fighting. Other than a small self-serving account by Gustavus Smith, the only full-length treatment of this important engagement is Steven H. Newton, *The Battle of Seven Pines* (Lynchburg, VA: H.E. Howard, 1993).

30. Salt, by 1862, had become such an important commodity because of its short supply that the discovery of salt deposits were of tremendous financial benefit to whomever could develop the site. For more information, see Ella Lonn, *Salt as a Factor in the Confederacy* (University, AL: University of Alabama Press, 1965).

31. This is a reference to the great number of refugees beginning to stream into the upper part of the state from Charleston and the neighboring sea islands.

32. "In silent desperation."

33. Palmetto Guards, Co. G, 27th Regt., SCV; Evans' report, *OR* 14, 34.

34. Federal forces commenced operations south of Charleston in an attempt to strengthen and enlarge their holdings around the Beaufort-Hilton Head area with an eye towards pushing their advantage as close to Charleston as possible.

35. This is probably typhoid fever, an ailment which is said to have caused a quarter of all of the deaths in the Southern armies. W. B. Blanton, *Medicine in Virginia in the Nineteenth Century* (Richmond, VA: Private Printing , 1933) 296.

36. More commonly known in military circles as "trench mouth," this painful malady was caused by poor hygiene practice and if left unchecked, led to peridontal disease.

37. Logan is referring to the opening of the Seven Days Battles around the Confederate capital. There are few scholarly works on this massive and fascinating series of battles. A best modern single volume treatment is Stephen Sears: *To The Gates of Richmond: The Peninsula Campaign* (New York, NY: Ticknor & Fields, 1992). A multi-volume collection of scholarly, original essays on virtually every aspect of this campaign may be found in Miller, ed., *The Peninsula Campaign of 1862: Yorktown to the Seven Days*. To date, three volumes have been published in this series.

38. After passage of the Conscription Act in April 1862, military organizations with enlistment terms of 12 months were reorganized for the war and the men were allowed to reelect their own officers. At this time nearly all those men over the age of 35 left the service, albeit only temporarily.

39. Federal forces had been active on James Island, south of Charleston, for several days. On this day, however, they unexpectedly withdrew.

40. Logan is referring to The Seven Days Battles.

41. Logan had two brothers in the battles around Richmond, Ben and Marion, both in Co. E, Cleveland Guards, 12th North Carolina Infantry. This regiment was a part of Brig. Gen. Alfred Iverson's Brigade.

42. This is a reference to the pants Logan received as a member of the Jasper Light Infantry in 1861. He resigned from this company and later helped form the Carolina Rifles.

43. A brief biography of A. S. Jefferies is provided in the appendix.

44. The "Great fight" is a reference to the Battle of Secessionville on James Island south of Charleston on June 16, 1862. This action, which was larger and more important than most students of the war realize, marked the only major attempt by Federal forces to take Charleston by land from the south. See generally, Brennan, *Secessionville*.

45. W. P. McFadden owned a store in the southeastern part of York County, south of present-day Rock Hill, near the community of Catawba.

46. Adams Run was about midway between Savannah and Charleston between the railroad and Federal forces on Editso Island. As such, it served as the headquarters for Confederate forces in the Second Military District of South Carolina, Department of South Carolina, Georgia and Florida.

47. A "sulkey" is a light, two-wheeled carriage.

48. A number of skirmishes took place in Arkansas during late June and early July 1862.

49. The early optimism in the Confederacy was that it would be recognized by the European nations, which would then intervene on the South's behalf. Despite fevered attempts throughout the war by Confederate diplomats in Europe, the Confederacy failed to achieve official recognition as an independent nation. See David Pase Crook, *The North, The South, and The Powers, 1861-1865* (NY: John Wiley and Sons, 1974); and Frank Lawrence Owsley, *King Cotton Diplomacy: Foreign Relations of the Confederate States* (Chicago: University of Chicago Press, 1959).

50. The last major battle of the Seven Days Battles was fought at Malvern Hill on July 1. Casualties for the campaign were staggering. The Confederates under Robert E. Lee suffered over 20,000 casualties, while McClellan's Federals lost almost 16,000 men. The vicious attacks launched by Lee, however, convinced McClellan to pull back his corps from near Richmond to the James River, where McClellan sought the protection of his gunboats.

51. On July 9-10, Union troops launched a reconnaissance in force at Pocataliago in an attempt to cut the Savannah & Charleston Railroad. The thrust was unsuccessful.

Chapter Two: Second Manassas

1. Edwards, *A Condensed History of the Seventeenth Regiment*.

2. Brigadier-General Maxcy Gregg's Brigade was composed of the 1st, Orr's Rifles, 12th, 13th and 14th regiments and served in the Army of Northern Virginia as part of Ambrose P. Hill's famous "Light Division." Gregg was later killed at the Battle of Fredericksburg on December 13, 1862.

3. Union General John Pope's newly-formed Army of Virginia was moving south into central Virginia toward Lee's army. Lee dispatched Thomas J. Jackson and his corps to keep an eye on Pope while the balance of Lee's army prepared to follow. Robert K. Krick, "Army of Northern Virginia," in Richard N. Current, ed., *Encyclopedia of the Confederacy* (NY: Simon and Schuster, 1993), p. 78.

4. Confederate forces attacked several Union camps while Southern artillery dueled with Federal ships between Shirley and Harrison's Landing.

5. Apparently, this "night attack on the yankee fleet" was the skirmishing that preceeded General McClellan's movement of men from the Army of the Potomac to reinforce General Pope's Army of Virginia, which was forming in northern Virginia.

6. The 5th, 6th and Palmetto Sharpshooters were a part of General Micah Jenkins' Brigade. Most of these men were from York and Chester counties. Jenkins was from Yorkville.

7. Skirmishing of July 31 on the James River east of Petersburg.

8. This was a good size skirmish as Confederate forces continued to push McClellan's Federals back once more on the Peninsula. For more on this see, Sears, *To The Gates of Richmond*, p. 354.

9. Logan is referring to a continuation of the skirmishing at Malvern Hill. James M. Gadberry commanded the 18th SCV, while Capt. Peter F. Stevens led the Holcombe Legion.

10. Sallie had gone to stay with the Logan family, either at the house in Shelby or on the plantation just outside the town.

11. Logan is referring to the Battle of Cedar (Slaughter) Mountain, a sharply-fought engagement on August 9 between Thomas J. "Stonewall" Jackson and Nathaniel Banks, who was leading a segment of Pope's Army of Northern Virginia. Contrary to what Logan asserts, Jackson was almost driven from the field, and was indeed fortunate to hold his ground against Banks' assaults. The best work on this subject is Robert K. Krick, *Stonewall Jackson at*

Cedar Mountain (Chapel Hill, 1990). See also, Daniel A. Grimsley *Battles in Culpepper County, 1861-1865* (Culpepper, VA: Exponent Printing Office, 1900).

12. Logan's mention of a "Genl Price" is actually a reference to Federal Brig. Gen. Henry Prince, who was captured in the fighting at Cedar Mountain on August 9, 1862. Prince suffered from ill health later in life and committed suicide in a hotel room in London in 1892. Patricia Faust, ed., *Historical Times Illustrated History of the Civil War* (Harper & Row: New York, 1986), 603. Brig. Gen. Charles Winder, who was commanding Jackson's Division, was mortally wounded at Cedar Mountain by a direct hit from a Federal artillery round. Ibid., 835-836.

13. Casualties at Cedar Mountain were as follows: The Union force lost 320 killed, 1,466 wounded and 617 captured or missing, for a total of 2,403, while the Confederates lost 314 killed, 1,062 wounded and 42 captured or missing, a total of 1,418. Krick, *Cedar Mountain*, 372, 374.

14. Instead of a major battle, Pope pulled his forces back in the face of continued pressure from Lee's Confederates. The finest work on the Second Manassas Campaign, which contains good information on the role played by Nathan Evans' Brigade, is John Hennessy's *Return to Bull Run: The Campaign and Battle of Second Manassas* (New York: Simon and Shuster, 1993).

15. For more information on the role of the South Carolinians at Second Manassas, see General Evans' report in *OR* 12, pt. 2, 627-629. See also, Col. F. W. McMaster's report, ibid., 632-634. The "Fire Zouaves" were officially the 11th New York Volunteers. The unit was recruited from the membership of the New York City Fire Department by Elmer E. Ellsworth, who afterwards became the regiment's colonel. The regiment was known for and easily recognized by its colorful uniforms.

16. Although smallpox vaccinations were in existence since the 1720s, most rural recruits had not been immunized. This was one reason so many recruits feared even the mention of the presence of the disease in camp. Among the hospitals of Virginia, in a thirty month period, 2,513 cases of the disease were reported with 1,020 fatalities. H. H. Cunningham, *Doctors in Gray* (Baton Rouge: Louisiana State University Press, 1968), 196. For more on the disease and camp-life in general, see James I. Robertson, Jr. *Soldiers Blue and Gray* (Columbia: University of South Carolina Press, 1988) and Bell Irvin Wiley, *The Life of Johnny Reb* (Baton Rouge: Louisiana State University Press, 1993).

17. Colonel John H. Means, to whom Logan refers, was the colonel of the 17th South Carolina and but one of nearly 600 men in Evans' Brigade who were either killed, wounded or captured at Second Manassas.Hennessy, *Return to Bull Run, 211; Ellison Capers, Confederate Military History: South Carolina* (Wilmington: Broadfoot Pub. Co., 1990), 133.

Chapter Three: Kinston and Courts Martials

1. The "Bermuda Line" refers to the trade in cotton being sent out of the Confederacy to Bermuda and the goods and supplies being shipped into the Confederacy through the port of Wilmington. The link between Wilmington and Bermuda became so important, particularly from 1863 on, that the route between the two was known as the "Bermuda Line." For more on this see Samuel N. Thomas, Jr, "Far Hope Dawns at Last: The Cape Fear and The Bermuda Line, 1861-1865 (Master's Thesis, Winthrop University, 1990), and Stephen R. Wise, *Lifeline of the Confederacy: Blockade Running During the Civil War* (Columbia: University of South Carolina Press, 1988).

2. Logan is referring to Maj. Gen. John G. Foster, the Federal commander of the Department of North Carolina. Faust, *Illustrated Encyclopedia of the Civil War*, 282. The gunboat to which Logan refers is the *CSS Neuse*. For detailed information on this ironclad, see generally, Leslie Bright, William H. Rowland, and James C. Bardon, *C.S.S. Neuse: A Question of Iron and Time* (Raleigh, NC: Division of Archives and History, N.C. Department of Cultural Resources, 1981).

3. Company C.

4. Company K.

5. The Emancipation Proclamation was issued September 22, 1862 to take effect on January 1, 1863. The decree pertained only to those states (and parts of states) still in rebellion. The Emancipation Proclamation arguably changed the focus of the war from one being fought to preserve the Union into one in which the abolition of slavery was the goal. See John Hope Franklin, *The Emancipation Proclamation* (Garden City, NY: Anchor Books, 1963); and Bell I. Wiley, *Southern Negroes, 1861-1865* (Baton Rouge: Louisiana State University Press, 1974)

6. Harrest's Chapel.

7. In his official report of the action at Kinston to Maj. Gen. Henry W. Halleck, general-in-chief in Washington, D.C., Maj. Gen. John Foster lists his forces as numbering 10,000 infantry, 640 cavalry and 40 guns. *OR* 18, 54-59.

8. The Battle of Fredericksburg, December 13, 1862, pitted Federal Maj. Gen. Ambrose Burnside and the Army of the Potomac against Robert E. Lee and the Army of Northern Virginia. Burnside crossed the Rappahannock River

on December 12 and launched a two-prong attack that was bloodily beaten back with heavy losses (nearly 13,000 men). Lee's army lost slightly more than 5,000. To date no scholarly volume has appeared on this important and largely overlooked major battle. For an excellent collection of essays, see generally, *Blood on the Rappahannock: The Battle of Fredericksburg,* an entire theme issue of *Civil War Regiments: A Journal of the American Civil War* (Campbell, CA, 1995), Volume Four, No. 4. Similarly, see Gary Gallagher, ed., *The Fredericksburg Campaign* (Chapel Hill: NC, 1996). Two older and less reliable sources include Alfred M. Scales, *The Battle of Fredericksburg* (Washington, DC, 1884), and Vorin E. Whan, Jr., *Fiasco at Fredericksburg* (State College, PA: Pennsylvania State University Press, 1961).

9. Flux was a common complaint for many who served in the ranks during the war. The disease was an intestinal disorder characterized by chronic diarrhea, sometimes with blood in the bowels. This was also known as dysentery. It was caused by a variety of bacteria and viruses, as well as inadequate and poorly cooked food. The improper placement of latrines and subsequent contamination of drinking water in conjunction with a reluctance to use latrines exacerbated the situation. See Cunningham, *Doctors in Gray,* 168.

10. Logan is referring to Southwest Creek. For more information on the fighting at Kinston and the Goldsborough Campaign, see the reports in *OR* 18, 106-122.

11. Union forces under Maj. Gen. William S. Rosecrans and Confederates under Gen. Braxton Bragg fought the three-day battle of Stones' River on December 31, 1862 through January 2, 1863, outside Murfreesboro, Tennessee. Bragg's devastating early-morning attack on the first day almost destroyed an entire wing of "old Rosie's" army, but the Federals remained on the field and counterattacked. Bragg eventually withdrew, abandoning most of Middle Tennessee in the process. Union losses were 12,700, while the Confederates lost 9,870 men. Two good books on the subject include: Peter Cozzens, *The Battle of Stone's River: No Better Place To Die* (Chicago: University of Chicago Press, 1990); and James Lee McDonough, *Stone's River: Bloody Winter in Tennessee* (Knoxville: University of Tennessee Press, 1980).

12. This "Card" is obviously a reference to Logan's writings. See his response later in this chapter.

13. This penciled note on the original article clipping in the Logan Scrapbook was added by either David or Sallie.

14. This article, found in Sallie's scrapbook, was penned by Logan, but apparently published in a North Carolina newspaper.

15. Early in the war the idea of digging trenches and creating earthworks was frowned upon, the predominant belief being that manual labor was beneath the dignity of the soldiers. Those who did engage in fortification work were often given the epithet of "dirt diggers." Throughout the war the Confed-

eracy, whenever able, relied upon slave labor to construct its forts and trenches. As the war progressed, however, the Confederacy relied more heavily upon earthen fortifications—and the men quickly realized the value of erecting them quickly. See O. E. Hunt, "Entrenchments and Fortifications," and "Forts and Artillery" in Volume Five of *The Photographic History of the Civil War*, 10 vols., (NY, 1959).

16. Three early churches with strong York County and surrounding area connections. Antioch, still an active church in what is now Cherokee County, South Carolina had strong Logan connections. David's father, John Randolph taught school here for a number of years. Shiloh was an early Presbyterian Church just across the state line in Cleveland County, North Carolina. Bethesda Presbyterian Church in the southern part of York County was founded in 1769 and is one of the oldest churches in the County. Sallie's family were members of Bethesda.

17. Two early forms of baseball.

18. David and Sallie bought the Pagan House on the south end of Yorkville in 1860. They lived there while in town.

19. On January 31, 1863, in command of the *CSS Palmetto State* and accompanied by the *CSS Chicora*, Commander Duncan N. Ingraham and his crews steamed boldly out of Charleston harbor and attacked the Union blockading vessels. The unexpected action scattered the blockaders and lifted, albeit briefly, the Union blockade of the port city. See Francis B. C. Bradlee, *A Forgotten Chapter in Naval History: A Sketch of the Career of Duncan Nathaniel Ingraham* (Salem, MA, 1923); and J. Thomas Scharf, *History of the Confederate States Navy* (NY, 1977), 675; Raimondo Luraghi, *A History of the Confederate Navy* (Annapolis, MD: Naval Institute Press, 1996), 209-210.

Chapter Four: Wilmington and Charleston

1. The *Isaac Smith* was disabled by Confederate land batteries and captured January 30, 1863. It was renamed the *Stono*. It ran aground in the breakwaters off Fort Moultrie at Charleston and was destroyed in June 1863; Stephen R. Wise, *Lifeline of the Confederacy* (Columbia, SC: University of South Carolina Press, 1988), 104.

2. The *Cornubia* was a sidewheel steamer which operated as a blockade runner by the Confederate government. The *Cornubia* was one of the most widely used and successful of the vessels plying the waters of the Bermuda Line having made at least nine trips into the blockaded port during 1863 alone. The *Cornubia's* luck finally ran out when it ran aground off New Inlet below Wilmington but was towed off by Union vessels, November 8, 1863. See Wise, *Lifeline*, 233-236; and Thomas, "Far Hope Dawns at Last."

3. Although Evans was acquitted of the charges, the men of the 17th remained unified in their belief that he was, in fact, drunk at the time of the Federal attack at Kinston. His men had very little respect for him for the remainder of the time he was in command of the Tramp Brigade. For more on Evans, see Ezra J. Warner, *Generals in Gray: Lives of the Confederate Commanders* (Baton Rouge: Louisiana State University Press, 1959), 83-84, and Douglas S. Freeman, *Lee's Lieutenants: A Study in Command* 3 vols., (NY, 1942-1944).

4. See the Appendix, Henry Laurens Benbow.

5. Apparently the letter David mentioned as having written "yesterday" was either never received by Sallie or was lost over the intervening years.

6. The "small note" Logan refers to has not been found. This expedition was in response to Gen. P. G. T. Beauregard's belief that Federal troops on Folly and Seabrook Islands would try to make a serious demonstration against Charleston from the south. However, the main attack came from north of the city near Bull's Bay, about 20 miles above Charleston. The seriousness of this perceived threat caused Beauregard to shift part of the brigade to the Charleston defenses. For more information on the Charleston theater of war, see E. Milby Burton. *The Siege of Charleston, 1861-1865* (Columbia, SC: University of South Carolina Press, 1970) 148-149; Walter J. Fraser, Jr., *Charleston! Charleston! The History of a Southern City* (Columbia: University of South Carolina Press, 1989).

7. Logan was indeed correct about the "running of the blockade," which was a euphemistic term for going AWOL.

8. Logan's brothers were members of the 12th North Carolina Infantry, part of Alfred Iverson's North Carolina Brigade. This brigade had just recently taken part in the Battle of Chancellorsville. See John Bigelow, *The Campaign of Chancellorsville* (Dayton, Ohio; Morningside Books, 1983), 133.

Chapter Five: Vicksburg, Jackson and The Army of Relief

1. Robert J. Stevens, *Captain Bill* (Richburg, SC: The Chester District Genealogical Society, 1985), 15.

2. Ibid., 15.

3. West Point was (and still is) a small town in western Georgia near the Alabama state line.

4. The "Palmetto Regiment" was a famous organization of South Carolinians, including some from York County, which saw extensive service in the War with Mexico. The Palmetto Regiment's flag was the first banner raised over the walls of Chapultepec. At that battle, the regiment lost 42% of its men, while the remainder of the American army lost an average of 15%. For more informa-

tion on this subject, see Jack Allen Meyer, *South Carolina in the Mexican War: A History of the Palmetto Regiment of Volunteers, 1846-1917* (Columbia, SC: Dept. Of Archives and History, 1996).

5. For more on the Vicksburg Campaign and surrounding environs see Edwin C. Bearss, *The Vicksburg Campaign*, 3 vols (Dayton, OH, 1985-1986); Peter F. Walker, *Vicksburg: A People at War, 1860-1865* (Chapel Hill: University of North Carolina Press, 1960); and Earl S. Miers, *The Web of Victory: Grant at Vicksburg* (NY, 1965; rept., Baton Rouge: Louisiana State University Press, 1984).

6. For more information on the city of Jackson and its role in the Vicksburg Campaign, see generally, Bearss, *The Vicksburg Campaign*, and John K. Bettersworth, *Confederate Mississippi: The People and Policies of a Cotton State in War Time* (Baton Rouge: Louisiana State University Press, 1943).

7. While Federal losses in the campaign were heavy—especially after Grant's two assaults against the city's defenses on May 19 and 22; Logan's figure of 40,000 Union casualties is wildly exaggerated.

8. The murder to which Logan refers is that of Maj. Gen. Earl Van Dorn by irate husband Dr. Peters, on May 7, 1863; The phrase "caught or not" is Logan's tactful way of asking Sallie whether or not she is pregnant.

9. The 26th South Carolina Volunteers was organized at Charleston, SC, in September of 1862 and was transferred west to support Johnson's effort to lift the siege of Vicksburg. It was assigned to Evans' Tramp Brigade at this time. Crute, *Units of the Confederate States Army*, 266.

10. Colonel McMaster was acquitted of the court martial charges of cowardice in the face of the enemy, which were filed by General Evans after McMaster distributed a petition against Evans following the Battle of Kinston.

11. Logan's mention of "good news from Virginia" is probably a reference to the early and error-filled reports filtering South that Lee had waged and won a major battle in Pennsylvania. Of course, the Battle of Gettysburg, fought on July 1-3, 1863, was a disaster for the Confederacy.

12. For more information on this fighting, see the report of Lt. Charles D. Myers, AAG, French's Division, July 16, 1863, in *OR* 24, pt. 2, 657-658.

13. "The battles in PA," refers to the fighting at Gettysburg. The retreating Army of Northern Virginia traveled south by way of Hagerstown, Maryland, where skirmishing occurred on July 6. Edwin B. Coddington, *The Gettysburg Campaign: A Study in Command* (NY: Scribners, 1968), is still the best single volume treatment of the campaign and battle.

14. John Randolph Logan was appointed Tax Collector of Cleveland County by the Confederate authorities. This position ultimately required him

to request a special pardon from the Andrew Johnson Administration following the war, which he did on November 10, 1865.

Chapter Six: Charleston, Again

1. For more information on these vessels, see W. A. Swanberg, *First Blood: The Story of Fort Sumter* (NY: Scribners, 1957), and Paul H. Silverstone, *Warships of the Civil War Navies* (Annapolis, MD: Naval Institute Press, 1989).

2. During two days of desperate fighting on Morris Island south of Charleston, the Federals finally succeeded in capturing the Confederate rifle pits in front of Battery Wagner, further increasing the pressure on the beleagured Confederate bastion. The best modern treatment of this action and the actions in this theater for the year 1863 is Stephen Wise, *Gate of Hell* (Columbia, SC: University of South Carolina, 1995). Other sources include Jack Sutor, "Charleston, South Carolina During the Civil War Era, 1858-1865" (M.A. Thesis, Duke University, 1942); and H. D. D. Twiggs, "The Defence of Battery Wagner," in *Southern Historical Society Papers*, 20 (1892), 166-183 (Wilmington, NC, 1990).

3. The men of the Tramp Brigade were among those being shuffled periodically back and forth to garrison Fort Sumter. On August 30, Union guns inflicted so much damage that the garrison was forced to dig its guns out from under the rubble. Shortly thereafter, the men were transferred back to the city. Sutor, "Charleston, South Carolina During the Civil War Era, 1858-1865."

4. Throughout this period, the companies and regiments in the Charleston theater were shifted between Fort Sumter, Battery Wagner and the city. In order to keep fresh troops in Battery Wagner to oppose the Federal advance, the Confederate hierarchy devised and conducted a risky endeavor of moving troops in and out the "back door" of the fort under cover of darkness. Ibid.

5. Logan is making reference to the fact that as the Confederacy's territorial boundries shrank, Federal legal tender notes and fractional currency steadily increased in appearance in the South. By war's end, the distrust of local money had so intensified that even Confederate troops insisted upon being paid in Union currency. For more information on these and other economic issues, see Douglas B. Ball, *Financial Failure and Confederate Defeat* (Urbana: University of Illinois Press, 1991).

6. Logan is comparing Columbus and it's commercial and manufacturing activities with that of Lowell, or Waltham, Massachusetts, where a complete operation (known as the Lowell System) began with the creation of the country's first all-inclusive textile industry in 1813.

7. As the war dragged on and spirits flagged, the rate of desertion for both sides increased dramatically. However, given the superiority in numbers, the

Union Army was better able to absorb such losses. For Confederate soldiers the granting of furloughs by the fall of 1863 had been largely curtailed, either because the men simply could not be spared or because furloughed men all too frequently failed to return. The number of furloughs was often tied to the number of men present for duty, a policy intended to give every soldier interested in leave a stake in the whole regiment's attendence record. For more on this interesting topic, see Ella Lonn, *Desertion During the Civil War* (Gloucester, MA: Peter Smith, Inc., 1966); and Albert Moore, *Conscription and Conflict in the Confederacy* (1924; rept., NY: Hillary House, 1963).

8. The Polish born Casimir Pulaski came to the American colonies to join the fight for American Independence. While under the command of Benjamin Lincoln in the Southern Theater, Pulaski was fatally shot while leading an American attack on British forces at Savannah, Georgia in October 1779.

9. The "Monsters" to which Logan refers are the two Confederate Ironclads stationed at Charleston, the *CSS Chicora* and *CSS Palmetto State*. For more information on these vessels, see William N. Still, Jr., *Iron Afloat: The Story of the Confederate Armorclads* (Nashville: Vanderbuilt University Press, 1971).

10. The *USS New Ironsides*, mounting fourteen 11-inch guns, was considered one of the most powerful warships in the Federal Navy; Burton, *Siege of Charleston*, 135. During the Union naval attack on Fort Sumter in April 1863, the monitor *USS Keokuk* ventured too close to Confederate guns. Pierced by 19 shots below the water line, and suffering the effects of some 90 direct hits, the *Keokuk* sank the next morning off Morris Island. *Official Records of the Union and Confederate Navies in the War of the Rebellion*, 30 vols. (Washington, DC: US Government), vol. 23. Hereinafter cited as *ORN*. Much to the embarrassment of the Federal authorities, Confederate forces succeeded in recovering the two 11-inch guns from the ship and remounting them in the city. *ORN* 14, 25, 257, 277, 300, 438.

11. Logan's September 14, 1863, request for a leave of absence reads as follows: "Sir, I would respectfully solicit through you, a leave of absence to visit my family in York Dist., S.C. to remain at home ten days. I have only received one furlough of ten days, at home, since the 8th of Nov 1862. I have been present for duty with my Company during the whole time, with the exception of a few days. My health has not been good during the last three weeks. All the Officers of my Company are present for duty! D. J. Logan 1st Lieut, Company F 17th S.C.V., Evans Brigade." His request was approved and forwarded by his company's commanding officer, Capt. J. W. Avery four days later. "Leaves of absences are granted for the following named officers. Lieut. D. J. Logan Co. "F" 17th Regt S. C. V. for 10 (ten) days on Surgeons certificate." Moore Collection, Historical Center of York County.

12. Salt, always an extremely important commodity to an army in the field, was "harvested" at a number of works along the coast. The substance became so important to the war effort that the state of North Carolina took over its production during the war. Lonn, *Salt as a Factor in the Confederacy*.

13. At this time the 18th South Carolina Infantry, Evans' Brigade, was on detached duty in Florida. Logan considered this "a pretty good sign" because if heavy fighting was expected, or if a tranfer was in the works, the regiment would likely not be allowed to remain on detached service.

14. Evans was undergoing a Court Martial for his conduct during the fighting at Kinston, NC, eleven months earlier.

15. Logan is referring to Brig. Gen. William Booth Taliaferro. This veteran of several of Stonewall Jackson's battles and campaigns left a checkered career behind him in Virginia, where he was known as a stern disciplinarian and intriguer. Still, he was a veteran commander and Gen. P. G. T. Beauregard welcomed his transfer to the Charleston theater. Faust, *Encyclopedia of the Civil War*, 740-741. The "Genl Anderson" mentioned by Logan is George Thomas Anderson, who commanded a brigade in James Longstreet's First Corps, which was detached and sent to North Georgia to support the Army of Tennessee. Ibid., 13.

16. The *USS Isaac P. Smith* had a habit of making excursions up the Stono River during 1862. Confederate forces, fed up with these forays into the Confederate defensive parameter, laid a trap for the vessel in January 1863. Placing masked batteries along the Stono at numerous points, the Confederates allowed the vessel to proceed unmolested as far up the river as she wanted, but on the return trip the batteries supported by units of sharpshooters, opened fire. Getting only as far as Legare's Point Place, the *Isaac P. Smith* was forced to drop its anchor after three well placed shots pierced the smoke stack, rendering the ship almost motionless. The entire crew of 119 men and officers were captured. The Confederates renamed the ship *CSS Stono*. Burton, *Siege of Charleston*, 120-122.

17. Logan is referring to the French naval vessel *Tisaphone*, which was commanded by Marivault. Evidently, the appearance of French ships this deep into Confederate territory created some diplomatic embarassment and consternation for the Federals, even though the French were there merely to pruchase goods such as tobacco. The French, like other European nations, never officially or diplomatically recognized the Confederacy as an independent nation. For more information on this subject, see Lynn M. Case and Warren F. Spencer, *The United States and France: Civil War Diplomacy* (Philadelphia: University of Pennsylvania Press, 1970).

18. "Greenbacks" were a popular name given for the paper currency issued by the United States Congress in 1862 under the Legal Tender Act to bolster the Federal government's credit.

19. After the Union occupied Morris Island with a force of some 6,000 troops, Maj. Gen. Quincy A. Gillmore began to actively bombard Fort Sumter in an attempt to pummel the fort into submission—or at least weaken it enough to be taken by storm. Charles E. Cauthen, *South Carolina Goes to War, 1860-1865* (Chapel Hill: University of North Carolina Press, 1950).

20. The greatest clothing shortages for both civilians and soldiers were boots and shoes. Prior to 1861 the South had depended upon the North and Europe to provide necessary footware. The Federal blockade significantly decreased such imports and leather was always in short supply in the Confederacy. Futhermore, few Southerners were skilled at tanning hides and shoe making. By 1863, many soldiers had neither shoes nor boots and barefooted men often marched miles over difficult roads. Indeed, during some battles, Confederate soldiers were prevented from pursuing the enemy because injured feet made further marching impossible. Mary Elizabeth Massey, *Ersatz in the Confederacy* (Columbia: University of South Carolina Press, 1952); and Bell I. Wiley, *The Life of Johnny Reb*.

21. The Battle of Secessionville took place on June 16, 1862. Union forces from James Island in Charleston Harbor had attacked the Confederate position at Secessionville, a small hamlet on the island. The battle, which revolved around the main Confederate defensive position of Fort Lamar, was a clear-cut Confederate victory and a sharp setback to Union operations seeking to control Charleston Harbor. For a full treatment of this campaign and battle, see Brennan, *Secessionville*.

22. For more on the importance of religion in the Confederate army, see generally, J. William Jones, *Christ in the Camp or Religion in the Confederate Army* (Harrisonburg, Sprinkle Publications, 1986).

23. General Braxton Bragg was in the midst of his Chattanooga Campaign against Union forces under the command of General Ulysses S. Grant. Several poor decisions by Bragg resulted in a stunning Union success atop Missionary Ridge that pushed the Confederate army out of southern Tennessee and into Georgia—and opened a direct route for a campaign against Atlanta. A good modern treatment of this campaign is Peter Cozzens, *The Shipwreck of Their Hopes: The Battles for Chattanooga* (Urbana: University of Illinois Press, 1994); See also, Thomas L. Connelly, *Autumn of Glory: The Army of Tennessee, 1862-1865* (Baton Rouge: Louisiana State University Press, 1971);

24. The bad news, of course, refers to the debacles of Lookout Mountain and Missionary Ridge (Chattanooga Campaign).

25. Logan is referring to the distance between Fort Moultrie, located opposite Fort Sumter on the tip of Sullivan's Island, and Fort Beauregard, located about one-half mile to the east.

26. "Memminger's proposition," named after the Confederate secretary of the treasury Christopher Memminger, concerns the Erlanger Loan, the Confed-

erate Government's loan from the French firm of Emile Erlanger & Co. with southern cotton as collateral. It was issued on March 19, 1863, in five European cities and raised £1,759,894 (a gold value of some $8,535,486) for Confederate use in Europe. See, generally, Douglas Ball, *Financial Failure and Confederate Defeat*, and Samuel Bernard Thompson, *Confederate Purchasing Operations Abroad* (Chapel Hill: University of North Carolina Press, 1935).

27. The family of Samuel Banks Meacham and his wife, Mary Elizabeth Henley, was increased by the arrival of twin girls, Sue Henley and Martha Banks Meacham. Joseph Hart Collection, Historical Center of York County.

28. Gutheriesville, or "Gutheries," and Smith's Turn Out, or "Smiths," are two small communities in southern York County near the line with Chester County.

29. More than 1,300 shells were lobbed at Fort Sumter and the surrounding Southern batteries between November 28 and December 4, 1863. E. B. Long, *The Civil War, Day by Day: An Almanac, 1861-1865* (NY: Doubleday, 1971), 440.

30. Logan is referring to William Moultrie and Francis Marion, two South Carolina heroes of the American Revolution.

31. The *Presto* was a blockade runner attempting to run the Union blockade on the night of November 1. Out Nassau, New Providence, in the Bahamas, the vessel was reported by Col. W. W. H. Davis, commander of the 104th Pennsylvania Volunteers stationed on Morris Island, as being loaded with "blankets, shoes, and salt beef." Davis further reported that the *Presto* ran aground between Forts Beauregard and Moultrie between 11 and 12 o'clock. *OR* 25, 467-468.

32. On February 9, a Federal force landed on Johns Island to reconnoiter the area, but was quickly pulled off two days later after skirmishing with Confederate troops stationed there. Long, *The Civil War Day by Day*, 462.

Chapter Seven: Side Trip to Wilmington

1. In the four day attack on Plymouth, North Carolina, April 17-20, 1864, Confederate forces under Brigadier General Robert F. Hoke, with support from the newly finished ironclad ram *CSS Albemarle*, succeeded in capturing the town. In the process, they sank the *USS Southfield* and captured 2,800 Federal troops, plus a large quantity of stores. This victory in eastern North Carolina was the first major success in the region since the war had begun and seemingly reversed three years of Confederate defeat and ineptitude in this sector. Such was not the case, however, and before year's end Plymouth would again be lost to the Federals. The best source for any study of Hoke and his contributions to the Confederacy is Daniel W. Barefoot, *General Robert F. Hoke: Lee's*

Modest Warrior (Winston-Salem, NC: John F. Blair, Publisher, 1996). For general references on the fighting at Plymouth, see John G. Barrett, *The Civil War in North Carolina* (Chapel Hill: University of North Carolina Press, 1963), and William R. Trotter, *Ironclads and Columbiads: The Civil War in North Carolina, The Coast* (Winston-Salem, NC: John F. Blair, 1989).

2. The coming fight would be the battle of the Wilderness fought on May 5 and 6. See Edward Steere, *The Wilderness Campaign: The Meeting of Grant and Lee* (1960; rept., Mechanicsburg, PA: Stackpole Books, 1994).

3. "Foot Cavalry" was a term used during the war to denote rapidly moving infantry. Indeed, this type of infantry moved so fast from one point to another that it covered nearly as much ground as cavalry. In 1862, during the Shenandoah Valley Campaign, General Stonewall Jackson's force of 16,000 Confederates marched more than 600 miles in thirty-five days, in the process fighting five major battles against four different Federal armies with a combined strength of over 63,000 men and defeated each of them. See Robert G. Tanner, *Stonewall in the Valley: Thomas J. 'Stonewall' Jackson's Shenandoah Valley Campaign, Spring 1862* (Garden City, NY: Doubleday & Company, Inc., 1976).

4. With the advance of Union General Benjamin Butler at Bermuda Hundred east of Petersburg, there was an increased height of fear that the Federals might be able to cut the Weldon Railroad which connected Petersburg to Weldon, North Carolina. This rail line was the main artery for supplies from the port of Wilmington to the Army of Northern Virginia in Richmond. It was also one of the few avenues available for troops to be carried quickly back and forth from Virginia. See Robert C. Black, III, *The Railroads of the Confederacy* (Chapel Hill: University of North Carolina Press, 1952); and Allen W. Trelease, *The North Carolina Railroad, 1849-1871, and The Modernization of North Carolina* (Chapel Hill: University of North Carolina Press, 1991).

5. The mention of "Ocean Steamers [blockade runners] of a suspicious color" refers to the practice of painting the ships neutral colors such as light blue or a greenish gray. This paint scheme would render the vessel nearly invisible at night to the Union blockaders off shore. See Kevin Foster, "Phantoms, Banshees, Will of Wisps and The Dare; or The Search for Speed Under Steam: The Design of Blockade Running Steamships" M.A. Thesis, East Carolina University, 1991); Thomas, "Far Hope Dawns at Last"; and Wise, *Lifeline of the Confederacy*.

6. North Carolina operated a number of salt works on the coast above Wilmington. These salt works were constant targets of Union seaborne raids. See Lonn, *Salt as a Factor in the Confederacy*.

7. A reference to Major General William Dorsey Pender (1834-1863). See Walter A. Montgomery, *Life and Character of Major-General W. D. Pender* (Raleigh, NC: Edwards & Broughton, 1894).

8. Brigadier General Evander McNair (1820-1902). See H. G. Burns, "Gen. Evander McNair," *Confederate Veteran*, 11 (1903), 265-266.

9. For more information on Hoke, see specific references in Barefoot, *Lee's Modest Warrior*.

10. The "Genl Jenkins" to whom Logan refers was Brig. Gen. Micah Jenkins, a South Carolinian who was mortally wounded by his own men while riding with Maj. Gen. James Longstreet and several other officers. Longstreet was critically wounded by the same volley.

11. Belle Boyd (1844-1900) was a lovely spy and one of the most famous Confederate operatives. For general information on Boyd, see Ruth Scarborough, *Belle Boyd: Siren of the South* (Macon, GA: Mercer University Press, 1982).

12. While the heavy loss of Federal casualties in the Wilderness and at Spotsylvania did indeed indicate that Lee had administered a "severe drubbing" against the Federals, figures can be deceiving. Although Grant had lost many thousands of soldiers, Lee's Army of Northern Virginia had likewise suffered proportionally similar losses. While Grant could make good most of his casualties, the Confederacy could ill-afford such a bloodletting. The staggering wave of casualties prompted the Northern press to label Grant "The Butcher." By the time the opposing armies departed the Spotslyvania area on May 20, the Confederates had sustained losses of almost 20,000 men, while the Federals left behind some 36,000 killed, wounded and missing. See generally, Gordon Rhea, *The Battle of the Wilderness* (Baton Rouge: LSU, 1995); Gordon Rhea, *The Battle of Spotsylvania Court House* (Baton Rouge: LSU, 1997), and William D. Matter, *If It Takes All Summer: The Battle of Spotsylvania* (Chapel Hill: University of North Carolina Press, 1988).

13. The brigade was now commanded by Brig. Gen. William Stephen Walker. Walker spent most of the war serving in various military districts along the Southeast Atlantic in South Carolina. For more on this officer, see the Biographical Directory in this book.

Chapter Eight: Petersburg

1. Better known as the battle of Ware Bottom Church (Howlett's House) where Confederate General P.G.T. Beauregard blocked the advance of Union troops under General Butler.

2. Confederate veterans often referred to the July 30, 1864, Federal attempt to tunnel beneath Southern lines and detonate tons of explosives as the "great blow-up." It is more commonly known as the Battle of the Crater. See Michael Cavanaugh and William Marvel, *The Petersburg Campaign: The Battle of the Crater - "The Horrid Pit," June 25-August 6, 1864* (Lynchburg, VA:

H.E. Howard, 1989); and Thomas J. Howe, *The Petersburg Campaign: Wasted Valor, June 15-18, 1864* (Lynchburg, VA: H.E. Howard, 1988).

3. Brigadier General Alfred H. Colquitt's Brigade consisted of the 6th, 19th, 23rd, 27th, and 28th Georgia Volunteers; *OR* 36, 208. See also, Warner, *Generals in Gray*.

4. James G. Martin's Brigade included the 17th, 42nd, and 66th North Carolina regiments, while Henry A. Wise's Brigade was composed of the 26th, 34th, 46th, and 59th Virginia regiments; *OR* 36, 208; See also, Warner, *Generals in Gray*; Ellsworth Eliot, Jr., *West Point in the Confederacy* (NY: G.A. Baker & Co., 1941); and Craig M. Simpson, *A Good Southerner: The Life of Henry A. Wise of Virginia* (Chapel Hill: University of North Carolina, 1985).

5. Logan is refering to the Battle of North Anna and the subsequent maneuvering leading up to the Battle of Cold Harbor (June 1-3), which Grant and Lee fought some ten miles northeast of Richmond. The 5th and 12th South Carolina Volunteers, both of which were engaged in these actions, contained many members from York District. The primary Federal attack at Cold Harbor on June 3 cost Grant about 7,000 men, while Lee lost perhaps 1,500. See Noah Andre' Trudeau, *Bloody Roads South: The Wilderness to Cold Harbor, May-June 1864* (Boston: Little, Brown & Co., 1989). For good firsthand accounts of the fighting, see Richard Wheeler, *On Fields of Fury: From The Wilderness to The Crater: An Eyewitness History* (NY: Harper Collins, 1991). Stephen Elliott's report dated June 2, 1864, is found in *OR* 36, pt. 2, 265-266.

6. The second day's fighting at the Battle of Cold Harbor, June 2. Troop movements, ammunition supply problems and other issues prevented Grant from launching his attack, which was postponed for June 3.

7. Brigadier General Robert Ransom's Brigade consisted of the 24th, 25th, 35th, 49th, and 56th North Carolina regiments. See D. H. Hill, Jr., "North Carolina," *Confederate Military History*, vol. 4 (Atlanta, 1899).

8. In addition to Ransom, Logan is referring to the brigades of Henry A. Wise and Bushrod R. Johnson.

9. Stephen Elliott was originally colonel of the Holcombe Legion and served most of the war on the South Carolina coast. For more on this officer, see the Biographical Directory in this book.

10. Logan was listening to the Union charge at Cold Harbor. During this charge, which Grant later regretted ordering, the Army of the Potomac lost a staggering number of men in a very brief timespan. See note 5 above.

11. Brigade and Brigadier General Bushrod Rust Johnson's Brigade was composed of the 17th, 23rd, 25th, 44th, and 63rd Tennessee infantry regiments. Johnson, a native of Ohio, was a graduate of West Point and a veteran of the Mexican War. After a solid career with the Army of Tennessee, he transferred east and took part in the Petersburg Campaign, serving thereafter with the Army of Northern Virginia. He was commissioned a major general to

rank from May 21, 1864. Johnson's Division was all but destroyed at Sayler's Creek, although he managed to escape and surrender at Appomattox Court House. Warner, *Generals in Gray*, 157-158.

12. "The Beast" is Union Maj. Gen. Benjamin Butler's nickname, which was given to him by the residents of New Orleans when he commanded the occupying forces of the city in early 1862. The name came about largely because of his harsh policies directed toward the citizens of the Crescent City. See Robert S. Holzman, *Stormy Ben Butler* (NY: Macmillan, 1954).

13. The two officers to whom Logan refers are Laurence Massillon Keitt and Olin M. Dantzler. Keitt, a former member of the United States Congress, was mortally wounded at Cold Harbor on June 2, 1864, and died two days later. As the senior colonel of Joseph Kershaw's leaderless veteran brigade, Keitt had assumed command and recklessly ridden his horse into his first battle. When he rode forward to rally his broken regiment, he was shot from the saddle. Dantzler, the colonel of the 22nd South Carolina Infantry, was killed in action at Bermuda Hundred on June 2, 1864. Krick, *Lee's Colonels*, 110, 220. (For additional information on these officers, see the Biographical Directory in this book).

14. Typescript copy of the diary of Samuel Cosmo Lowry, Historical Center of York County. When Logan was killed, leadership of Company F passed to Lowry, who was himself killed the following month during the July 30, 1864, Battle of the Crater.

Chapter Nine: Postscript

1. A photocopy of the Funeral Discourse delivered by Rev. Tilman R. Gaines on August 12, 1866, is in the Moore Family Papers, Historical Center of York County.

2. Logan Scrapbook, Moore Family Papers, Historical Center of York County.

3. Ibid.

Appendix: Biographical Roster

1. Ellison Capers, South Carolina Vol. 5 of *Confederate Military History*. Edited by Clement A. Evans (Atlanta, 1899; rept, Secaucus, NJ: The Blue & Grey Press, n.d.), 400.

2. Robert P. Hamby, Brief Baptist Biographies, *Vol. 2: 1707-1982*; photocopied pages found in Logan family file, Historical Center of York County.

Bibliography

MANUSCRIPT SOURCES

Historical Center of York County
  Confederate Soldiers File
  Joseph Hart Collection
  David Moore Collection
  Lowry Family Collection

DISSERTATIONS AND THESES

Foster, Kevin. "Phantoms, Banshees, Will of Wisps and the Dare; or the Search for Speed Under Steam: The Design of Blockade Running Steamships." M.A. Thesis, East Carolina University, 1991.

Sutor, Jack. "Charleston, South Carolina During the Civil War Era, 1858-1865." M.A. Thesis, Duke University, 1942.

Thomas, Samuel N., Jr. "Far Hope Dawns at Last: The Cape Fear and the Bermuda Line, 1861-1865." M. A. Thesis, Winthrop University, 1990.

OFFICIAL PUBLICATIONS

U.S. War Department. *The War of the Rebellion: A Compilation of the Official Records of the Union and Confederate Armies*. 129 vols. Washington, D.C: Government Printing Office, 1880-1900.

U.S. War Department. *The War of the Rebellion: Official Records of the Union and Confederate Navies*, 29 vols. Washington, D.C: Government Printing Office, 1894-1921.

BOOKS AND ARTICLES

Amann, William Frayne. *Personnel of the Civil War*. New York: T. Yoseloff, 1961.

Ball, Douglas B. *Financial Failure and Confederate Defeat*. Urbana: University of Illinois Press, 1991.

Barefoot, Daniel W. *General Robert F. Hoke: Lee's Modest Warrior*. Winston-Salem: John F. Blair, Publisher, 1996.

Barrett, John G. *The Civil War in North Carolina*. Chapel Hill: University of North Carolina Press, 1963.

Bearss, Edwin C. *The Vicksburg Campaign*. Dayton, OH: Private Printing, 1986.

Beers, Henry Putney. *The Confederacy: A Guide to the Archives of the Government of the Confederate States of America*. Washington, DC: National Archives and Records Administration, 1986.

Bellows, Barbara L. *Benevolence Among Slaveholders: Assisting the Poor in Charleston, 1670-1860*. Baton Rouge: Louisiana State University Press, 1993.

Bettersworth, John K. *Confederate Mississippi: The People and Policies of a Cotton State in War Time*. Baton Rouge: Louisiana State University Press, 1943.

Bigelow, John. *The Campaign of Chancellorsville*. Dayton, OH: Private Printing, 1983.

Black, Robert C., III. *The Railroads of the Confederacy*. Chapel Hill: University of North Carolina Press, 1952.

Blanton, W. B. *Medicine in Virginia in the Nineteenth Century*. Richmond, VA: Private printing, 1933.

Bradlee, Francis B. C. *A Forgotten Chapter in Our Naval History: A Sketch of the Career of Duncan Nathaniel Ingraham*. Salem, MA: The Essex Institute, 1923.

Brennan, Patrick. *Secessionville: Assault on Charleston*. Campbell, CA: Savas Publishing Company, 1996.

Bright, Leslie, William H. Rowland, and James C. Bardon. *C.S.S. Neuse: A Question of Iron and Time*. Raleigh, NC: North Carolina Department of Cultural Resources, Division of Archives and History, 1981.

Burns, H. G. "Gen. Evander McNair," *Confederate Veteran*. 11 (1903).

Burton, E. Milby. *The Siege of Charleston, 1861-1865*. Columbia, SC: University of South Carolina Press, 1971.

Capers, Ellison. *Confederate Military History Extended Edition*. Wilmington, NC: Broadfoot Publishing Co., 1987.

Case, Lynn M. and Warren F. Spencer. *The United States and France: Civil War Diplomacy*. Philadelphia: University of Pennsylvania Press, 1970.

Castel, Albert. *General Sterling Price and the Civil War in the West*. Baton Rouge: Louisiana State University Press, 1968.

Cauthen, Charles E. *South Carolina Goes to War, 1860-1865*. Chapel Hill: University of North Carolina Press, 1950.

Cavanaugh, Michael and William Marvel. *The Petersburg Campaign: The Battle of the Crater—"The Horrid Pit," June 25–August 6, 1864*. Lynchburg, VA: H. E. Howard, 1989.

Clark, Walter, ed. *Histories of the Several Regiments and Battalions from North Carolina in the Great War, 1861-1865*. Wendell, NC: Broadfoot's Bookmark, 1982.

Cleveland County Historical Association. *The Heritage of Cleveland County, Volume 1 - 1982*. Winston-Salem, NC: Hunter Publishing, 1982.

Coddington, Edwin B. *The Gettysburg Campaign: A Study in Command*. NY: Scribners, 1968.

Connelly, Thomas L. *Autumn of Glory: The Army of Tennessee, 1862-1865*. Baton Rouge: Louisiana State University Press, 1971.

Cozzens, Peter. *The Battle of Stone's River: No Better Place to Die*. Chicago: University of Chicago Press, 1990.

——. *The Shipwreck of Their Hopes: The Battles for Chattanooga*. Urbana: University of Illinois Press, 1995.

Crook, David Paul. *The North, The South, and The Powers, 1861-1865*. NY: John Wiley and Sons, 1974.

Cullen, Joseph P. *The Peninsula Campaign, 1862: McClellan and Lee Struggle For Richmond*. Harrisburg, PA: Stackpole Books, 1973.

Cunningham, H. H. *Doctors in Gray: The Confederate Medical Service*. Baton Rouge: Louisiana State University Press, 1958.

Current, Richard E., ed. *The Encyclopedia of the Confederacy*. 4 vols. NY: Simon & Schuster, 1993.

Davis, Nora M. *Military and Naval Operations in South Carolina, 1860-1865: Chronological List, With Reference to Sources of Further Information*. Columbia, SC: South Carolina Archives Department, 1959.

Davis, William C. *The Battle of Bull Run*. NY: Doubleday, 1977.

—— *The Image of War, 1861-1865: The Embattled Confederacy*. Garden City, NY: Doubleday & Company, Inc., 1982

——. *The Image of War, 1861-1865: The Guns of '62*. Garden City, NY: Doubleday & Company, Inc., 1982.

Eaton, Clement. *A History of the Old South*. Prospect Heights, IL: Waveland Press, 1975.

Edwards, W. H. *A Condensed History of the Seventeenth Regiment, S. C. V., C. S. A.* [Privately Printed], 1908.

Eliot, Ellsworth, Jr. *West point in the Confederacy*. NY: G. A. Baker & Co., 1841.

Ellsworth, Eliot, Jr. *West Point in the Confederacy*. NY: G.A. Baker & Co., 1941.

Faust, Patricia. *Historical Times Illustrated Encyclopedia of the Civil War*. NY: Harper & Row, 1986.

Ford, Arthur Peronneau. *Life in the Confederate Army; Being Personal Experiences of a Private Soldier in the Confederate Army*. Washington, DC: The Neal Publishing Co., 1905.

Ford, Lacy K., Jr. *Origins of Southern Radicalism: The South Carolina Upcountry, 1800-1860*. NY: Oxford University Press, 1988.

Franklin, John Hope. *The Emancipation Proclamation*. Garden City, NY: Anchor Books, 1963.

Fraser, Walter J. *Charleston! Charleston!: The History of a Southern City*. Columbia: University of South Carolina Press, 1989.

Freeman, Douglas S. *Lee's Lieutenants: A Study in Command*. 3 Vols. NY: Charles Scribner's Sons, 1942-1944.

Gallagher, Gary, ed. *The Fredericksburg Campaign*. Chapel Hill: University of North Carolina Press, 1996.

Gardner, P. Cleveland. "Roster of the Fifteen Military Companies of Cleveland County in the Civil War." Cleveland County Memorial Library, Shelby, NC.

Gibbons, Tony. *Warships and Naval Battles of the Civil War*. NY: Gallery Books, 1989.

Gragg, Rod. *Confederate Goliath: The Battle of Fort Fisher*. NY: HarperCollins Publishers, 1991.

Grimsley, Daniel A. *Battles in Culpepper County, 1861-1865*. Culpepper, VA: Exponent Printing Office, 1900.

Hart, Joseph E., Jr. *Supplement to Confederate Veterans Enrollment Book of York County, S.C, 1902*. York, SC: Privately Printed, 1984.

Hassler, Warren W., Jr. *Crisis at the Crossroads: The First Day at Gettysburg*. University, AL: University of Alabama Press, 1970.

Hennessy, John. *Return to Bull Run: The Battle and Campaign of Second Manassas*. NY: Simon and Schuster, 1993.

——. *The First Battle of Manassas: An End to Innocence*. Lynchburg: H. E. Howard, 1989.

Hill, D. H., Jr. *North Carolina*. Volume Five. *Confederate Military History*. Wilmington, NC: Broadfoot, 1987.

Holzman, Robert S. *Stormy Ben Butler*. NY: Macmillan, 1954.

Howe, Thomas J. *The Petersburg Campaign: Wasted Valor, June 15-18, 1864*. Lynchburg, VA: H.E. Howard, 1988.

Hudson, Joshua Hilary. *Sketches and Reminiscences*. Columbia, SC: The State Co., 1903.

Hunt, O. E. "Entrenchments and Fortifications," and "Forts and Artillery." Volume Five. *The Photographic History of the Civil War*. NY: Castle Books, 1957.

Jackson, Carlton. *A Social History of the Scotch-Irish*. NY: Madison Books, 1993.

Jervey, Theodore Dehon. *Charleston During the Civil War*. Washington, DC: [private printing], 1915.

Johnson, John. *The Defense of Charleston Harbor, Including Fort Sumter and the Adjacent Islands, 1863-1865*. Charleston, SC: Walker, Evans & Cogswell Co., 1890.

Jones, Samuel. *The Siege of Charleston and the Operations on the South Atlantic Coast in the War Among the States*. NY: The Neale Publishing Co., 1911.

Jones, William. *Christ in Camp: Religion in the Confederate Army*. Harrisonburg, PA: Sprinkle Publications, 1986.

Jordan, Weymouth T., Jr., comp. *North Carolina Troops, 1861-1865, A Roster*. Raleigh, NC: North Carolina Department of Cultural Resources, Division of Archives and History, 1975.

Ketchen, Smith. "Smith Ketchen Diary While in the War, 1861-1865," *The Bulletin*. 13 [Chester District Genealogical Society, 1990] 8-15, 64-71, 96-103, 128-135.

Krick, Robert K. *Stonewall Jackson at Cedar Mountain*. Chapel Hill: University of North Carolina Press, 1990.

Long, E. B. *The Civil War Day by Day: An Almanac, 1861-1865*. Garden City, NY: Doubleday & Company, Inc., 1971.

Lonn, Ella. *Salt as a Factor in the Confederacy*. University, AL: University of Alabama Press, 1965.

———. *Desertion During the Civil War*. Glocester, MA: Peter Smith, Inc., 1966.

Luraghi, Raimondo. *A History of the Confederate Navy*. Annapolis, MD: Naval Institute Press, 1996.

Massey, Mary Elizabeth. *Ersatz in the Confederacy*. Columbia: University of South Carolina Press, 1952.

Matter, William D. *If It Takes All Summer: The Battle of Spotsylvania*. Chapel Hill: University of North Carolina Press, 1988.

McDonough, James Lee. *Stone's River: Bloody Winter in Tennessee*. Knoxville: University of Tennessee Press, 1980.

Merrill, James M. "Notes on the Yankee Blockade of the South Atlantic Seaboard, 1861-1865," *Civil War History* (December 1958).

Meyer, Jack Allen. *South Carolina in the Mexican War: A History of the Palmetto Regiment of Volunteers, 1846-1917*. Columbia: SC Department of Archives and History, 1996.

Miers, Earl S. *The Web of Victory: Grant at Vicksburg*. Baton Rouge: Louisiana State University Press, 1984.

Miller, Francis Trevelyan., ed. *The Photographic History of the Civil War: Forts and Artillery*. NY: Castle Books, 1957.

Miller, William J., ed. *The Peninsula Campaign of 1862: Yorktown to the Seven Days*, Vols. 1-3. Campbell, CA. Savas Publishing Company. 1997.

Montgomery, Walter A. *Life and Character of Major-General W. D. Pender*. Raleigh, NC: Edwards & Broughton, 1894.

Moore, Albert. *Conscription and Conflict in the Confederacy*. NY: Hillary House, 1963.

Newton, Steven. H. *The Battle of Seven Pines*. Lynchburg, VA: H. E. Howard, 1993.

Owens, Jo Robert and Ruth Dickson Thomas, ed. *Confederate Veterans Enrollment Book of York County, S.C., 1902*. Clover, SC: Westmoreland Printers Inc., 1983.

Owsley, Frank Lawrence. *King Cotton Diplomacy: Foreign Relations of the Confederate States*. Chicago: University of Chicago Press, 1959.

Porter, James D. *Tennessee*. Volume Ten. *Confederate Military History*. Wilmington, NC: Braodfoot, 1987.

Rhea, Gordon. *The Battle of the Wilderness*. Baton Rouge: Louisiana State University Press, 1995.

———. *The Battle of Spotsylvania Court House*. Baton Rouge: Louisiana State University Press, 1997.

Ripley, Warren. *Siege Train: The Journal of a Confederate Artilleryman in the Defense of Charleston*. Columbia, SC: University of South Carolina Press, 1986.

Robertson, James I., Jr. *Soldiers Blue and Gray*. Columbia, SC: University of South Carolina Press, 1988.

Rose, Willie Lee. *Rehearsal for Reconstruction: The Port Royal Experiment*. Indianapolis, IN: Bobbs-Merrill, 1964.

Salley, A. S. *South Carolina Troops in Confederate Service*. Columbia, SC: The R. L. Bryan Co., 1913.

Scales, Alfred M. *The Battle of Fredericksburg*. Washington, DC, 1884.

Scarborough, Ruth. *Belle Boyd: Siren of the South*. Macon, GA: Mercer University Press, 1983.

Scharf, J. Thomas. *History of the Confederate Navy*. NY: Rogers & Sherwood, 1887.

Sears, Stephen. *To The Gates of Richmond: The Peninsula Campaign*. NY: Ticknor & Fields, 1992.

Shankman, Arnold, et al. *York County, South Carolina: Its People and Its Heritage*. Norfolk, VA: The Donning Company, 1983.

Sifakis, Stewart. *Compendium of The Confederate Armies: North Carolina*. NY: Facts on File, 1992.

———. *Compendium of The Confederate Armies: South Carolina and Georgia*. NY: Facts on File, 1995.

———. *Who was Who in the Civil War*. NY: Facts on File Publications, 1988.

Silverman, Jason H., and Susan R. Murphy. "'Our Separation is Like Years': The Civil War Letters of Deopold Daniel Louis," *South Carolina Historical Magazine* 87 (July) 1986.

Silverstone, Paul H. *Warships of the Civil War Navies*. Annapolis, MD: Naval Institute Press, 1989.

Simpson, Craig M. *A Good Southerner: The Life of Henry A. Wise of Virginia*. Chapel Hill: University of North Carolina Press, 1985.

Steere, Edward. *The Wilderness Campaign: The Meeting of Grant and Lee*. Mechanicsburg, PA: Stackpole Books, 1994.

Stevens, Robert J. *Captain Bill*. Richburg, SC: The Chester District Genealogical Society, 1985.

Still, William N. *Iron Afloat: The Story of the Confederate Armorclads*. Columbia: University of South Carolina Press, 1985.

Swanberg, W. A. *First Blood: The Story of Fort Sumter*. NY: Scribners, 1957.

Tanner, Robert G. *Stonewall in the Valley: Thomas J. 'Stonewall' Jackson's Shenandoah Valley Campaign, Spring 1862*. Garden City, NY: Doubleday & Company, 1976.

Thomas, Samuel N., Jr., and Paul C. Whitesides. *Under the Leaves of the Palmetto: York County's Confederate Veterans Vols. 1-2*. York, SC: Historical Center of York County, York County Historical Commission, 1994, 1996.

Thompson, Samuel Bernard. *Confederate Purchasing Operations Abroad*. Chapel Hill: University of North Carolina Press, 1935.

Trelease, Allen W. *The North Carolina Railroad, 1849-1871, and the Modernization of North Carolina*. Chapel Hill: University of North Carolina Press, 1991.

Trotter, William R. *Ironclads and Columbiads: The Civil War in North Carolina, The Coast*. Winston-Salem, NC: John F. Blair, 1989.

Trudeau, Noah Andre'. *Bloody Roads South: The Wilderness to Cold Harbor, May-June 1864*. Boston: Little, Brown & Co., 1989.

Twiggs, H. D. D. "The Defense of Battery Wagner," *Southern Historical Society Papers*. 20 (1892) 166-183.

Walker, Peter F. *Vicksburg: A People at War, 1860-1865*. Chapel Hill: University of North Carolina Press, 1960.

Warner, Ezra J. *Generals in Grey: Lives of the Confederate Commanders*. Baton Rouge: Louisiana State University Press, 1959.

Whan, Vorin E., Jr. *Fiasco at Fredericksburg*. State College, PA: Pennsylvania State University Press, 1961.

Wheeler, Richard. *On Fields of Fury: From The Wilderness to The Crater: An Eyewitness History*. NY: Harper Collins, 1991.

Wiley, Bell Irvin. *Southern Negroes, 1861-1865*. Baton Rouge: Louisiana State University Press, 1974.

——. *The Life of Johnny Reb: The Common Soldier of the Confederacy*. Baton Rouge: Louisiana State University Press, 1993.

Wise, Stephen R. *Lifeline of the Confederacy: Blockade Running During the Civil War*. Columbia: University of South Carolina Press, 1989.

——. *Gate of Hell: Charleston, 1863*. Columbia, SC: University of South Carolina, 1995.

INDEX

Adams Run, SC., 32-35
Adickes, Henning F., 175
Aiken, Col. William, 175
Alabama River, 96
Albemarle, CSS, 228
Albemarle River, 85
Anderson, Rev. ?., 137-138
Anderson's Brigade, 123
Anderson, Gen. George T., 226
Anderson, Rev. John M., 175
Anderson, Gen. Richard H., 176
Anthony, Capt. S.H., 1, 16
Appomattox Court House, VA., surrender at, 171, 182, 186, 193, 197, 203-204, 208, 232
Appomattox River, 156, 160
Arkansas Troops, *4th Infantry,* 199
Army of Northern Virginia, 2, 37, 45, 89, 104, 143, 176, 182, 189, 192, 203, 217, 219, 229-231
Army of Tennessee, 143
Army of the Potomac, 37-38, 89, 143, 148, 179, 197, 203, 217, 219
Army of Relief, 90, 93, 193
Army of Tennessee, 67, 179, 185, 187, 190, 193, 195, 231
Army of the Cumberland, 143
Army of the James, 148
Army of the Ohio, 143
Army of the Tennessee, 143
Army of Virginia, 203, 217
Ashe, Pvt. Andrew F., 129, 176
Ashe, Pvt. John J., Jr. 176
Ashley River, 5, 37
Atlanta Campaign, 190, 193, 195
Atlanta, Ga., 100

Atlantic & North Carolina Railroad, 51
Augusta, Ga., 100
Avery, Dr. E.T., 1
Avery, Col. John W., 4, 6, 15, 21, 30-32, 39, 41, 55-56, 59, 61-62, 80, 87-88, 90, 98-99, 102, 104, 111, 130, 131, 133, 137-138, 141-142, 156, 163, 173, 176, 225

Banks, Gen. Nathaniel, 217
Barnette, Pvt. David F., 108, 131, 176
Barnwell District, SC., 5, 213
Battery Island, SC., 20, 24, 125
Battery Wagner, SC., 113, 124, 193, 224
Beamgrard, Pvt., Samuel, 16
Beatty, Pvt. E.A., 34, 176
Beatty, Pvt., E.G., 35, 176
Beatty, Capt. James C., 131, 164, 176
Beaufort Artillery, 21
Beaufort, SC., 22
Beauregard, Gen. Pierre G.T., ii, 124, 126, 145, 156, 176-177, 179, 203, 205, 207, 222, 226, 230, 192
Beheeler, Pvt. A., 16
Beheeler, Pvt. Henry, 16
Beheeler, Pvt. W.T., 16
Benbow, Col. Henry L., 86, 177
Benham, Col. Henry, 27
Bentonville, NC., Battle of, 178, 189, 193, 206

Ku Klux Klan, 176, 188

Lacy Guards, xix, 4, 180-183, 193,
  200, 202-205, 209, 213
Ladies Christian Association, 5
Lancaster County, 215
Lancaster Tigers, 206, 213
Lancaster, S.C. 5
Latham, Pvt. J. G., 16, 30
Lavaughn, Col. —, 61, 193
Lee, Gen. Robert E., 37-38, 45, 51,
  89, 93, 104, 143, 148, 151, 153,
  158, 161, 163-164, 171, 176,
  191-192, 215-216, 219-220, 223,
  230-231
Lee, Gen. W. H. F., 192
Legares Point, 122
Legares, S.C. 6
Lenoir County, NC., 50
Lincoln, Abraham, xviii, 1, 67, 117,
  126, 197, 214
Lincolnton, NC., 49
Lochart, Pvt. —, 129
Lockhart, Pvt. Edmond M., 193
Lockhart, Pvt. J. Alexander, 160, 193
Lockhart, Pvt. Robert A., 193
Logan & Meacham, xvi
Logan, Lt. Benjamin F., 34, 172,
  193, 212, 216
Logan, Lt. David J., ii-x, xiii-xiv,
  xix-xx, 1-2, 4, 6, 13, 15, 190-191,
  193-196, 199, 207, 210, 214,
  216, 218, 220, 222-223, burial
  173-174, death of 166-167, let-
  ters to wife, Feb 21, 1861, 2,
  Nov. 28, 1861, 8, Dec. 19, 1861,
  9, March 27, 1862, 13, April 10,
  1862, 17, April 17, 1862, 18,
  June 6, 1862, 23, undated, June
  1862, 24, June 11, 1862, 25, June
  21, 1862, 27, June 28, 1862, 29,

July 3, 1862, 31, July, 18, 1862,
  35, August 3, 1862, 42, August
  12, 1862, 45, August 29, 1862,
  46, Sept. 12, 1862, 49, Dec. 18,
  1862, 58, Dec. 23, 1862, 58, Jan.
  4, 1863, 65, Jan. 30, 1863, 79,
  Feb. 5, 1863, 80, March 3, 1863,
  85, April 6, 1863, 87, April 7,
  1863, 88, April 26, 1863, 89,
  May 13, 1863, 90, May 28, 1863,
  97, June 2, 1863, 99, June 21,
  1863, 102, June 24, 1863, 103,
  July 8, 1863, 104, July 30, 1863,
  110, Aug 27, 1863, 114, Aug 30,
  1863, 114, Oct. 12, 1863, 122,
  Nov. 26, 1863, 127, Dec. 10,
  1863, 131, Dec. 19, 1863, 132,
  Feb. 6, 1864, 137, Feb. 9, 1864,
  138, Mar. 22, 1864, 141, May 1,
  1864, 144, May 12, 1864, 149,
  May 16, 1864, 151, June 2, 1864,
  158, June 5, 1864, 162, June 8,
  1864, 164, June 8, 1864, 165,
  wounding of, 48, 51
Logan, Lt. Henry G., 122, 194
Logan, James S., 128, 194
Logan, Jeff, 102, 104, 111, 132-133,
  138, 145, 150, 162, 166
Logan, Jim, 162, 164
Logan, Pvt. John "Pink," 39, 49,
  171-173, 214, 194-195, 221, 223
Logan, Pvt. Leonidas M., 194
Logan, Lula M., 194
Logan, Marion, 35, 216
Logan, Sarah C. Rowell, iii, v-vi,
  xiii, xix, xv, 1, 2-3, 8-9, 13, 17-
  18, 23-25, 27, 29, 35, 42, 45-46,
  49, 58, 65, 67, 79-80, 85, 87-90,
  97, 99, 102-104, 110, 114, 122,
  127, 131-132, 134, 137-138, 140-
  141, 144, 149, 151, 158, 162,